Refined & Relaxed Ranch Home Plans is a collection of best-selling ranch homes in a variety of styles and sizes. These plans cover a broad range of architectural styles as well as a wide variety of lifestyles and budgets. Each design page features floor plans, a front view of the house, interior square footage of the home, number of bedrooms, baths, garage size and foundation types. All floor plans show room and exterior dimensions.

Technical Specifications - At the time the construction drawings were prepared, every effort was made to ensure that these plans and specifications meet nationally recognized building codes (BOCA, Southern Building Code Congress and others). Because national building codes change or vary from area to area some drawing modifications may be necessary to comply with your local codes or to accomodate specific building site conditions. We advise you to consult with your local building official for information regarding codes governing your area.

Blueprint Ordering - Fast and easy - Your ordering is made simple by following the instructions on page 480. See page 479 for more information on which types of blueprint packages are available and how many plan sets to order.

Your Home, Your Way - The blueprints you receive are a master plan for building your new home. They start you on your way to what may well be the most rewarding experience of your life.

Refined & Relaxed Ranch Home Plans is published by HDA, Inc. (Home Design Alternatives) 4390 Green Ash Drive, St. Louis, MO 63045. All rights reserved. Reproduction in whole or in part without written permission of the publisher is prohibited. Printed in the U.S.A. © 2004.

COVER HOME
The home featured on the cover is Plan #581-065D-0041 located on page 256. Courtesy of Studer Residential Design, photo courtesy of Exposures Unlimited, Ron and Donna Kolb; photographers

Current Printing   5   4   3   2   1

YO-BWW-966

Refined & Relaxed RANCH HOME PLANS

Features

Step Inside Our Cover Home...

This home is filled with every amenity both inside and out making it perfect for the most exciting entertaining possiblities.

*E*xtending from the sun-filled breakfast room is an exceptional covered deck featuring the latest trend in the home design industry - a stone covered outdoor fireplace and grill area (photo, above). This unique outdoor kitchen will especially be enjoyed by the chef of the house because it takes the "chore" out of cooking and creates a whole new dimension of culinary fun.

*L*ooking from the rear yard, it is easy to see how well the outdoor kitchen merges the indoors with the outdoors. It is truly an extension of the indoor living space and can be enjoyed year-round by the entire family.

*S*tanding in the foyer and looking beyond the hall into the great room is the perfect place to take in the view of the lavish surroundings (photo, left). A beautiful window wall, multiple decorative columns and gorgeous hardwood floors help create a feeling of richness and splendor to this home. Other wonderful additions include the arched soffit entrance into the great room and the functional, yet inviting openness of this floor plan in general. The staircase in the foreground leads to an optional lower level which includes two bedrooms and a full bath that is perfect for guests. The lower level living area also has a spectacular wet bar with seating, a state-of-the-art media room and a recreation area with enough space for billiards.

*T*his is another angle of the elegant great room (photo, right). This view spotlights the beautiful woodwork and cabinetry surrounding the fireplace. Special details have been added to achieve a custom, one-of-a-kind look. Built-in cabinetry helps eliminate a cluttered look by neatly stowing away all collectibles from view while enhancing the overall appearance of the room.

A stylish kitchen was easily accomplished with the addition of many artistic elements (photo, left). Rich wood details immediately draw the eye to the tile embellished range, while the lighted windowed cabinetry demands equal attention from those who enter the space. A comfortable and friendly snack bar with seating invites visitors to stay and relax for awhile.

*E*nter double-doors from the master bedroom to find this sophisticated dressing area (photo, below). The oversized whirlpool tub is centered between the vanities making it an enticing and hard to ignore rejuvenating retreat. Stunning stained glass windows surround the tub softening the light from the outdoors creating a warm, inviting feel.

A glorious bay window expands the length of the master bedroom filling it with sunlight while creating a natural sitting area (photo, above). A coffered ceiling and exceptional moulding complete the room while maintaining an ultimate formal feel to the space.

For more information on this home, please see page 256.
Plan courtesy of Studer Residential Design.
Photos courtesy of Exposures Unlimited, Ron and Donna Kolb; photographers.
Photos shown may vary slightly from the actual working drawings.
Please refer to the floor plan for accurate layout.

*P*lan #581-007D-0002

3,814 total square feet of living area

Special features

◆ Massive sunken great room with vaulted ceiling includes exciting balcony overlook of towering atrium window wall

◆ Breakfast bar adjoins open "California" kitchen

◆ Seven vaulted rooms for drama and four fireplaces for warmth

◆ Master bath complemented by colonnade and fireplace surrounding sunken tub and deck

◆ 3 bedrooms, 2 1/2 baths, 3-car side entry garage

◆ Walk-out basement foundation

◆ 3,566 square feet on the first floor and 248 square feet on the lower level atrium

Price Code G

Rear View

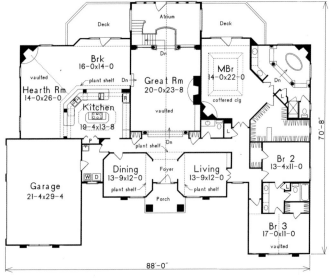

Quick & Easy Customizing
Make Changes To Your Home Plan In 4 Steps

Here's an affordable and efficient way to make changes to your plan.

1. **Select the house plan that most closely meets your needs.** Purchase of a reproducible master is necessary in order to make changes to a plan.

2. **Call 1-800-373-2646 or e-mail customize@hdainc.com to place your order.** Tell the sales representative you're interested in customizing a plan. A $50 nonrefundable consultation fee will be charged. You will then be instructed to complete a customization checklist indicating all the changes you wish to make to your plan. You may attach sketches if necessary. If you proceed with the custom changes the $50 will be credited to the total amount charged.

3. **FAX the completed customization checklist** to our design consultant. Within 24-48* business hours you will be provided with a written cost estimate to modify your plan. Our design consultant will contact you by phone if you wish to discuss any of your changes in greater detail.

4. **Once you approve the estimate,** a 75% retainer fee is collected and customization work gets underway. Preliminary drawings can usually be completed within 5-10* business days. Following approval of the preliminary drawings your design changes are completed within 5-10* business days. Your remaining 25% balance due is collected prior to shipment of your completed drawings. You will be shipped five sets of revised blueprints or a reproducible master, plus a customized materials list if required.

Sample Modification Pricing Guide

The average prices specified below are provided as examples only. They refer to the most commonly requested changes, and are subject to change without notice. Prices for changes will vary or differ, from the prices below, depending on the number of modifications requested, the plan size, style, quality of original plan, format provided to us (originally drawn by hand or computer), and method of design used by the original designer. To obtain a detailed cost estimate or to get more information, please contact us.

Categories	Average Cost*
Adding or removing living space	Quote required
Adding or removing a garage	Starting at $400
Garage: Front entry to side load or vice versa	Starting at $300
Adding a screened porch	Starting at $280
Adding a bonus room in the attic	Starting at $450
Changing full basement to crawl space or vice versa	Starting at $220
Changing full basement to slab or vice versa	Starting at $260
Changing exterior building material	Starting at $200
Changing roof lines	Starting at $360
Adjusting ceiling height	Starting at $280
Adding, moving or removing an exterior opening	$65 per opening
Adding or removing a fireplace	Starting at $90
Modifying a non-bearing wall or room	$65 per room
Changing exterior walls from 2"x4" to 2"x6"	Starting at $200
Redesigning a bathroom or a kitchen	Starting at $120
Reverse plan right reading	Quote required
Adapting plans for local building code requirements	Quote required
Engineering and Architectural stamping and services	Quote required
Adjust plan for handicapped accessibility	Quote required
Interactive Illustrations (choices of exterior materials)	Quote required
Metric conversion of home plan	Starting at $400

*Prices and Terms are subject to change without notice.

Convenient Wet Bar

Plan #581-026D-0122

1,850 total square feet of living area

Special features

- ◆ Oversized rooms throughout
- ◆ Great room spotlights fireplace with sunny windows on both sides
- ◆ Master bedroom has private sky-lighted bath
- ◆ Interesting wet bar between kitchen and dining area is an added bonus when entertaining
- ◆ 3 bedrooms, 2 baths, 2-car garage
- ◆ Basement foundation

Price Code C

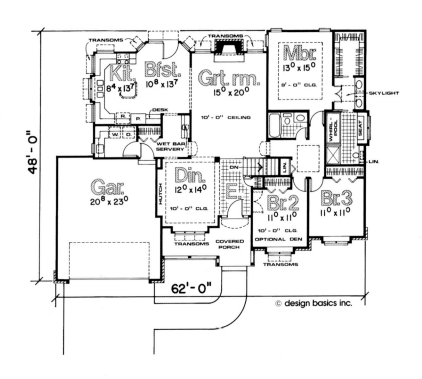

© design basics inc.

© 2003, Garrell Associates, Inc.

Christine Canova 2/02

Plan #581-056D-0005

2,111 total square feet of living area

Special features

◆ 9' ceilings throughout first floor

◆ Formal dining room has columns separating it from other areas while allowing it to maintain an open feel

◆ Master bedroom has privacy from other bedrooms

◆ 3 bedrooms, 2 baths, 2-car side entry garage

◆ Basement foundation

Price Code H

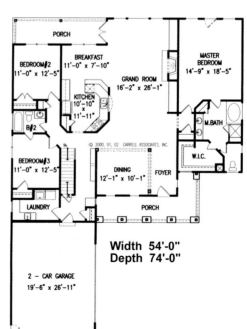

First Floor
2,111 sq. ft.

Width 54'-0"
Depth 74'-0"

Optional
Second Floor
345 sq. ft.

PAINT - BY - NUMBER WALL MURALS

Choose from over 100 designs!

All Aboard #76503

Flamingo Island #76703

Photo colors may vary from kit colors.

Create a unique room for your child with 🖰 WALL ART.™
Patent Pending

Your children will be the envy of all their friends when you decorate their room with a Paint-By-Number Wall Mural.® Choose from over 100 custom designs and transform your child's room into a kid-friendly paradise.

You don't have to be an artist to paint a Wall Art mural. The whole family can participate in this fun and easy weekend project. Your Wall Art Kit includes everything but the wall!

Wall Art murals are available in a variety of sizes starting at $49.97.

It's Easy As 1 - 2 - 3.

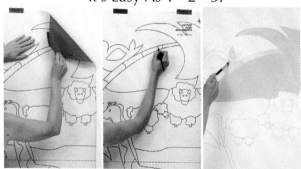

1. Tape   2. Trace   3. Paint

**To order or request a catalog, call toll free
1-877-WALLMURAL (925-5687)
24 hours a day, 7 days a week,
or buy online at
www.wallartdesigns.com**

Order Today! www.wallartdesigns.com

*P*lan #581-055D-0088

2,261 total square feet of living area

Special features

◆ Efficiently designed kitchen with work island and snack bar

◆ Master bath has double vanities, whirlpool tub and two walk-in closets

◆ Spacious laundry room

◆ 4 bedrooms, 3 1/2 baths, 2-car side entry garage

◆ Slab or crawl space foundation, please specify when ordering foundation

Price Code D

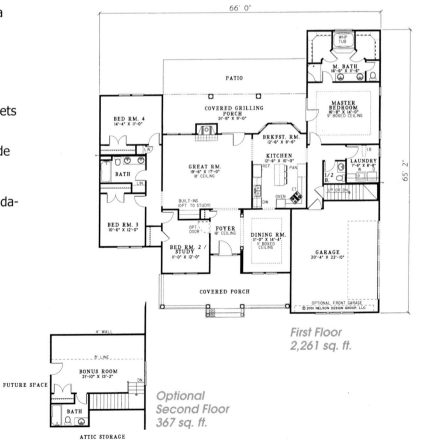

First Floor
2,261 sq. ft.

Optional
Second Floor
367 sq. ft.

Plan #581-001D-0007

2,874 total square feet of living area

Special features

- ◆ Large family room with sloped ceiling and wood beams adjoins the kitchen and breakfast area with windows on two walls
- ◆ Spacious foyer opens to family room with massive stone fireplace and open stairs to the basement
- ◆ Private master bedroom with raised tub under the bay window, dramatic dressing area and a huge walk-in closet
- ◆ 4 bedrooms, 2 1/2 baths, 2-car side entry garage
- ◆ Basement foundation

Price Code E

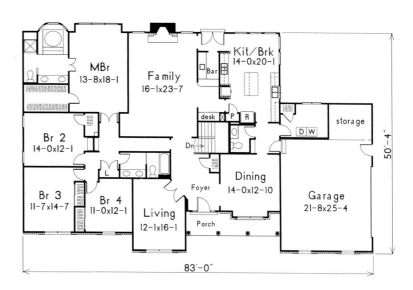

Arts And Crafts Style Facade

*P*lan #581-011D-0007

1,580 total square feet of living area

Special features

◆ A covered porch extends the great room to the outdoors

◆ Secluded master bedroom enjoys a vaulted ceiling, private bath with double vanity and a large walk-in closet

◆ Built-in bookshelves flank one wall of the dining room and are perfect for collectibles or cookbooks

◆ 3 bedrooms, 2 1/2 baths, 2-car garage

◆ Crawl space foundation

Price Code C

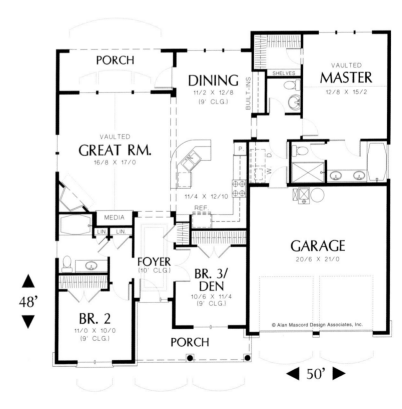

An Elegant Southern Home

Plan #581-028D-0005

1,856 total square feet of living area

Special features

◆ Kitchen is well-positioned between the formal dining room and the casual breakfast area

◆ Master bedroom has a luxurious bath with all the amenities

◆ Home office or bedroom #4 has its own private bath

◆ 4 bedrooms, 3 baths, 2-car side entry garage

◆ Crawl space or slab foundation, please specify when ordering

Price Code C

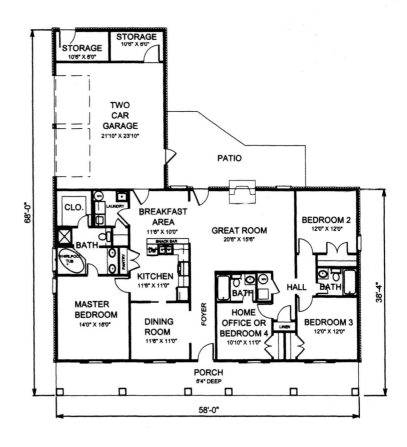

Plan #581-065D-0005

1,782 total square feet of living area

Special features

- ◆ Outstanding breakfast area accesses the outdoors through French doors
- ◆ Generous counterspace and cabinets combine to create an ideal kitchen
- ◆ The master bedroom is enhanced with a beautiful bath featuring a whirlpool tub and double-bowl vanity
- ◆ 3 bedrooms, 2 baths, 2-car garage
- ◆ Basement foundation

Price Code B

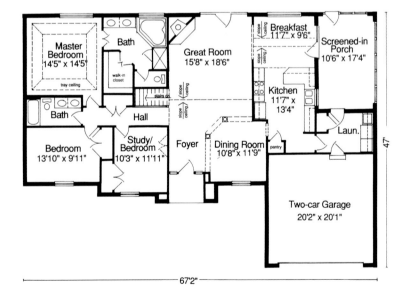

Angled Hallway

*P*lan #581-011D-0013

2,001 total square feet of living area

Special features

◆ Large wrap-around counter in kitchen is accessible from dining area

◆ Double-doors keep den secluded from other living areas maintaining privacy

◆ Decorative columns adorn the entry leading into the great room

◆ 3 bedrooms, 2 baths, 2-car garage

◆ Crawl space foundation

Price Code D

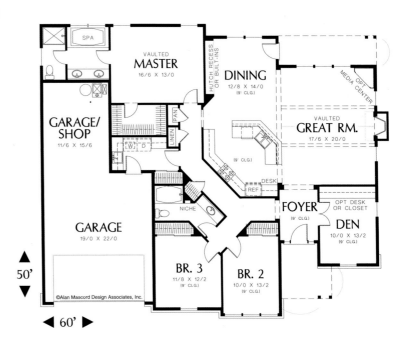

Plan #581-007D-0062

2,483 total square feet of living area

Special features

- A large entry porch with open brick arches and palladian door welcomes guests
- The vaulted great room features an entertainment center alcove and the ideal layout for furniture placement
- The dining room is extra large with a stylish tray ceiling
- Study can easily be converted to a fourth bedroom
- 3 bedrooms, 2 baths, 2-car side entry garage
- Basement foundation

Price Code D

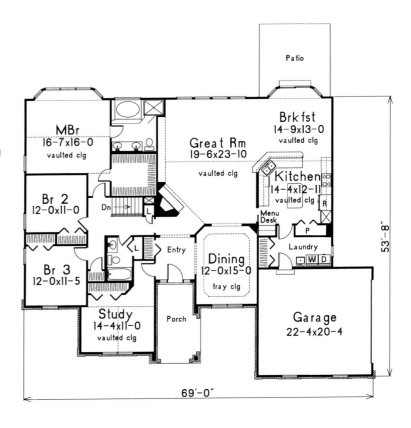

Plan #581-062D-0053

1,405 total square feet of living area

Special features

- An expansive wall of glass gives a spectacular view to the great room and accentuates the high vaulted ceilings throughout the design
- Great room is warmed by a wood-stove and is open to the dining room and L-shaped kitchen
- Triangular snack bar graces kitchen
- 3 bedrooms, 2 baths
- Basement or crawl space foundation, please specify when ordering

Price Code A

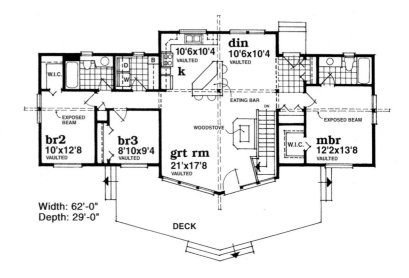

Width: 62'-0"
Depth: 29'-0"

Plan #581-013D-0021

1,982 total square feet of living area

Special features

- ◆ Large screened porch creates a great casual living area and connects to a covered deck leading into the master suite
- ◆ Dramatic formal living room has a sunny bay window and high ceilings
- ◆ Master suite has a private sitting area as well as a private luxury-filled bath
- ◆ 3 bedrooms, 2 1/2 baths, 3-car side entry garage
- ◆ Basement, crawl space or slab foundation, please specify when ordering

Price Code C

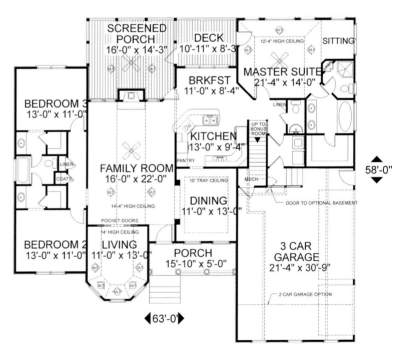

Plan #581-007D-0077

1,977 total square feet of living area

Special features

- Classic traditional exterior always in style
- Spacious great room boasts a vaulted ceiling, dining area, atrium with elegant staircase and feature windows
- Optional living area below consists of a family room, two bedrooms, two baths and a study
- 4 bedrooms, 2 1/2 baths, 3-car side entry garage
- Walk-out basement foundation

Price Code C

First Floor
1,977 sq. ft.

First Floor plan:
- 76'-0"
- 45'-0"
- MBr 14-6x15-5
- Br 2 10-7x10-0
- Br 3 11-4x11x8
- Br 4 11-8x12-8 vaulted
- Brk 11-8x13-0
- open to below
- Dn
- Deck
- Great Rm 16-4x24-2 vaulted
- Kit 11-3x12-4
- Dining
- Garage 23-4x29-4
- Porch

Optional Lower Level
1,416 sq. ft.

Lower Level plan:
- Br 5 15-3x15-6
- Up Atrium
- Study 10-9x13-2
- Family 18-4x23-6
- Br 6 11-5x12-7
- storage

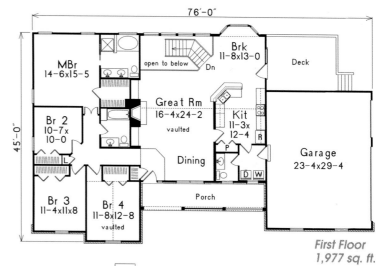

Plan #581-028D-0008

2,156 total square feet of living area

Special features

- ◆ Secluded master bedroom has spa-style bath with corner whirlpool tub, large shower, double sinks and a walk-in closet
- ◆ Kitchen overlooks rear patio
- ◆ Plenty of windows add an open, airy feel to the great room
- ◆ 4 bedrooms, 3 baths, 2-car side entry garage
- ◆ Basement, crawl space or slab foundation, please specify when ordering

Price Code C

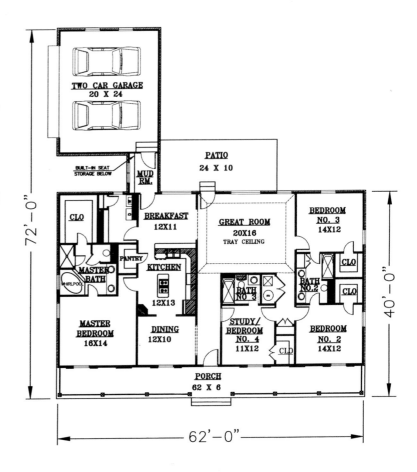

Plan #581-052D-0038

1,787 total square feet of living area

Special features

- Private master bedroom features an enormous tub, walk-in closet and close proximity to the laundry room
- A Jack and Jill style bath is shared by bedrooms #2 and #3
- 12' ceiling in foyer makes a dramatic entrance
- 3 bedrooms, 2 1/2 baths, 2-car garage
- Basement foundation

Price Code B

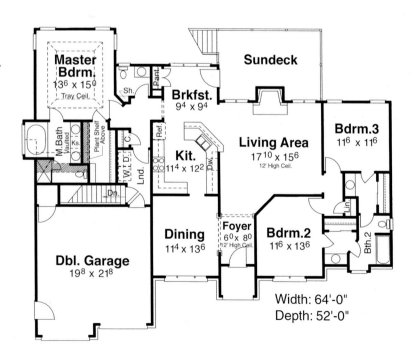

Master Bdrm. 13⁶ x 15⁰ Tray Ceil.

Sundeck

Brkfst. 9⁴ x 9⁴

Bdrm.3 11⁶ x 11⁶

M. Bath Vaulted

Plant Shelf Above

Kit. 11⁴ x 12²

Living Area 17¹⁰ x 15⁶ 12' High Ceil.

Lnd.

Dn.

Dining 11⁴ x 13⁶

Foyer 6⁰ x 8⁰ 12' High Ceil.

Bdrm.2 11⁶ x 13⁶

Bth.2

Dbl. Garage 19⁸ x 21⁸

Width: 64'-0"
Depth: 52'-0"

Plan #581-025D-0008

1,609 total square feet of living area

Special features

- ◆ Laundry area is adjacent to kitchen for convenience
- ◆ Two storage areas with one that can be accessed from the outdoors and another that can be reached from the garage
- ◆ Eating bar overlooks from kitchen into dining area
- ◆ 3 bedrooms, 2 baths, 2-car side entry garage
- ◆ Slab foundation

Price Code B

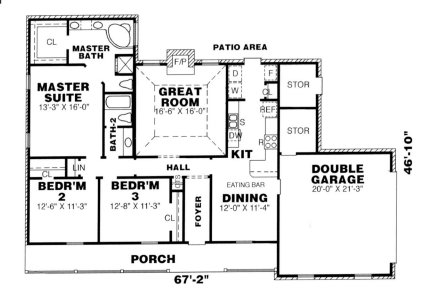

Plan #581-001D-0031

1,501 total square feet of living area

Special features

◆ Spacious kitchen with dining area is open to the outdoors

◆ Convenient utility room is adjacent to garage

◆ Master bedroom features a private bath, dressing area and access to the large covered porch

◆ Large family room creates openness

◆ 3 bedrooms, 2 baths, 2-car side entry garage

◆ Basement foundation, drawings also include crawl space and slab foundations

Price Code B

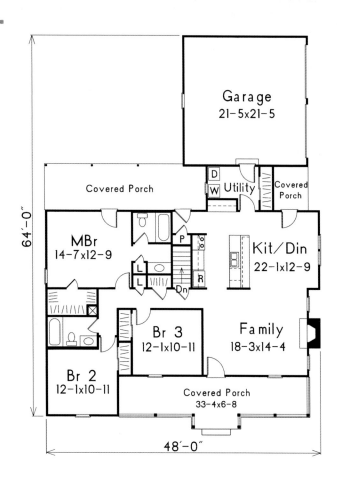

Garage
21-5x21-5

Covered Porch

D | Utility | Covered Porch
W

MBr
14-7x12-9

Kit/Din
22-1x12-9

P

Dn

Family
18-3x14-4

Br 3
12-1x10-11

Br 2
12-1x10-11

Covered Porch
33-4x6-8

64'-0"

48'-0"

*P*lan #581-038D-0033

1,312 total square feet of living area

Special features

◆ A beamed ceiling and fireplace create an exciting feel to the living room

◆ Box window behind double sink in kitchen is a nice added feature

◆ Private bath and generous closet space in the master bedroom

◆ 3 bedrooms, 2 baths, 2-car garage

◆ Basement or crawl space foundation, please specify when ordering

Price Code A

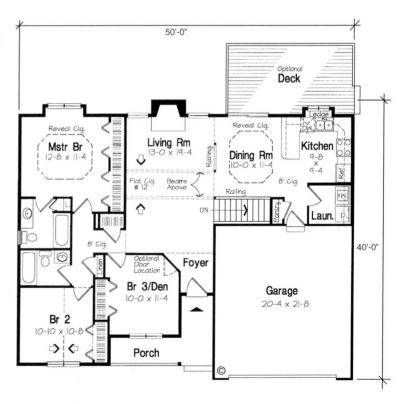

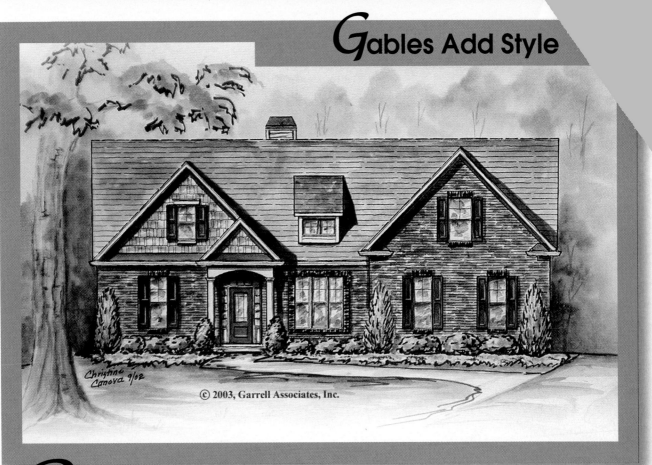

© 2003, Garrell Associates, Inc.

Plan #581-056D-0008

1,821 total square feet of living area

Special features

- ◆ 9' ceilings throughout first floor
- ◆ Master suite is secluded for privacy and has a spacious bath
- ◆ Sunny breakfast room features bay window
- ◆ 3 bedrooms, 2 baths, 2-car side entry garage
- ◆ Basement or slab foundation, please specify when ordering

Price Code E

Optional Second Floor 191 sq. ft.

BONUS ROOM
11'-5" x 15'-3"

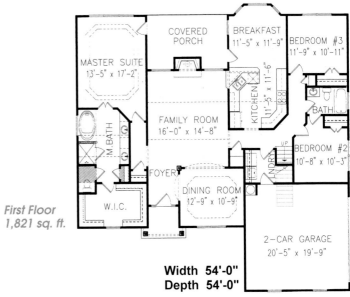

First Floor 1,821 sq. ft.

COVERED PORCH

BREAKFAST
11'-5" x 11'-9"

BEDROOM #3
11'-9" x 10'-11"

MASTER SUITE
13'-5" x 17'-2"

KITCHEN
11'-5" x 11'-6"

BATH

M.BATH

FAMILY ROOM
16'-0" x 14'-8"

BEDROOM #2
10'-8" x 10'-3"

FOYER

W.I.C.

DINING ROOM
12'-9" x 10'-9"

2-CAR GARAGE
20'-5" x 19'-9"

Width 54'-0"
Depth 54'-0"

Plan #581-007D-0117

2,695 total square feet of living area

Special features

- A grandscale great room features a fireplace with flanking shelves, handsome entry foyer with staircase and opens to large kitchen and breakfast room
- Roomy master bedroom has a bay window, huge walk-in closet and bath with a shower built for two
- Bedrooms #2 and #3 are generously oversized with walk-in closets and a Jack and Jill style bath
- 3 bedrooms, 2 1/2 baths, 2-car side entry garage
- Basement foundation

Price Code E

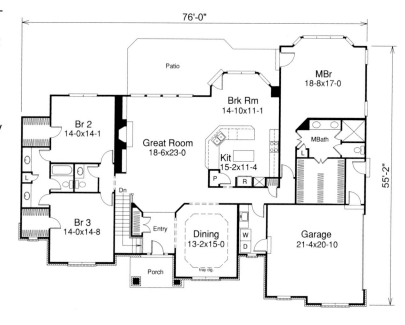

*S*pacious Ranch Home

*P*lan #581-065D-0038

1,663 total square feet of living area

Special features

- ◆ The open great room, dining area and kitchen combine to form the main living area
- ◆ An 11' ceiling tops the great room and foyer for added openness
- ◆ The rear covered porch provides a cozy and relaxing atmosphere
- ◆ The master bedroom enjoys a sloped ceiling and a private entrance to the covered porch
- ◆ 3 bedrooms, 2 baths, 2-car side entry garage
- ◆ Basement foundation

Price Code B

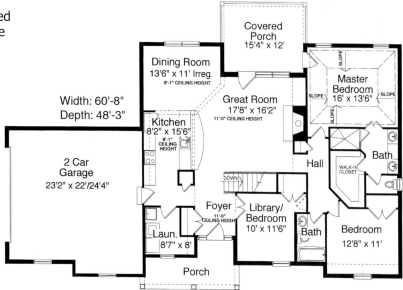

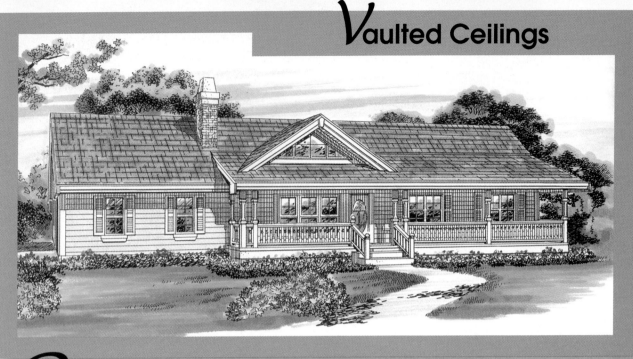

*P*lan #581-062D-0050

1,408 total square feet of living area

Special features

- ◆ A bright country kitchen boasts an abundance of counterspace and cupboards
- ◆ The front entry is sheltered by a broad verandah
- ◆ A spa tub is brightened by a box bay window in the master bath
- ◆ 3 bedrooms, 2 baths, 2-car side entry garage
- ◆ Basement or crawl space foundation, please specify when ordering

Price Code A

Width: 70'-0"
Depth: 28'-0"

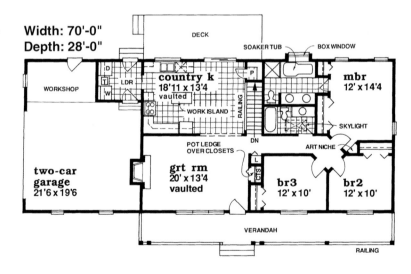

Pillared Front Porch

Plan #581-017D-0007

1,567 total square feet of living area

Special features

- The living room flows into the dining room shaped by an angled pass-through into the kitchen
- Cheerful, windowed dining area
- Master bedroom is separated from other bedrooms for privacy
- 3 bedrooms, 2 baths, 2-car side entry garage
- Basement foundation, drawings also include slab foundation

Price Code C

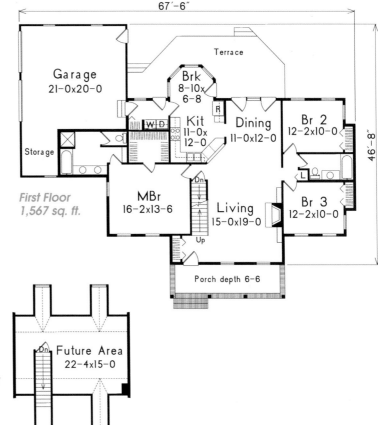

67'-6"

Terrace

Garage
21-0x20-0

Brk
8-10x
6-8

Kit
11-0x
12-0

Dining
11-0x12-0

Br 2
12-2x10-0

Storage

W D

R

46'-8"

*First Floor
1,567 sq. ft.*

MBr
16-2x13-6

Living
15-0x19-0

Br 3
12-2x10-0

Dn

Up

Porch depth 6-6

Dn Future Area
22-4x15-0

*Optional
Second Floor
338 sq. ft.*

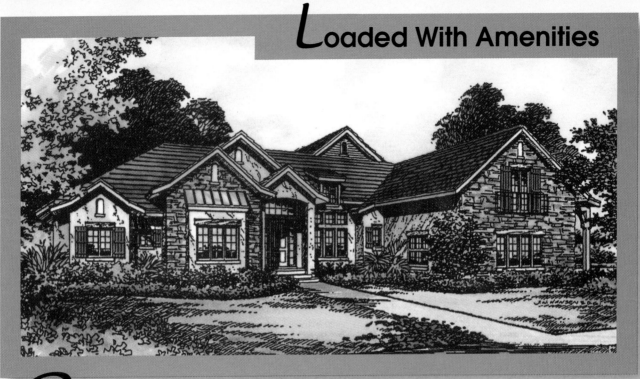

Plan #581-047D-0062

3,359 total square feet of living area

Special features

◆ A covered patio wraps around the rear of the home providing extra outdoor living area

◆ Master suite is separated from other bedrooms for privacy

◆ Framing - only concrete block available

◆ 4 bedrooms, 3 1/2 baths, 3-car side entry garage

◆ Slab foundation

Price Code G

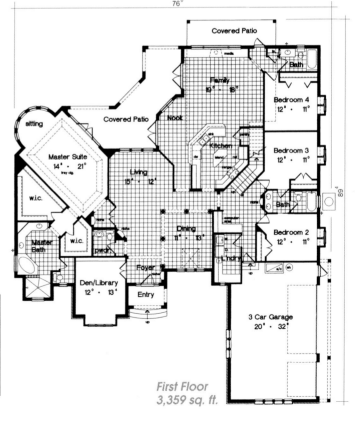

*Optional
Second Floor
459 sq. ft.*

*First Floor
3,359 sq. ft.*

© 2003, Garrell Associates, Inc.

Plan #581-056D-0023

1,277 total square feet of living area

Special features

◆ Both the family room and master bedroom have direct access to an outdoor deck

◆ Compact, yet efficient kitchen

◆ Columns add distinction between dining and family rooms

◆ 3 bedrooms, 2 baths, 2-car garage

◆ Slab foundation

Price Code E

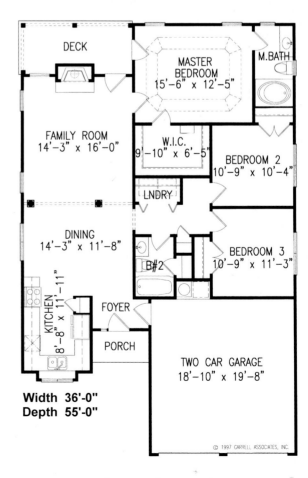

DECK

MASTER BEDROOM
15'-6" x 12'-5"

M.BATH

FAMILY ROOM
14'-3" x 16'-0"

W.I.C.
9'-10" x 6'-5"

BEDROOM 2
10'-9" x 10'-4"

LNDRY

DINING
14'-3" x 11'-8"

BEDROOM 3
10'-9" x 11'-3"

B#2

KITCHEN
8'-8" x 11'-11"

FOYER

PORCH

TWO CAR GARAGE
18'-10" x 19'-8"

Width 36'-0"
Depth 55'-0"

© 1997 GARRELL ASSOCIATES, INC.

Country Flavor With Atrium

Plan #581-007D-0101

2,384 total square feet of living area

Special features

- ◆ Bracketed box windows create an exterior with country charm
- ◆ Massive-sized great room features a majestic atrium, fireplace, box window wall, dining balcony and vaulted ceilings
- ◆ An atrium balcony with large bay window off sundeck is enjoyed by the spacious breakfast room
- ◆ 3 bedrooms, 2 1/2 baths, 2-car side entry garage
- ◆ Walk-out basement foundation

Price Code D

Optional Lower Level 1,038 sq. ft.

First Floor 2,384 sq. ft.

Brick Ranch Has It All

*P*lan #581-055D-0108

2,671 total square feet of living area

Special features

- ◆ Spacious master suite has luxurious bath with whirlpool tub, oversized shower and walk-in closet
- ◆ Great room and breakfast room both access the grilling porch perfect for entertaining
- ◆ Laundry room is conveniently located near all secondary bedrooms
- ◆ 4 bedrooms, 2 1/2 baths, 2-car side entry garage
- ◆ Crawl space or slab foundation, please specify when ordering

Price Code E

Plan #581-007D-0017

1,882 total square feet of living area

Special features

- ◆ Handsome brick facade
- ◆ Spacious great room and dining room combination brightened by unique corner windows and patio access
- ◆ Well-designed kitchen incorporates breakfast bar peninsula, sweeping casement window above sink and walk-in pantry island
- ◆ Master bedroom features large walk-in closet and private bath with bay window
- ◆ 4 bedrooms, 2 baths, 2-car side entry garage
- ◆ Basement foundation

Price Code C

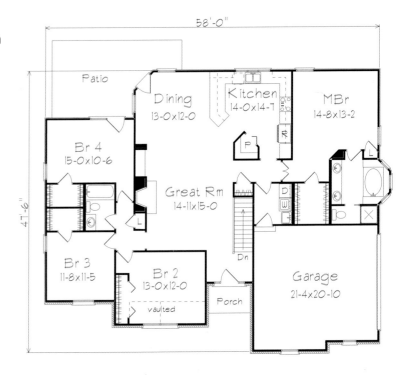

Plan #581-062D-0054

1,375 total square feet of living area

Special features

◆ Open U-shaped kitchen shares an eating bar with the dining room

◆ Two secondary bedrooms share a full bath

◆ Master bedroom provides a walk-in closet and private bath

◆ 3 bedrooms, 2 baths

◆ Basement or crawl space foundation, please specify when ordering

Price Code A

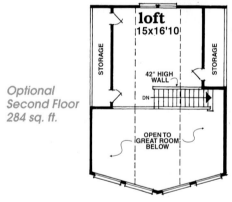

Optional Second Floor 284 sq. ft.

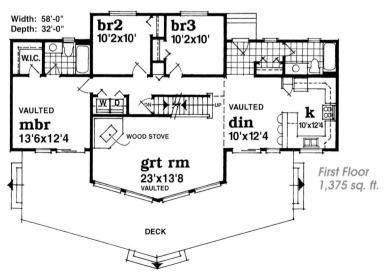

Width: 58'-0"
Depth: 32'-0"

First Floor 1,375 sq. ft.

Country Elegance

*P*lan #581-007D-0085

1,787 total square feet of living area

Special features

- ◆ Large great room with fireplace and vaulted ceiling features three large skylights and windows galore

- ◆ Cooking is sure to be a pleasure in this L-shaped well-appointed kitchen which includes bayed breakfast area with access to rear deck

- ◆ Every bedroom offers a spacious walk-in closet with a convenient laundry room just steps away

- ◆ 415 square feet of optional living area available on the lower level

- ◆ 3 bedrooms, 2 baths, 2-car drive under garage

- ◆ Walk-out basement foundation

Price Code B

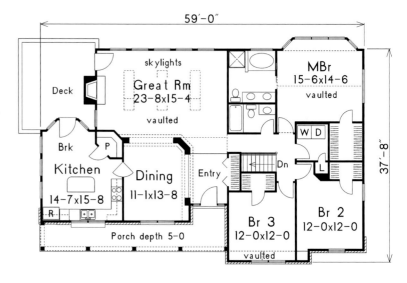

Plan #581-065D-0044

2,203 total square feet of living area

Special features

- The spacious great room with fireplace and entertainment alcove, dining area and kitchen combine to offer a large family gathering place
- Three sets of French doors provide an abundance of warm natural light
- A spectacular covered porch with fireplace provides an exceptional entertaining area
- The private master bedroom enjoys a 10' ceiling and deluxe dressing room with a whirlpool tub and two walk-in closets
- 3 bedrooms, 2 1/2 baths, 2-car garage
- Basement foundation

Price Code D

Plan #581-028D-0002

1,377 total square feet of living area

Special features

- ◆ Master bedroom has double-door access onto screened porch
- ◆ Cozy dining area is adjacent to kitchen for convenience
- ◆ Great room includes fireplace
- ◆ 3 bedrooms, 1 bath
- ◆ Crawl space or slab foundation, please specify when ordering

Price Code A

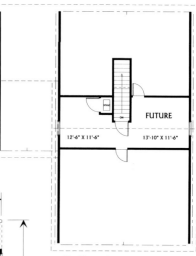

*Optional
Second Floor
349 sq. ft.*

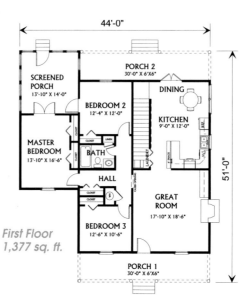

*First Floor
1,377 sq. ft.*

© 2003, Garrell Associates, Inc.

Plan #581-056D-0007

1,985 total square feet of living area

Special features

- ◆ 9' ceilings throughout home
- ◆ Master suite has direct access into sunroom
- ◆ Sunny breakfast room features bay window
- ◆ 3 bedrooms, 3 baths, 2-car side entry garage
- ◆ Slab foundation

Price Code G

Optional Second Floor 191 sq. ft.

OPT BONUS ROOM 11'-5" x 15'-3"

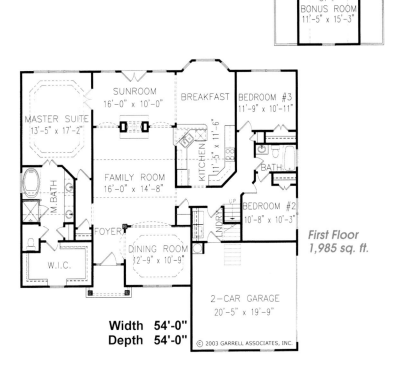

First Floor 1,985 sq. ft.

Width 54'-0"
Depth 54'-0"

© 2003 GARRELL ASSOCIATES, INC.

$\mathcal{S}$ensational Cottage Retreat

$\mathcal{P}$lan #581-007D-0043

647 total square feet of living area

Special features

- Large vaulted room for living/sleeping has plant shelves on each end, stone fireplace and wide glass doors for views
- Roomy kitchen is vaulted and has a bayed dining area and fireplace
- Step down into a sunken and vaulted bath featuring a 6'-0" whirlpool tub-in-a-bay with shelves at each end for storage
- A large palladian window adorns each end of the cottage giving a cheery atmosphere throughout
- 1 living/sleeping room, 1 bath
- Crawl space foundation

Price Code AAA

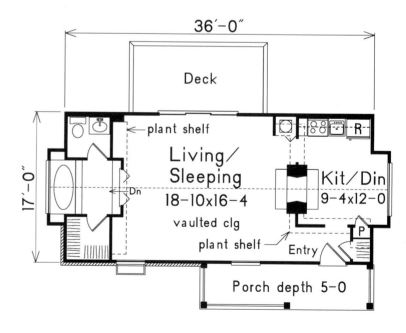

*P*lan #581-024D-0004

1,500 total square feet of living area

Special features

- ◆ Living room features corner fireplace adding warmth
- ◆ Master bedroom has all the amenities including a walk-in closet, private bath and porch access
- ◆ Sunny bayed breakfast room is cheerful and bright
- ◆ 3 bedrooms, 2 baths, 2-car garage
- ◆ Slab foundation

Price Code B

Width: 64'-0"
Depth: 45'-0"

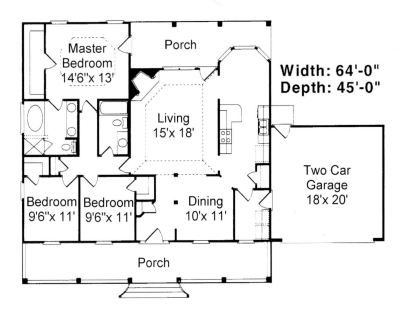

*P*lan #581-007D-0058

4,826 total square feet of living area

Special features

- Brightly lit entry connects to great room with balcony and massive bay-shaped atrium

- Kitchen has island/snack bar, walk-in pantry, computer area and an atrium overlook

- Master bedroom has sitting area, walk-in closets, atrium overlook and luxury bath with private courtyard

- Family room/atrium, home theater area with wet bar, game room and guest bedroom comprise the lower level

- 4 bedrooms, 3 1/2 baths, 3-car side entry garage

- Walk-out basement foundation with lawn and garden workroom

Price Code G

First Floor
3,050 sq. ft.

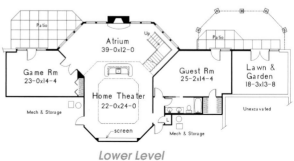

Lower Level
1,776 sq. ft.

Plan #581-010D-0006

1,170 total square feet of living area

Special features

- Master bedroom enjoys privacy at the rear of this home
- Kitchen has an angled bar that overlooks great room and breakfast area
- Living areas combine to create a greater sense of spaciousness
- Great room has a cozy fireplace
- 3 bedrooms, 2 baths, 2-car garage
- Slab foundation

Price Code AA

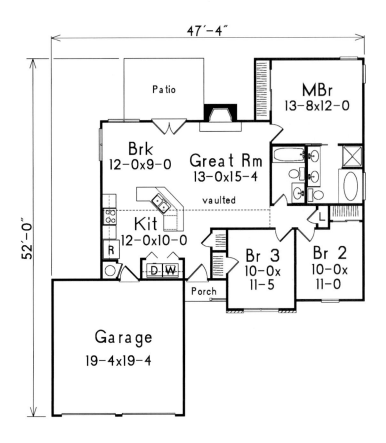

*B*uilt-In Computer Desk

*P*lan #581-055D-0017

1,525 total square feet of living area

Special features

- Corner fireplace is highlighted in the great room
- Unique glass block window over whirlpool tub in master bath brightens interior
- Open bar overlooks both the kitchen and great room
- Breakfast room leads to an outdoor grilling and covered porch
- 3 bedrooms, 2 baths, 2-car garage
- Basement, walk-out basement, crawl space or slab foundation, please specify when ordering

Price Code B

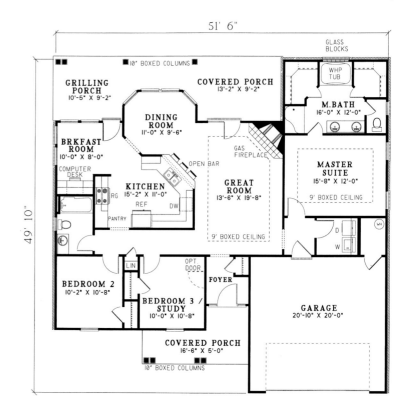

Plan #581-022D-0026

1,993 total square feet of living area

Special features

- Spacious country kitchen with fire-place and plenty of natural light from windows
- Formal dining room features large bay window and steps down to sunken living room
- Master bedroom features corner windows, plant shelves and deluxe private bath
- Entry opens into vaulted living room with windows flanking the fireplace
- 3 bedrooms, 2 baths, 2-car garage
- Basement foundation

Price Code D

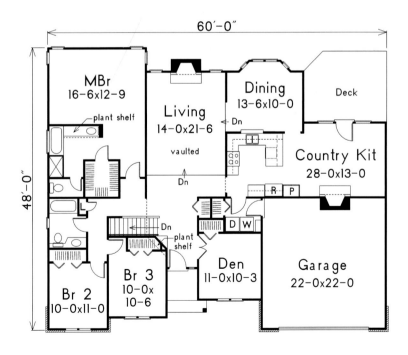

Plan #581-007D-0068

1,384 total square feet of living area

Special features

- ◆ Wrap-around country porch for peaceful evenings
- ◆ Vaulted great room enjoys a large bay window, stone fireplace, pass-through kitchen and awesome rear views through atrium window wall
- ◆ Master bedroom features double entry doors, walk-in closet and a fabulous bath
- ◆ 2 bedrooms, 2 baths, 1-car side entry garage
- ◆ Walk-out basement foundation

Price Code B

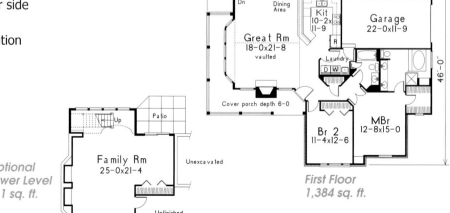

Rear View

First Floor
1,384 sq. ft.

55'-8"

46'-0"

Atrium below

Dn

Dining Area

Kit
10-2x
11-9

Garage
22-0x11-9

Great Rm
18-0x21-8
vaulted

Laundry

D W

Cover porch depth 6-0

Br 2
11-4x12-6

MBr
12-8x15-0

Optional
Lower Level
611 sq. ft.

Up

Patio

Family Rm
25-0x21-4

Unexcavated

Unfinished Basement

Plan #581-070D-0008

2,083 total square feet of living area

Special features

- ◆ A handy server counter located between the kitchen and formal dining room is ideal for entertaining
- ◆ Decorative columns grace the entrance into the great room
- ◆ A large island in the kitchen aids in food preparation
- ◆ 3 bedrooms, 2 1/2 baths, 2-car garage
- ◆ Basement foundation

Price Code C

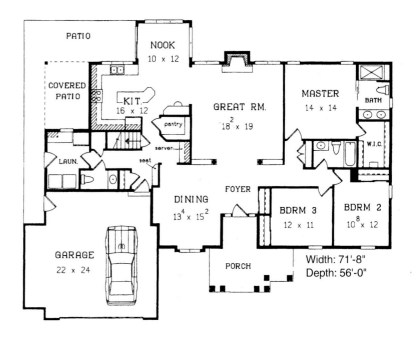

Three Bedroom Luxury

Plan #581-007D-0107

1,161 total square feet of living area

Special features

- Brickwork and feature window add elegance to home for a narrow lot
- Living room enjoys a vaulted ceiling, fireplace and opens to kitchen
- U-shaped kitchen offers a breakfast area with bay window, snack bar and built-in pantry
- 3 bedrooms, 2 baths
- Basement foundation

Price Code AA

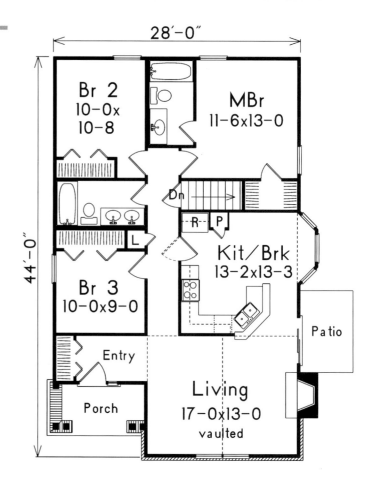

Handsome, Compact Ranch

Plan #581-013D-0003

1,296 total square feet of living area

Special features

- Two secondary bedrooms share a bath and have convenient access to the laundry room
- Family room has a large fireplace flanked by sunny windows
- Master bedroom includes privacy as well as an amenity-full bath
- 3 bedrooms, 2 baths, 2-car garage
- Basement, crawl space or slab foundation, please specify when ordering

Price Code B

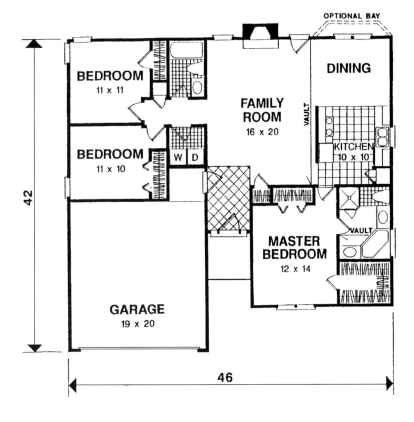

Plan #581-055D-0032

2,439 total square feet of living area

Special features

- ◆ Enter columned gallery area just before reaching family room with see-through fireplace
- ◆ Master suite has a corner whirlpool tub
- ◆ Double-door entrance into study
- ◆ 4 bedrooms, 3 baths, 2-car garage
- ◆ Slab, crawl space, basement or walk-out basement foundation, please specify when ordering

Price Code D

Plan #581-006D-0003

1,674 total square feet of living area

Special features

◆ Vaulted great room, dining area and kitchen all enjoy central fireplace and log bin

◆ Convenient laundry/mud room located between garage and family area with handy stairs to basement

◆ Easily expandable screened porch and adjacent patio with access from dining area

◆ Master bedroom features full bath with tub, separate shower and walk-in closet

◆ 3 bedrooms, 2 baths, 2-car garage

◆ Basement foundation, drawings also include crawl space and slab foundations

Price Code B

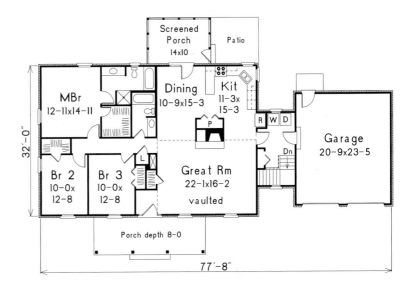

Screened Porch 14x10

Patio

MBr 12-11x14-11

Dining 10-9x15-3

Kit 11-3x 15-3

R W D

Garage 20-9x23-5

32'-0"

Br 2 10-0x 12-8

Br 3 10-0x 12-8

L

Great Rm 22-1x16-2 vaulted

Dn

Porch depth 8-0

77'-8"

Plan #581-007D-0119

1,621 total square feet of living area

Special features

◆ The front exterior includes an attractive gable-end arched window and extra-deep porch

◆ A grand-scale great room enjoys a coffered ceiling, fireplace, access to the wrap-around deck and is brightly lit with numerous French doors and windows

◆ The master bedroom suite has a sitting area, double walk-in closets and a luxury bath

◆ 3 bedrooms, 2 baths, 2-car drive under side entry garage

◆ Basement foundation

Price Code B

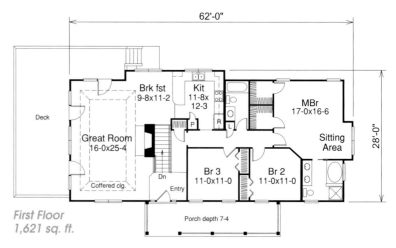

First Floor
1,621 sq. ft.

Lower Level
With Optional Laundry Area
223 sq. ft.

Plan #581-011D-0002

1,557 total square feet of living area

Special features

◆ Vaulted dining room extends off the great room and features an eye-catching plant shelf above

◆ Double closets adorn the vaulted master bedroom which also features a private bath with tub and shower

◆ Bedroom #3/den has the option to add double-doors creating the feeling of a home office if needed

◆ 3 bedrooms, 2 baths, 2-car garage

◆ Crawl space foundation

Price Code C

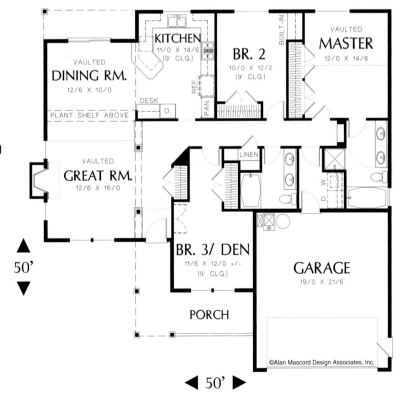

KITCHEN
11/0 X 14/6
(9' CLG.)

VAULTED
DINING RM.
12/6 X 10/0

PLANT SHELF ABOVE

DESK

BR. 2
10/0 X 12/2
(9' CLG.)

BUILT-IN

VAULTED
MASTER
12/0 X 14/6

REF.

PAN.

VAULTED
GREAT RM.
12/6 X 16/0

LINEN

D. W.

BR. 3/ DEN
11/6 X 12/0 +/-
(9' CLG.)

GARAGE
19/0 X 21/6

PORCH

50'

50'

©Alan Mascord Design Associates, Inc.

Plan #581-007D-0053

2,334 total square feet of living area

Special features

- ◆ Roomy front porch gives home a country flavor
- ◆ Vaulted great room boasts a fireplace, TV alcove, pass-through snack bar to kitchen and atrium featuring bayed window wall and an ascending stair to family room
- ◆ Oversized master bedroom and bath features a vaulted ceiling, double entry doors and large walk-in closet
- ◆ 3 bedrooms, 2 baths, 2-car garage
- ◆ Walk-out basement foundation

Price Code D

Rear View

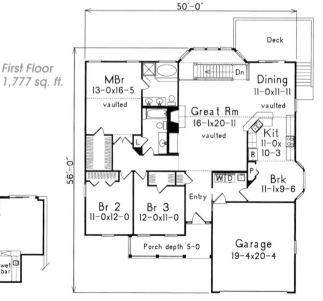

First Floor 1,777 sq. ft.

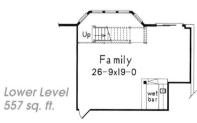

Lower Level 557 sq. ft.

Plan #581-028D-0014

2,340 total square feet of living area

Special features

- Great room shares a see-through fireplace with the dining room
- Bedrooms #2 and #3 share a split bath
- Enormous sitting area in master bedroom could easily be converted to a study or even a nursery
- 3 bedrooms, 2 1/2 baths, 2-car side entry garage
- Crawl space or slab foundation, please specify when ordering

Price Code D

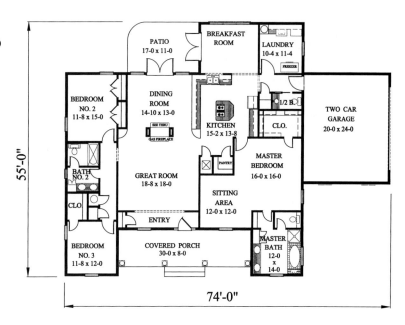

Plan #581-016D-0040

1,595 total square feet of living area

Special features

- Large great room features a tray ceiling and French doors to a screened porch
- Dining room and bedroom #2 have bay windows
- Master bedroom has a tray ceiling and a bay window
- 3 bedrooms, 2 baths, 2-car side entry garage
- Basement, crawl space, slab or walkout basement foundation, please specify when ordering

Price Code C

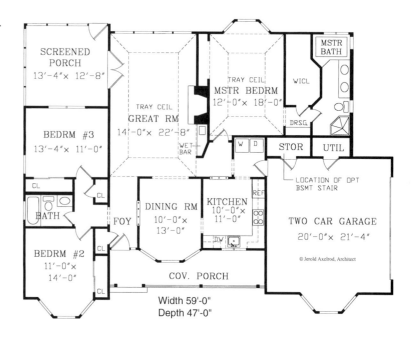

Width 59'-0"
Depth 47'-0"

Plan #581-022D-0018

1,368 total square feet of living area

Special features

◆ Entry foyer steps down to open living area which combines great room and formal dining area

◆ Vaulted master bedroom includes box bay window, large vanity, separate tub and shower

◆ Cozy breakfast area features direct access to the patio and pass-through kitchen

◆ Handy linen closet located in hall

◆ 3 bedrooms, 2 baths, 2-car garage

◆ Basement foundation

Price Code A

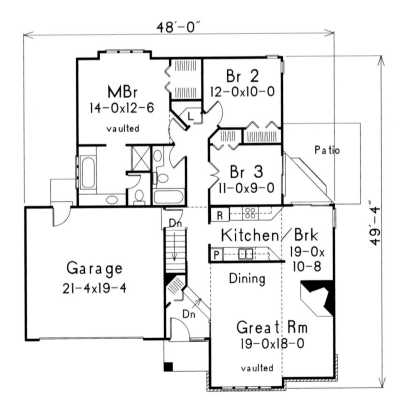

48'-0"

49'-4"

MBr
14-0x12-6
vaulted

Br 2
12-0x10-0

Br 3
11-0x9-0

Patio

Kitchen/Brk
19-0x
10-8

Dining

Garage
21-4x19-4

Dn

Dn

Great Rm
19-0x18-0

vaulted

A Cottage With Class

Plan #581-007D-0029

576 total square feet of living area

Special features

◆ Perfect country retreat features vaulted living room and entry with skylights and plant shelf above

◆ Double-doors enter a vaulted bedroom with bath access

◆ Kitchen offers generous storage and pass-through breakfast bar

◆ 1 bedroom, 1 bath

◆ Crawl space foundation

Price Code AAA

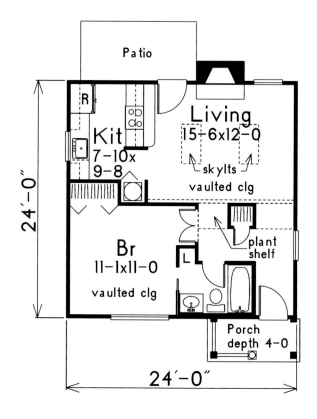

Plan #581-007D-0056

3,199 total square feet of living area

Special features

- Grand-scale kitchen features bay-shaped cabinetry built over atrium that overlooks two-story window wall
- A second atrium dominates the master bedroom which boasts a sitting area with bay window as well as a luxurious bath which has a whirlpool tub open to the garden atrium and lower level study
- 3 bedrooms, 2 1/2 baths, 3-car side entry garage
- Walk-out basement foundation

Price Code E

Rear View

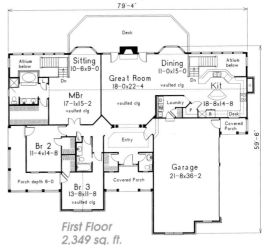

First Floor
2,349 sq. ft.

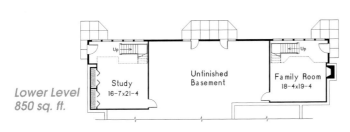

Lower Level
850 sq. ft.

*P*lan #581-025D-0019

2,074 total square feet of living area

Special features

- Unique sewing room is ideal for hobby enthusiasts and has counter-space for convenience
- Double walk-in closets are located in the luxurious master bath
- A built-in bookcase in the great room adds charm
- 3 bedrooms, 2 baths, 2-car side entry garage
- Slab foundation

Price Code C

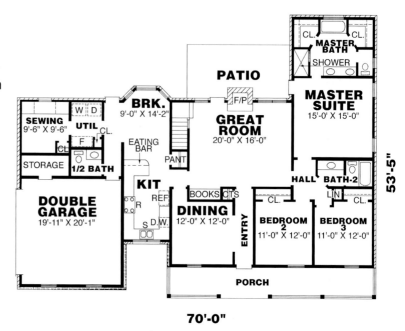

Plan #581-007D-0037

1,403 total square feet of living area

Special features

- ◆ Impressive living areas for a modest-sized home
- ◆ Special master/hall bath has linen storage, step-up tub and lots of window light
- ◆ Spacious closets everywhere you look
- ◆ 3 bedrooms, 2 baths, 2-car drive under garage
- ◆ Basement foundation

Price Code A

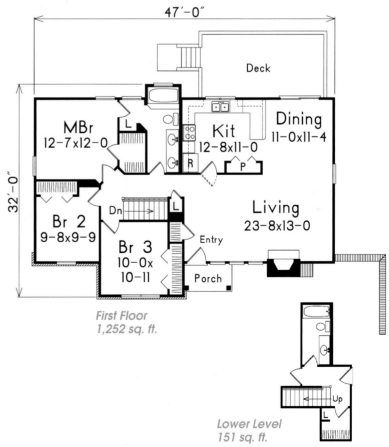

47'-0"

32'-0"

Deck

MBr
12-7x12-0

L

Kit
12-8x11-0

Dining
11-0x11-4

R

P

Br 2
9-8x9-9

Dn

L

Living
23-8x13-0

Br 3
10-0x
10-11

Entry

Porch

First Floor
1,252 sq. ft.

Up

L

Lower Level
151 sq. ft.

*F*ireplace In Great Room

*P*lan #581-038D-0040

1,642 total square feet of living area

Special features

- ◆ Built-in cabinet in dining room adds a custom feel
- ◆ Secondary bedrooms share an over-sized bath
- ◆ Master bedroom includes private bath with dressing table
- ◆ 3 bedrooms, 2 baths, 2-car garage
- ◆ Crawl space foundation

Price Code B

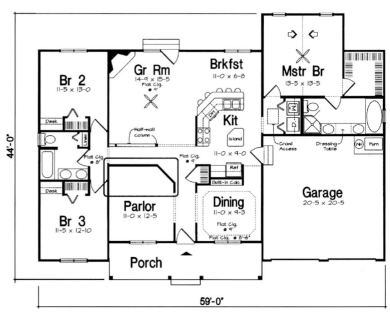

Optional Basement Stairs

Plan #581-007D-0049

1,791 total square feet of living area

Special features

◆ Vaulted great room and octagon-shaped dining area enjoy views of covered patio

◆ Kitchen features a pass-through to dining area, center island, large walk-in pantry and breakfast room with large bay window

◆ Master bedroom is vaulted with sitting area

◆ 4 bedrooms, 2 baths, 2-car garage with storage

◆ Basement foundation, drawings also include crawl space and slab foundations

Price Code C

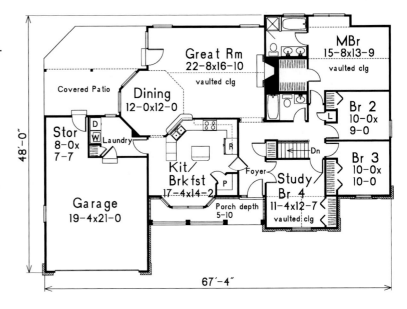

Plan #581-021D-0006

1,600 total square feet of living area

Special features

◆ Energy efficient home with 2" x 6" exterior walls

◆ Impressive sunken living room features a massive stone fireplace and 16' vaulted ceiling

◆ Dining room is conveniently located next to kitchen and divided for privacy

◆ Special amenities include sewing room, glass shelves in kitchen and master bath and a large utility area

◆ Sunken master bedroom features a distinctive sitting room

◆ 3 bedrooms, 2 baths, 2-car side entry garage

◆ Slab foundation, drawings also include crawl space and basement foundations

Price Code C

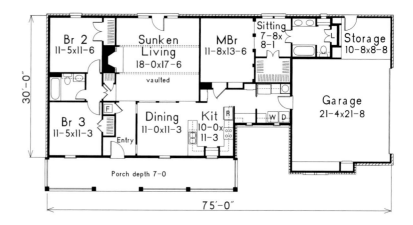

Plan #581-022D-0011

1,630 total square feet of living area

Special features

- ◆ Crisp facade and full windows front and back offer open viewing
- ◆ Wrap-around rear deck is accessible from breakfast room, dining room and master bedroom
- ◆ Vaulted ceilings in living room and master bedroom
- ◆ Sitting area and large walk-in closet complement master bedroom
- ◆ 3 bedrooms, 2 baths, 2-car garage
- ◆ Basement foundation

Price Code B

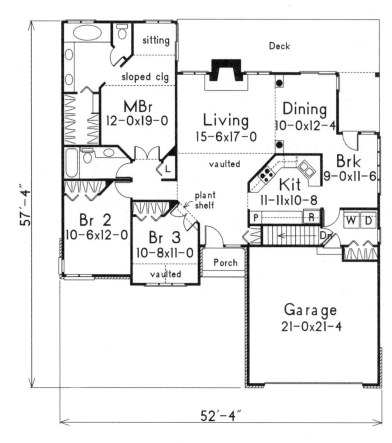

*P*lan #581-001D-0001

1,605 total square feet of living area

Special features

◆ Vaulted ceilings in great room, kitchen and breakfast area

◆ Spacious great room features large bay window, fireplace, built-in book-shelves and a convenient wet bar

◆ Dine in formal dining room or breakfast area overlooking rear yard, perfect for entertaining or everyday living

◆ Master bedroom has a spacious master bath with oval tub and separate shower

◆ 3 bedrooms, 2 baths, 2-car garage

◆ Basement foundation, drawings also include slab and crawl space foundations

Price Code B

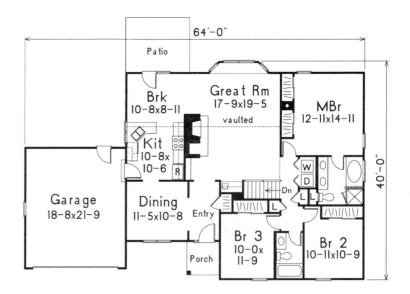

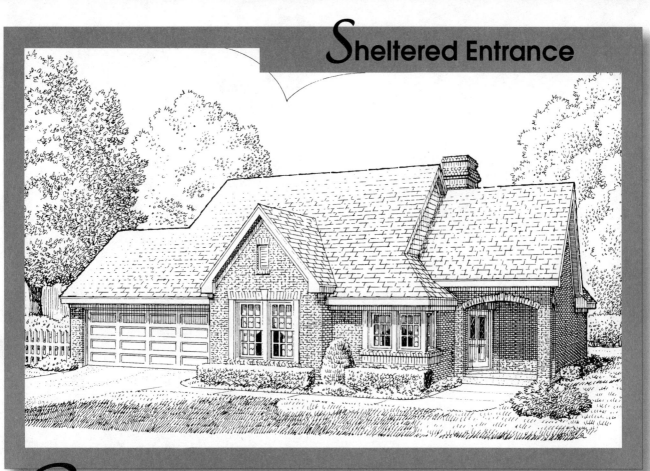

Plan #581-037D-0012

1,661 total square feet of living area

Special features

◆ Large open foyer with angled wall arrangement and high ceiling adds to spacious living room

◆ Kitchen and dining area have impressive cathedral ceilings and French door allowing access to the patio

◆ Utility room is conveniently located near the kitchen

◆ Secluded master bedroom has large walk-in closets, unique brick wall arrangement and 10' ceiling

◆ 3 bedrooms, 2 baths, 2-car garage

◆ Slab foundation

Price Code B

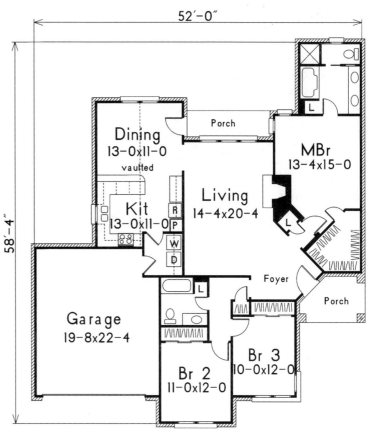

*D*ramatic Appeal

*P*lan #581-040D-0009

2,468 total square feet of living area

Special features

- ◆ Open floor plan has family room with columns, fireplace, triple French doors and 12' ceiling
- ◆ Master bath features double walk-in closets and vanities
- ◆ Bonus room above garage has a private stairway and is included in the total square footage
- ◆ Bedrooms are separate from main living space for privacy
- ◆ 3 bedrooms, 2 1/2 baths, 2-car side entry garage
- ◆ Slab foundation

Price Code D

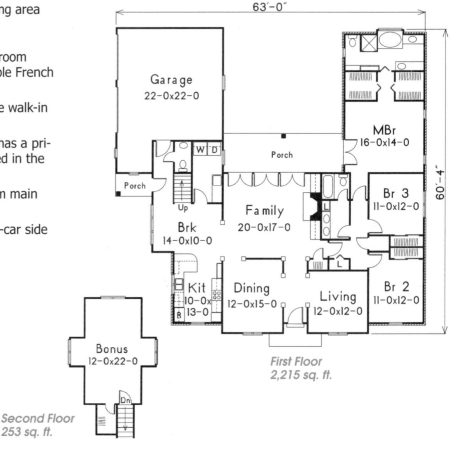

First Floor
2,215 sq. ft.

Second Floor
253 sq. ft.

Plan #581-001D-0069

1,504 total square feet of living area

Special features

◆ Private master bedroom features double walk-in closets, linen closet and bath

◆ Laundry room is conveniently located near garage

◆ Open great room and dining area create a spacious living atmosphere

◆ Generous closet space in secondary bedrooms

◆ Kitchen features breakfast bar, pantry and storage closet

◆ 3 bedrooms, 2 baths, 2-car garage

◆ Crawl space foundation, drawings also include basement and slab foundations

Price Code B

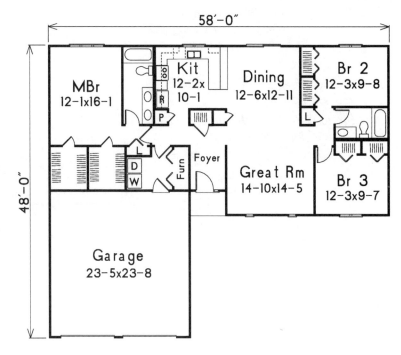

*P*lan #581-021D-0002

1,442 total square feet of living area

Special features

- ◆ Centrally located living room with recessed fireplace and 10' ceiling
- ◆ Large U-shaped kitchen offers an eating bar and pantry
- ◆ Expanded garage provides extra storage and work area
- ◆ Spacious master bedroom with sitting area and large walk-in closet
- ◆ 3 bedrooms, 2 baths, 2-car garage
- ◆ Slab foundation, drawings also include crawl space foundation

Price Code A

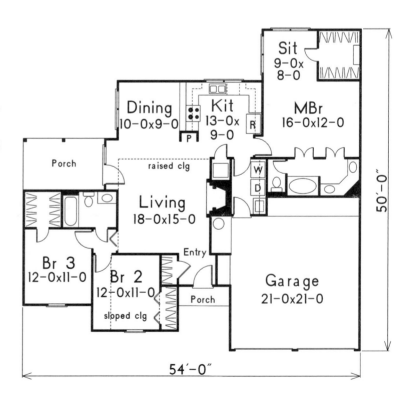

*P*lan #581-013D-0015

1,787 total square feet of living area

Special features

◆ Skylights brighten screened porch which connects to family room and deck outdoors

◆ Master bedroom features a comfortable sitting area, large private bath and direct access to screened porch

◆ Kitchen has serving bar which extends dining into family room

◆ 3 bedrooms, 2 baths, 2-car side entry garage

◆ Basement, crawl space or slab foundation, please specify when ordering

Price Code B

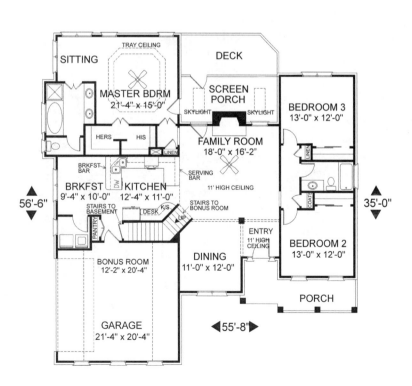

Plan #581-053D-0045

1,698 total square feet of living area

Special features

- ◆ Kitchen includes walk-in pantry and corner sink that faces living area
- ◆ Breakfast room is highlighted by an expanse of windows and access to the sun deck
- ◆ Recessed foyer opens into vaulted living room with fireplace
- ◆ Master bedroom features private bath with large walk-in closet
- ◆ 3 bedrooms, 2 baths, 2-car drive under garage
- ◆ Basement foundation

Price Code B

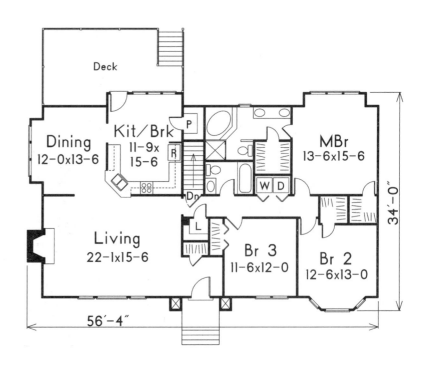

Plan #581-022D-0005

1,360 total square feet of living area

Special features

- ◆ Double-gabled front facade frames large windows
- ◆ Entry area is open to vaulted great room, fireplace and rear deck creating an open feel
- ◆ Vaulted ceiling and large windows add openness to kitchen/breakfast room
- ◆ Bedroom #3 easily converts to a den
- ◆ Plan easily adapts to crawl space or slab construction, with the utilities replacing the stairs
- ◆ 3 bedrooms, 2 baths, 2-car garage
- ◆ Basement foundation

Price Code A

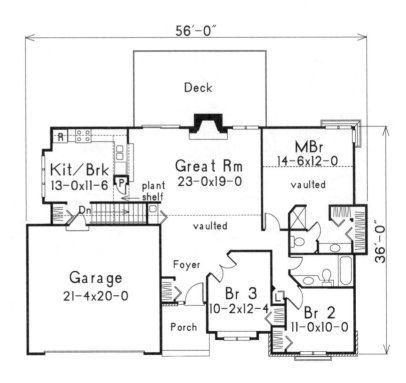

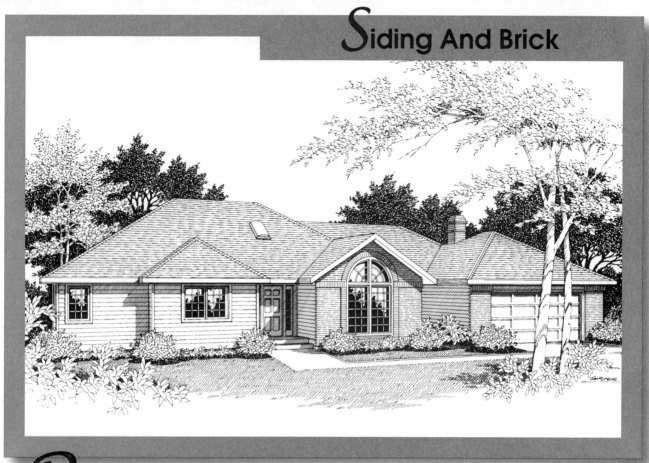

Plan #581-014D-0001

2,159 total square feet of living area

Special features

- ◆ Energy efficient home with 2" x 6" exterior walls
- ◆ Covered entry opens into large foyer with skylight and coat closet
- ◆ Master bedroom includes private bath with angled vanity, separate spa and shower and walk-in closet
- ◆ Family and living rooms feature vaulted ceilings and sunken floors for added openness
- ◆ Kitchen features an island counter and convenient pantry
- ◆ 3 bedrooms, 2 baths, 2-car garage
- ◆ Basement foundation, drawings also include crawl space and slab foundations

Price Code C

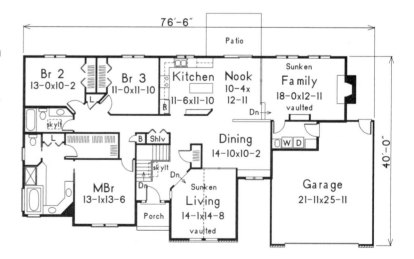

Mullioned Windows

Plan #581-053D-0004

1,740 total square feet of living area

Special features

- Coffered ceilings in dining room, specially treated ceilings in living room and master bedroom
- Master bedroom features large master bath with walk-in closet, double-vanity, separate shower and tub
- Both secondary bedrooms have ample closet space
- Large breakfast area convenient to the laundry, pantry and rear deck
- 3 bedrooms, 2 baths, 2-car drive under garage
- Basement foundation

Price Code B

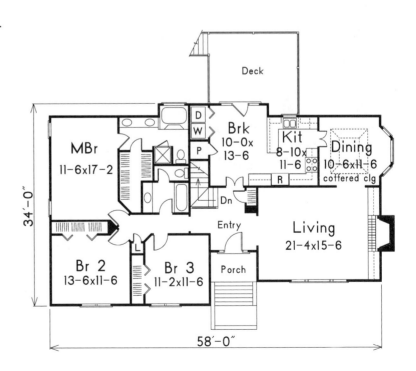

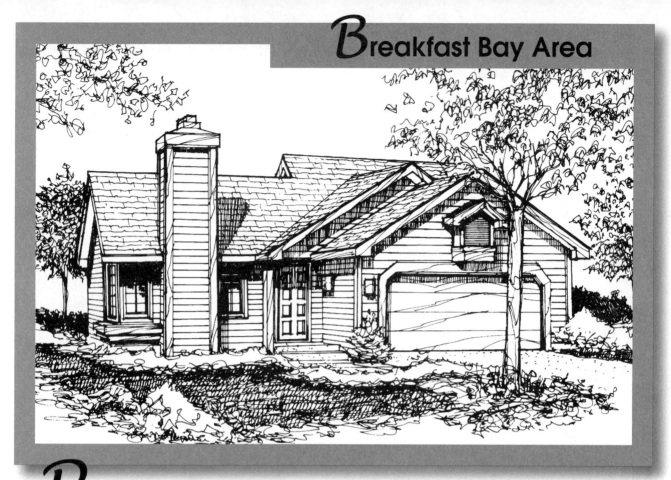

*P*lan #581-022D-0021

1,020 total square feet of living area

Special features

- ◆ Kitchen features open stairs, pass-through to great room, pantry and deck access
- ◆ Master bedroom features private entrance to bath, large walk-in closet and sliding doors to deck
- ◆ Informal entrance into home through the garage
- ◆ Great room has a vaulted ceiling and fireplace
- ◆ 2 bedrooms, 1 bath, 2-car garage
- ◆ Basement foundation

Price Code AA

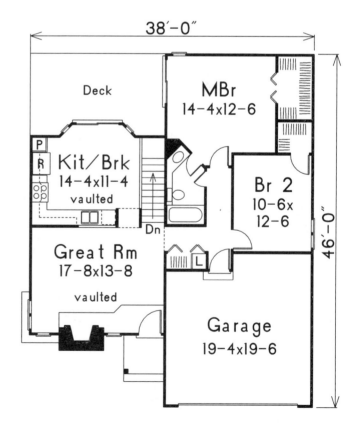

Plan #581-007D-0150

2,420 total square feet of living area

Special Features

◆ The huge great room has a fireplace with flanking shelves, a wide bay window and dining area surrounded with windows

◆ Many excellent features adorn the kitchen including a corner window sink, island snack bar, walk-in pantry and breakfast area with adjoining covered patio

◆ The apartment with its own exterior entrance and entry with coat closet accesses the dining and great rooms of the primary residence

◆ 4 bedrooms, 3 1/2 baths, 2-car garage

◆ Basement foundation

Price Code D

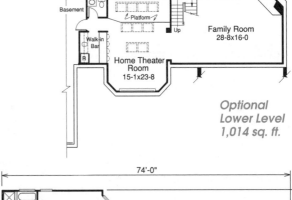

Optional Lower Level 1,014 sq. ft.

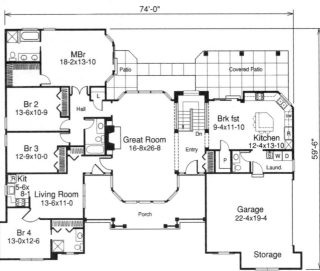

First Floor 2,420 sq. ft.

Cozy Breakfast Bay

Plan #581-037D-0030

2,397 total square feet of living area

Special features

◆ Varied ceiling heights throughout home

◆ All bedrooms boast walk-in closets

◆ Garage includes convenient storage area

◆ Angled kitchen counter overlooks spacious living room with fireplace

◆ Master bedroom has coffered ceiling and luxurious bath

◆ 4 bedrooms, 3 baths, 2-car side entry garage

◆ Slab foundation

Price Code D

Rear View

*I*deal For A Starter Home

*P*lan #581-001D-0088

800 total square feet of living area

Special features

- ◆ Master bedroom has walk-in closet and private access to bath
- ◆ Large living room features handy coat closet
- ◆ Kitchen includes side entrance, closet and convenient laundry area
- ◆ 2 bedrooms, 1 bath
- ◆ Basement foundation

Price Code AAA

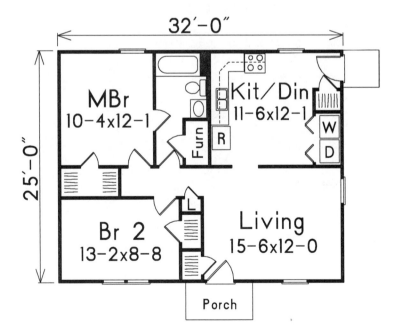

*P*lan #581-001D-0033

1,624 total square feet of living area

Special features

- Master bedroom has a private entry from the outdoors
- Garage is adjacent to the utility room with convenient storage closet
- Large family and dining area features a fireplace and porch access
- Pass-through kitchen opens directly to cozy breakfast area
- 3 bedrooms, 2 baths, 2-car side entry garage
- Basement foundation, drawings also include crawl space and slab foundations

Price Code B

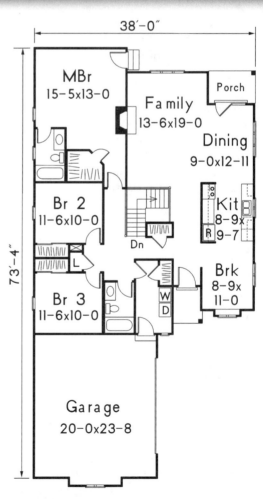

Plan #581-021D-0008

1,266 total square feet of living area

Special features

- ◆ Narrow frontage is perfect for small lots
- ◆ Energy efficient home with 2" x 6" exterior walls
- ◆ Prominent central hall provides a convenient connection for all main rooms
- ◆ Design incorporates full-size master bedroom complete with dressing room, bath and walk-in closet
- ◆ Angled kitchen includes handy laundry facilities and is adjacent to an oversized storage area
- ◆ 3 bedrooms, 2 baths, 2-car rear entry garage
- ◆ Crawl space foundation, drawings also include slab foundation

Price Code A

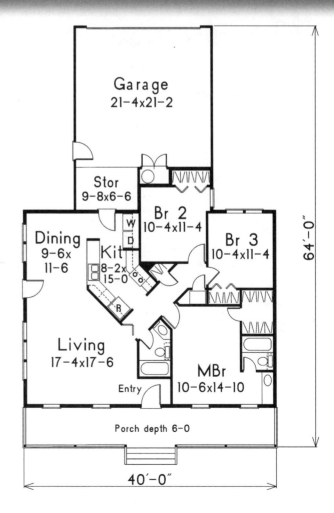

Covered Porch

Plan #581-040D-0015

1,655 total square feet of living area

Special features

- ◆ Master bedroom features a 9' ceiling, walk-in closet and bath with dressing area
- ◆ Oversized family room includes 10' ceiling and masonry see-through fireplace
- ◆ Island kitchen with convenient access to laundry room
- ◆ Handy covered walkway from garage to kitchen and dining area
- ◆ 3 bedrooms, 2 baths, 2-car garage
- ◆ Crawl space foundation

Price Code B

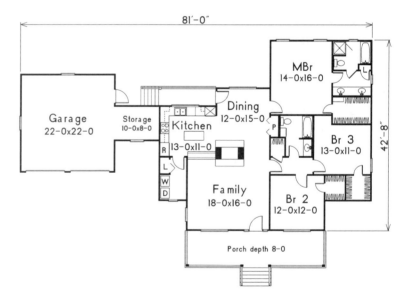

Plenty Of Detail

Plan #581-035D-0011

1,945 total square feet of living area

Special features

- ◆ Master suite is separated from other bedrooms for privacy
- ◆ Vaulted breakfast room is directly off great room
- ◆ Kitchen includes a built-in desk area
- ◆ Elegant dining room has an arched window
- ◆ 4 bedrooms, 2 baths, 2-car side entry garage
- ◆ Walk-out basement, crawl space or slab foundation, please specify when ordering

Price Code C

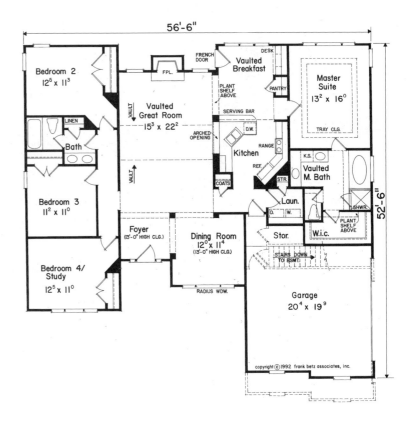

56'-6"

Bedroom 2
12⁵ x 11³

FPL.

FRENCH DOOR

DESK

Vaulted Breakfast

VAULT

Vaulted Great Room
15³ x 22²

PLANT SHELF ABOVE

PANTRY

Master Suite
13² x 16⁰

LINEN

SERVING BAR

D.W.

TRAY CLG.

Bath

ARCHED OPENING

Kitchen

RANGE

K.S.

VAULT

REF.

Vaulted M. Bath

Bedroom 3
11² x 11⁰

COATS

STR.

Laun.

D.   W.

SHWR.

PLANT SHELF ABOVE

Foyer
(13'-0" HIGH CLG.)

Dining Room
12⁰ x 11⁴
(13'-0" HIGH CLG.)

Stor.

W.i.c.

52'-6"

STAIRS DOWN TO BSMT.

Bedroom 4/ Study
12⁵ x 11⁰

RADIUS WDW.

Garage
20⁴ x 19⁹

copyright © 1992 frank betz associates, inc.

Plan #581-001D-0021

1,416 total square feet of living area

Special features

- ◆ Excellent floor plan eases traffic
- ◆ Master bedroom features private bath
- ◆ Foyer opens to both formal living room and informal family room
- ◆ Great room has access to the outdoors through sliding doors
- ◆ 3 bedrooms, 2 baths, 2-car garage
- ◆ Crawl space foundation, drawings also include basement foundation

Price Code A

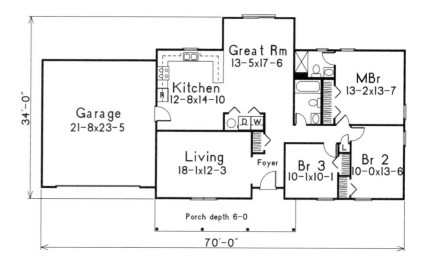

Plan #581-022D-0027

1,847 total square feet of living area

Special features

◆ Kitchen includes island cooktop and sunny breakfast area

◆ Master bedroom features vaulted ceilings and skylighted bath with large tub, separate shower and walk-in closet

◆ Service bar eases entertaining in vaulted dining and living rooms

◆ Family room, complete with corner fireplace, accesses outdoor patio

◆ 3 bedrooms, 2 baths, 2-car garage

◆ Slab foundation

Price Code C

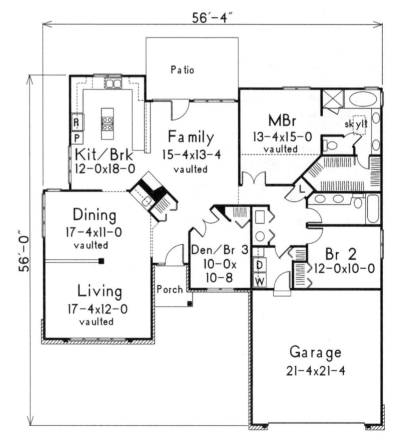

Plan #581-007D-0018

1,941 total square feet of living area

Special features

- Dramatic, exciting and spacious interior
- Vaulted great room is brightened by sunken atrium window wall and skylights
- Vaulted U-shaped gourmet kitchen with plant shelf opens to dining room
- First floor half bath features space for stackable washer and dryer
- 4 bedrooms, 2 1/2 baths, 2-car garage
- Walk-out basement foundation

Price Code C

Lower Level
945 sq. ft.

First Floor
996 sq. ft.

Plan #581-061D-0001

1,747 total square feet of living area

Special features

- ◆ Entry opens into large family room with coat closet, angled fireplace and attractive plant shelf
- ◆ Kitchen and master bedroom access covered patio
- ◆ Functional kitchen includes ample workspace
- ◆ 4 bedrooms, 2 baths, 2-car garage
- ◆ Slab foundation

Price Code B

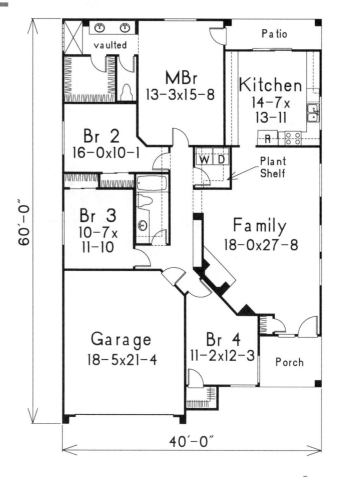

Three-Car Garage

Plan #581-007D-0139

1,348 total square feet of living area

Special features

- Ideal retirement home or lakeside retreat with a country flavor
- The living room has a stone corner fireplace and carefully planned shelving for a flat panel TV and components
- A luxury bath, huge walk-in closet and covered deck adjoin the master bedroom
- The lower level is comprised of a guest bedroom, hall bath and garage with space for two cars and a boat
- 2 bedrooms, 2 1/2 baths, 3-car rear entry garage
- Walk-out basement foundation

Price Code A

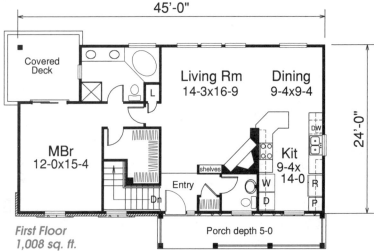

First Floor
1,008 sq. ft.

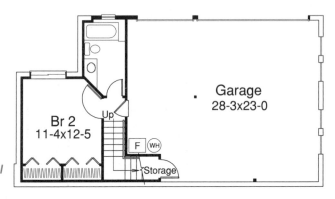

Lower Level
340 sq. ft.

Plan #581-053D-0055

1,803 total square feet of living area

Special features

- ◆ Master bedroom features raised ceiling and private bath with walk-in closet, large double-bowl vanity and separate tub and shower
- ◆ U-shaped kitchen includes corner sink and convenient pantry
- ◆ Vaulted living room complete with fireplace and built-in cabinet
- ◆ 3 bedrooms, 2 baths, 3-car drive under garage
- ◆ Basement foundation

Price Code C

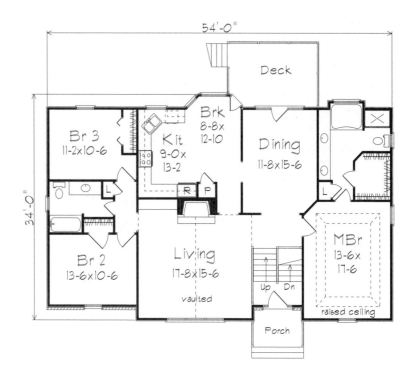

Plan #581-001D-0044

1,375 total square feet of living area

Special features

◆ Attractive gables highlight home's exterior

◆ Centrally located living room with bay area

◆ Master bedroom features patio access, double walk-in-closets and private bath

◆ Side entry garage includes handy storage area

◆ 3 bedrooms, 2 baths, 2-car side entry garage

◆ Crawl space foundation, drawings also include basement and slab foundations

Price Code A

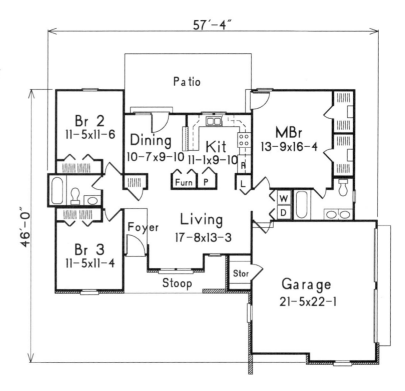

Plan #581-027D-0008

3,411 total square feet of living area

Special features

◆ Foyer opens to large study with raised ceiling

◆ Master bedroom features octagon-shaped raised ceiling and private bath with double vanity and corner whirlpool tub

◆ Expansive windows and a two-way fireplace in great room

◆ 3 bedrooms, 3 baths, 3-car garage

◆ Basement foundation

Price Code F

*First Floor
2,182 sq. ft.*

*Lower Level
1,229 sq. ft.*

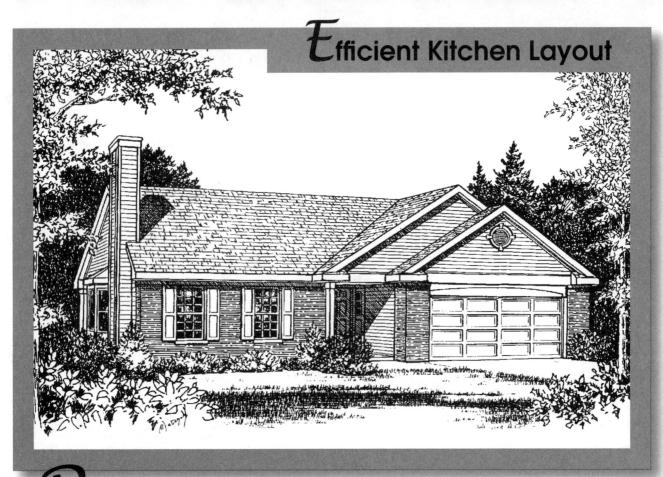

*P*lan #581-058D-0024

1,598 total square feet of living area

Special features

◆ Additional storage area in garage

◆ Double-door entry into master bedroom with luxurious master bath

◆ Entry opens into large family room with vaulted ceiling and open stairway to basement

◆ 3 bedrooms, 2 baths, 2-car garage

◆ Basement foundation

Price Code B

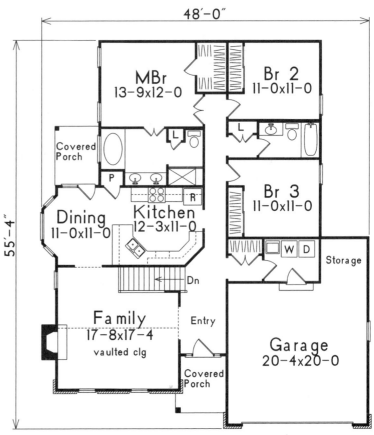

Plan #581-067D-0004

1,698 total square feet of living area

Special features

- ◆ Vaulted master bedroom has a private bath and a walk-in closet
- ◆ Decorative columns flank the entrance to the dining room
- ◆ Open great room is perfect for gathering family together
- ◆ 3 bedrooms, 2 1/2 baths, 2-car side entry garage with storage
- ◆ Basement, crawl space or slab foundation, please specify when ordering

Price Code B

Width 59'-0"
Depth 61'-0"

*P*lan #581-007D-0115

588 total square feet of living area

Special features

- ◆ May be built as a duplex, 4-car garage or apartment garage/vacation cabin as shown
- ◆ Very livable plan in a small footprint
- ◆ Living room features a functional entry, bayed dining area, corner fireplace and opens to kitchen with breakfast bar
- ◆ 1 bedroom, 1 bath, 2-car side entry garage
- ◆ Slab foundation
- ◆ 1,176 square feet of living area when built as a duplex

Price Code AAA

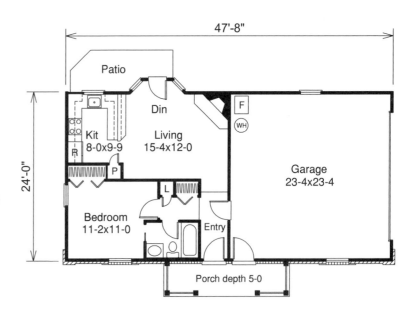

Quaint Box Window Seat

Plan #581-031D-0003

1,665 total square feet of living area

Special features

◆ Oversized family room has corner fireplace and double-doors leading to patio

◆ Bedroom locations give privacy from gathering areas

◆ 3 bedrooms, 2 baths, 2-car garage

◆ Slab foundation

Price Code B

Width: 50'-0"
Depth: 55'-0"

Plan #581-053D-0036

1,567 total square feet of living area

Special features

- Front gables and extended porch add charm to facade
- Large bay windows add brightness to breakfast and dining rooms
- The master bath boasts an oversized tub, separate shower, double sinks and large walk-in closet
- Living room features a vaulted ceiling and a prominent fireplace
- 3 bedrooms, 2 baths, 2-car drive under garage
- Basement foundation

Price Code B

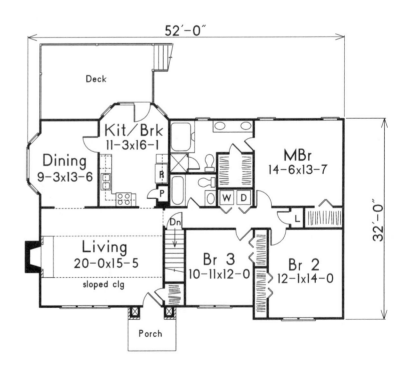

Plan #581-010D-0003

1,560 total square feet of living area

Special features

◆ Cozy breakfast room is tucked at the rear of this home and features plenty of windows for natural light

◆ Large entry has easy access to secondary bedrooms, laundry/utility, dining and living rooms

◆ Private master bedroom

◆ Kitchen overlooks living room with fireplace and patio access

◆ 3 bedrooms, 2 baths, 2-car garage

◆ Slab foundation

Price Code B

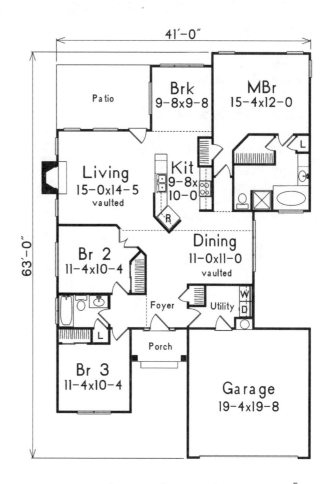

*P*lan #581-047D-0020

1,783 total square feet of living area

Special features

◆ Formal living and dining rooms in the front of the home

◆ Kitchen overlooks breakfast area

◆ Conveniently located laundry area near kitchen and master bedroom

◆ 3 bedrooms, 2 baths, 2-car garage

◆ Slab foundation

Price Code B

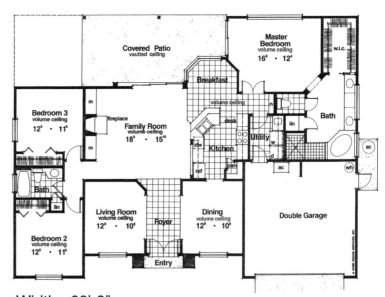

Width: 60'-0"
Depth: 45'-0"

*E*legant Brick Ranch

*P*lan #581-051D-0054

2,590 total square feet of living area

Special features

◆ Sunny bayed dining area leads to a wood deck

◆ Inviting entry is open and airy

◆ Enormous laundry area has a half bath, corner sink and a storage closet

◆ 3 bedrooms, 2 1/2 baths, 3-car side entry garage

◆ Basement or walk-out basement foundation, please specify when ordering

Price Code D

Lower Level
890 sq. ft.

First Floor
1,700 sq. ft.

*H*igh-Style Vaulted Ranch

*P*lan #581-014D-0007

1,453 total square feet of living area

Special features

- ◆ Decorative vents, window trim, shutters and brick blend to create dramatic curb appeal
- ◆ Energy efficient home with 2" x 6" exterior walls
- ◆ Kitchen opens to living area and includes salad sink in the island, pantry and handy laundry room
- ◆ Exquisite master bedroom is highlighted by a vaulted ceiling
- ◆ Dressing area with walk-in closet, private bath and spa tub/shower
- ◆ 3 bedrooms, 2 baths, 2-car garage
- ◆ Basement foundation, drawings also include crawl space foundation

Price Code A

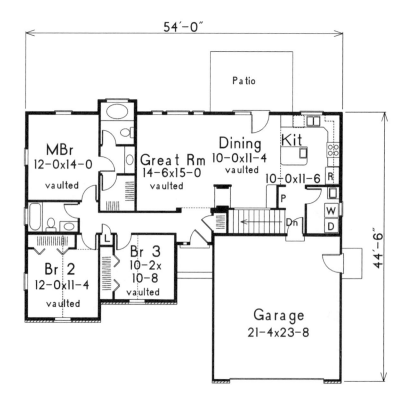

Plan #581-037D-0026

1,824 total square feet of living area

Special features

- ◆ Living room features 10' ceiling, fireplace and media center
- ◆ Dining room includes bay window and convenient kitchen access
- ◆ Master bedroom features large walk-in closet and double-doors leading into master bath
- ◆ Modified U-shaped kitchen features pantry and bar
- ◆ 3 bedrooms, 2 baths, 2-car detached garage
- ◆ Slab foundation

Price Code C

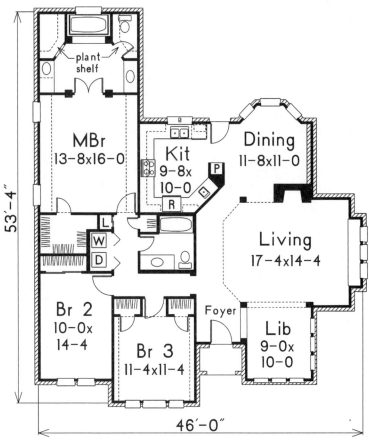

*P*lan #581-070D-0002

1,700 total square feet of living area

Special features

◆ Open and airy dining room
◆ Secondary bedrooms share a central bath
◆ 3 bedrooms, 2 baths, 2-car garage
◆ Basement foundation

Price Code B

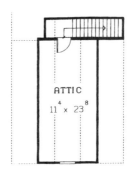

Optional Second Floor 268 sq. ft.

ATTIC
$11^4 \times 23^8$

First Floor 1,700 sq. ft.

Width: 58'-4"
Depth: 57'-4"

Plan #581-045D-0010

1,558 total square feet of living area

Special features

- Illuminated spaces created with access to outdoor living
- Vaulted master bedroom has private bath with whirlpool tub, separate shower and large walk-in closet
- Convenient laundry area has garage access
- U-shaped kitchen is adjacent to sunny breakfast area
- 2 bedrooms, 2 baths, 2-car rear entry garage
- Basement foundation

Price Code B

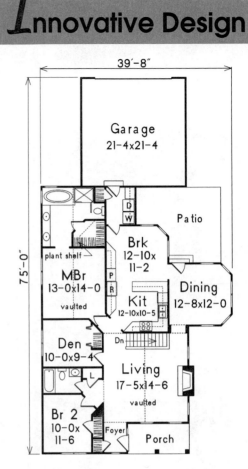

Plan #581-001D-0071

1,440 total square feet of living area

Special features

- Spaciousness is created with open living and dining areas
- Entry foyer features coat closet and half wall leading into living area
- Walk-in pantry adds convenience to U-shaped kitchen
- Spacious utility room adjacent to garage
- 3 bedrooms, 2 baths, 2-car side entry garage
- Crawl space foundation, drawings also include basement and slab foundations

Price Code A

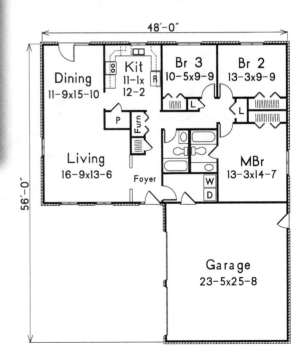

Plan #581-016D-0062

1,380 total square feet of living area

Special features

- Built-in bookshelves complement fireplace in great room
- Lots of storage space near laundry room and kitchen
- Covered porch has views of the backyard
- 3 bedrooms, 2 baths, optional 2-car side entry garage
- Basement, crawl space or slab foundation, please specify when ordering

Price Code A

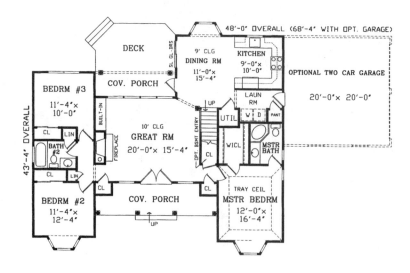

Circle-Top Window

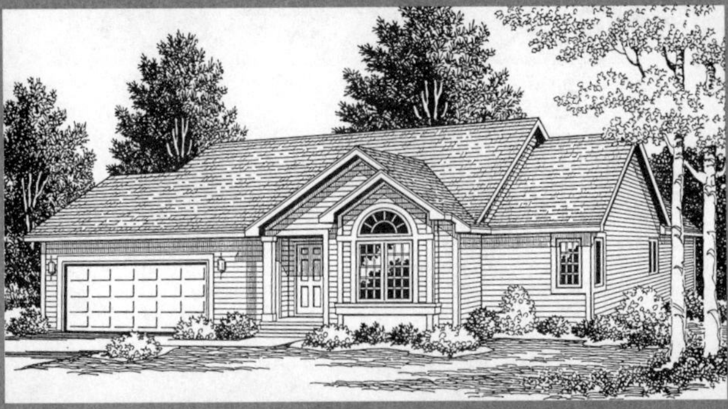

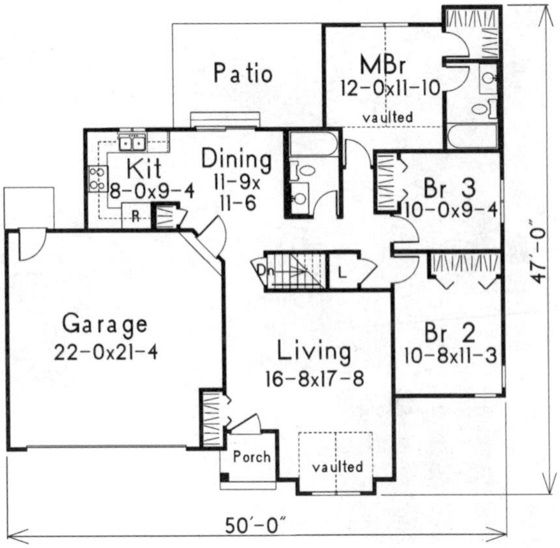

Plan #581-041D-0004

1,195 total square feet of living area

Special features

- Dining room opens onto the patio
- Master bedroom features vaulted ceiling, private bath and walk-in closet
- Coat closets located by both the entrances
- Convenient secondary entrance at the back of the garage
- 3 bedrooms, 2 baths, 2-car garage
- Basement foundation

Price Code AA

Country Home

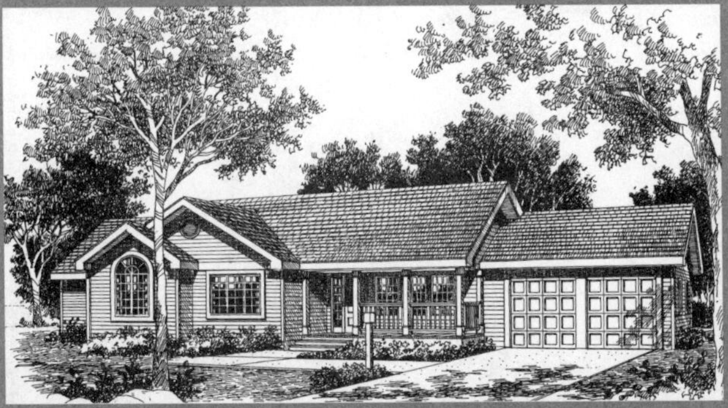

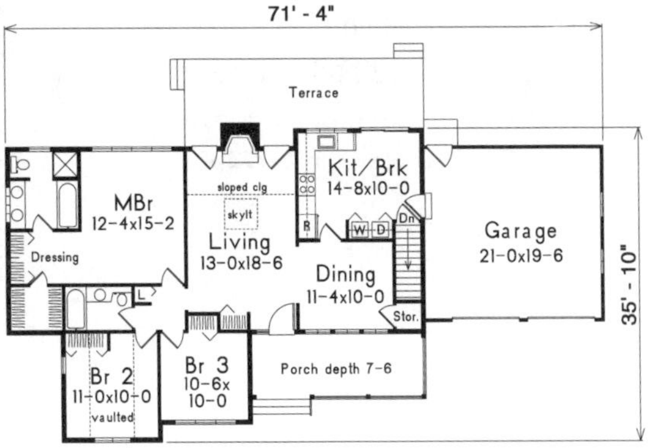

Plan #581-017D-0005

1,367 total square feet of living area

Special features

- Neat front porch shelters the entrance
- Dining room has full wall of windows and convenient storage area
- Breakfast area leads to the rear terrace
- Large living room with high ceiling, skylight and fireplace
- 3 bedrooms, 2 baths, 2-car garage
- Basement foundation, drawings also include slab foundation

Price Code B

*P*lan #581-020D-0003

1,420 total square feet of living area

Special features

- Energy efficient home with 2" x 6" exterior walls
- Living room has 12' ceiling, corner fireplace and atrium doors leading to covered porch
- Separate master suite has garden bath and walk-in closet
- 3 bedrooms, 2 baths, 2-car garage
- Slab foundation, drawings also include crawl space foundation

Price Code A

Plan #581-036D-0060

1,760 total square feet of living area

Special features

- ◆ Stone and brick exterior has old world charm
- ◆ Master bedroom includes a sitting area and is situated away from other bedrooms for privacy
- ◆ Great room has fireplace, built-in bookshelves and an entertainment center
- ◆ 3 bedrooms, 2 baths, 2-car side entry garage
- ◆ Slab foundation

Price Code B

Bay Windows

Plan #581-035D-0035

2,322 total square feet of living area

Special features

- ◆ Vaulted family room has fireplace and access to kitchen
- ◆ Decorative columns and arched openings surround dining area
- ◆ Master suite has a sitting room and grand scale bath
- ◆ Kitchen includes island with serving bar
- ◆ 3 bedrooms, 2 1/2 baths, 2-car side entry garage
- ◆ Walk-out basement, crawl space or slab foundation, please specify when ordering

Price Code D

High-Styled Master Bedroom

Plan #581-061D-0003

2,255 total square feet of living area

Special features

♦ Walk-in closets in all bedrooms

♦ Plant shelf graces hallway

♦ Large functional kitchen adjoins family room with fireplace and access outdoors

♦ Master bath comes complete with double vanity, enclosed toilet, separate tub and shower and cozy fireplace

♦ Living/dining room combine for a large formal gathering room

♦ 4 bedrooms, 2 1/2 baths, 3-car garage

♦ Slab foundation

Price Code D

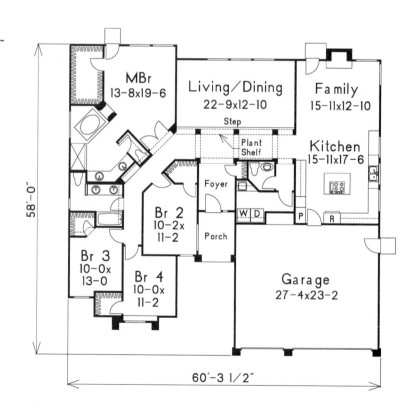

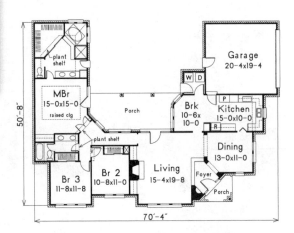

Plan #581-037D-0003

1,996 total square feet of living area

Special features

- Garden courtyard comes with large porch and direct access to master bedroom suite, breakfast room and garage
- Sculptured entrance has artful plant shelves
- Master bedroom boasts French doors, garden tub, desk with bookshelves and generous storage
- 3 bedrooms, 2 baths, 2-car side entry garage
- Slab foundation, drawings also include crawl space foundation

Price Code D

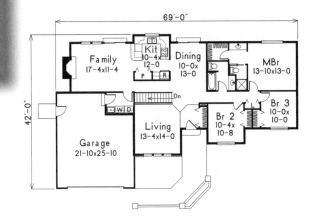

Plan #581-014D-0006

1,588 total square feet of living area

Special features

- Family and dining rooms access rear patio
- Angled walkway leads guests by a landscape area
- Master bedroom with separate dressing area, walk-in closet and private bath
- U-shaped kitchen has large pantry and eating bar
- 3 bedrooms, 2 baths, 2-car garage
- Basement foundation, drawings also include crawl space and slab foundations

Price Code B

*P*lan #581-058D-0012

1,143 total square feet of living area

Special features

- ◆ Enormous stone fireplace in family room adds warmth and character
- ◆ Spacious kitchen with breakfast bar overlooks family room
- ◆ Separate dining area great for entertaining
- ◆ Vaulted family room and kitchen create an open atmosphere
- ◆ 2 bedrooms, 1 bath
- ◆ Crawl space foundation

Price Code AA

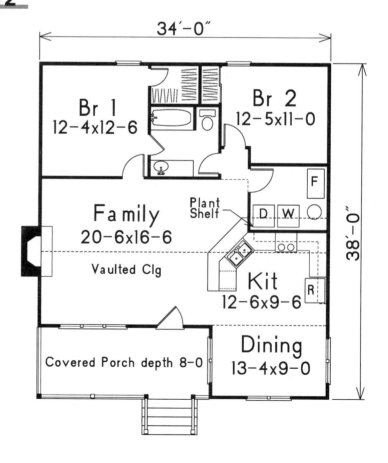

34'-0"

38'-0"

Br 1
12-4x12-6

Br 2
12-5x11-0

F

Family
20-6x16-6

Vaulted Clg

Plant Shelf

D W

Kit
12-6x9-6

R

Dining
13-4x9-0

Covered Porch depth 8-0

Plan #581-068D-0010

1,849 total square feet of living area

Special features

- Laundry/mud room has many extras
- Master bath has corner jacuzzi tub, double sinks, separate shower and walk-in closet
- Kitchen has wrap-around eating counter
- 3 bedrooms, 2 1/2 baths, 2-car side entry garage
- Slab foundation, drawings also include crawl space foundation

Price Code C

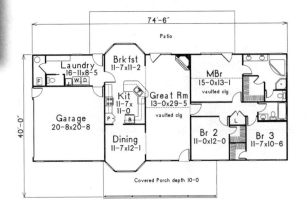

Plan #581-013D-0022

1,992 total square feet of living area

Special features

- Angled walls add drama to many of the living areas including family room, master bedroom and breakfast area
- Covered porch includes spa and an outdoor kitchen with sink, refrigerator and cooktop
- Enter master bath to find a dramatic corner oversized tub
- 4 bedrooms, 3 baths, 2-car side entry garage
- Basement, crawl space or slab foundation, please specify when ordering

Price Code C

Plan #581-007D-0044

1,516 total square feet of living area

Special features

- ◆ Spacious great room is open to dining area with a bay and unique stair location
- ◆ Attractive and well-planned kitchen offers breakfast bar and built-in pantry
- ◆ Smartly designed master bedroom enjoys patio views
- ◆ 3 bedrooms, 2 baths, 2-car garage
- ◆ Basement foundation

Price Code B

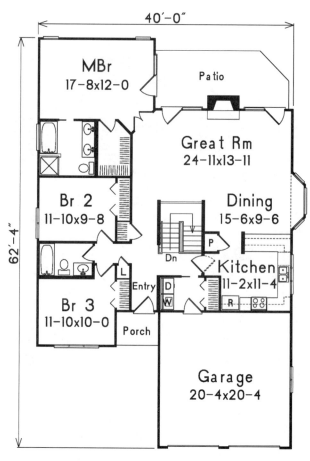

Plan #581-043D-0001

3,158 total square feet of living area

Special features

◆ Coffered ceiling in entry

◆ Vaulted ceilings in living room, master bedroom and family room

◆ Interior columns accent the entry, living and dining areas

◆ Kitchen island has eating bar adding extra seating

◆ 3 bedrooms, 2 1/2 baths, 3-car garage

◆ Crawl space foundation

Price Code E

Corner Fireplace

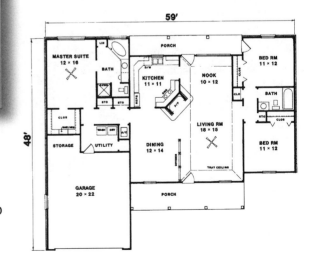

Plan #581-069D-0013

1,646 total square feet of living area

Special features

◆ Master suite has a luxury bath with a corner whirlpool tub

◆ Large living room connects to the breakfast nook adding spaciousness

◆ Secondary bedrooms are separate from master suite for privacy

◆ 3 bedrooms, 2 baths, 2-car garage

◆ Slab or crawl space foundation, please specify when ordering

Price Code B

Colossal Great Room

*P*lan #581-068D-0007

1,599 total square feet of living area

Special features

- ◆ Efficiently designed kitchen with large pantry and easy access to laundry room
- ◆ Bedroom #3 has a charming window seat
- ◆ Master bedroom has a full bath and large walk-in closet
- ◆ 4 bedrooms, 2 baths, 2-car garage
- ◆ Basement foundation, drawings also include crawl space and slab foundations

Price Code B

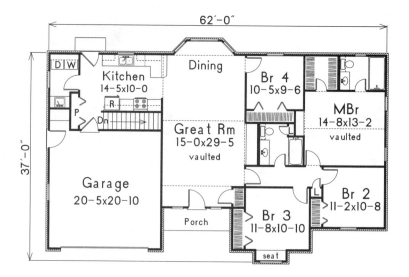

Plan #581-007D-0124

1,944 total square feet of living area

Special features

- ◆ Spacious surrounding porch, covered patio and stone fireplace create an expansive ponderosa appearance
- ◆ Large entry leads to a grand-sized great room featuring a vaulted ceiling, fireplace, wet bar and porch access
- ◆ The U-shaped kitchen is open to the hearth room and enjoys a snack bar, fireplace and patio access
- ◆ 3 bedrooms, 2 baths, 3-car detached garage
- ◆ Basement foundation

Price Code C

Plan #581-038D-0018

1,792 total square feet of living area

Special features

- ◆ Master bedroom has a private bath and large walk-in closet
- ◆ A central stone fireplace and windows on two walls are focal points in the living room
- ◆ Decorative beams and sloped ceilings add interest to the kitchen, living and dining rooms
- ◆ 3 bedrooms, 2 baths, 2-car drive under garage
- ◆ Basement foundation

Price Code B

*C*lassic Styling

*P*lan #581-024D-0018

2,246 total square feet of living area

Special features

◆ Enormous master bedroom and bath have all the amenities

◆ Covered rear porch is accessible to all parts of the home

◆ Kitchen features island with sink, large pantry and plenty of cabinet space

◆ 4 bedrooms, 2 1/2 baths, 2-car side entry garage

◆ Slab foundation

Price Code D

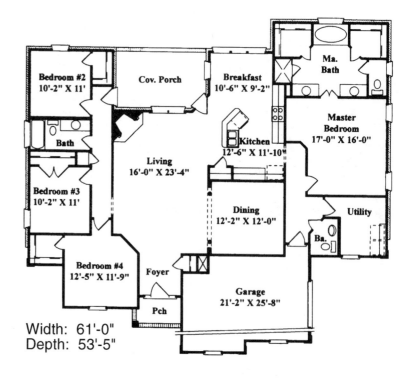

Bedroom #2
10'-2" X 11'

Bath

Bedroom #3
10'-2" X 11'

Cov. Porch

Living
16'-0" X 23'-4"

Bedroom #4
12'-5" X 11'-9"

Foyer

Pch

Breakfast
10'-6" X 9'-2"

Kitchen
12'-6" X 11'-10"

Dining
12'-2" X 12'-0"

Garage
21'-2" X 25'-8"

Ma. Bath

Master Bedroom
17'-0" X 16'-0"

Utility

Ba.

Width: 61'-0"
Depth: 53'-5"

Plan #581-007D-0149

1,929 total square feet of living area

Special features

- The grand room has a vaulted ceiling, brick and wood mantle fireplace and double-doors to rear patio
- The U-shaped kitchen has a built-in pantry, computer desk, breakfast bar and breakfast room with bay window
- The vaulted master bedroom has a large walk-in closet
- 4 bedrooms, 3 baths, 3-car garage
- Crawl space foundation, drawings also include slab and basement foundations

Price Code C

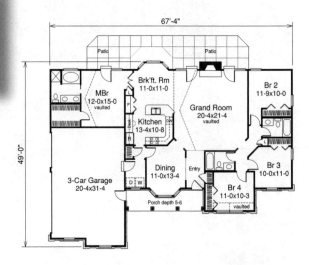

Plan #581-043D-0003

1,890 total square feet of living area

Special features

- Inviting covered porch
- Vaulted ceilings in living, dining and family rooms
- Kitchen is open to family room and nook
- Arch accented master bath has spa tub, double sinks and walk-in closet
- 3 bedrooms, 2 baths, 2-car garage
- Crawl space foundation

Price Code C

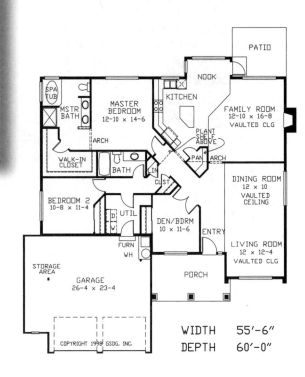

Dramatic Cathedral Ceilings

Plan #581-034D-0001

1,436 total square feet of living area

Special features

- Covered entry is inviting
- Kitchen has handy breakfast bar which overlooks great room and dining room
- Private master bedroom with bath and walk-in closet is separate from other bedrooms
- 3 bedrooms, 2 baths, 2-car garage
- Basement foundation

Price Code A

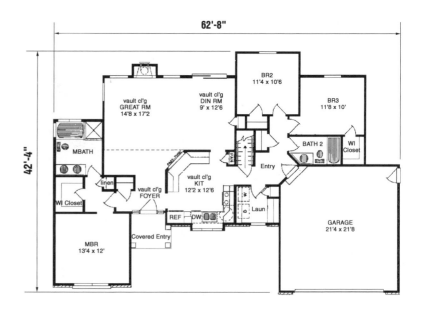

Plan #581-058D-0025

2,164 total square feet of living area

Special features

- Great design for entertaining with wet bar and see-through fireplace in great room
- Vaulted ceilings enlarge the master bedroom, great room and kitchen/breakfast area
- Great room features great view to the rear of the home
- 3 bedrooms, 2 1/2 baths, 2-car side entry garage
- Basement foundation

Price Code C

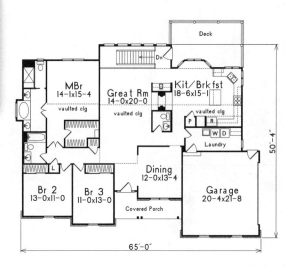

Plan #581-035D-0003

2,115 total square feet of living area

Special features

- Cozy living room/den has a double-door entry and makes an ideal office space
- Kitchen has serving bar which overlooks vaulted breakfast area and family room
- Master suite has all the amenities
- 3 bedrooms, 2 baths, 2-car side entry garage
- Walk-out basement, crawl space or slab foundation, please specify when ordering

Price Code C

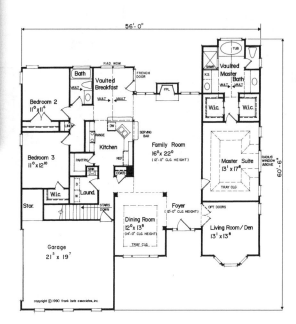

*I*nviting Vaulted Entry

*P*lan #581-013D-0025

2,097 total square feet of living area

Special features

- ◆ Angled kitchen, family room and eating area adds interest to this home
- ◆ Family room includes a T.V. niche making this a cozy place to relax
- ◆ Sumptuous master bedroom includes sitting area, double walk-in closet and a full bath with double vanities
- ◆ 3 bedrooms, 3 baths, 3-car side entry garage
- ◆ Crawl space or slab foundation, please specify when ordering

Price Code C

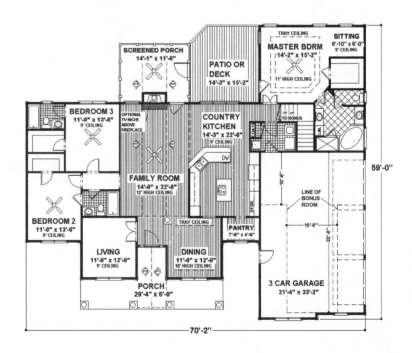

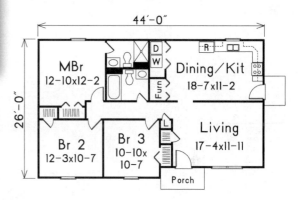

Plan #581-001D-0043

1,104 total square feet of living area

Special features

- ◆ Master bedroom includes private bath
- ◆ Convenient side entrance to dining area/kitchen
- ◆ Laundry area located near kitchen
- ◆ Large living area creates a comfortable atmosphere
- ◆ 3 bedrooms, 2 baths
- ◆ Crawl space foundation, drawings also include basement and slab foundations

Price Code AA

Traditional Elegance

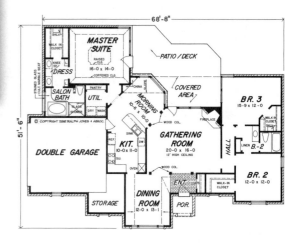

Plan #581-060D-0006

1,945 total square feet of living area

Special features

- ◆ Large gathering room has corner fireplace and 12' ceiling
- ◆ Master suite has a coffered ceiling and French door leading to the patio/deck
- ◆ Master bath has a cultured marble seat, separate shower and tub
- ◆ 3 bedrooms, 2 baths, 2-car side entry garage
- ◆ Slab or crawl space foundation, please specify when ordering

Price Code C

Front Porch Adds Style

Plan #581-040D-0010

1,496 total square feet of living area

Special features

- ◆ Master bedroom features a tray ceiling, walk-in closet and spacious bath
- ◆ Vaulted ceiling and fireplace grace family room
- ◆ Dining room is adjacent to kitchen and features access to rear porch
- ◆ Convenient access to utility room from kitchen
- ◆ 3 bedrooms, 2 baths, 2-car drive under garage
- ◆ Basement foundation

Price Code A

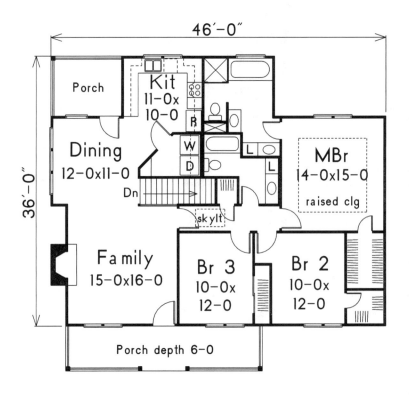

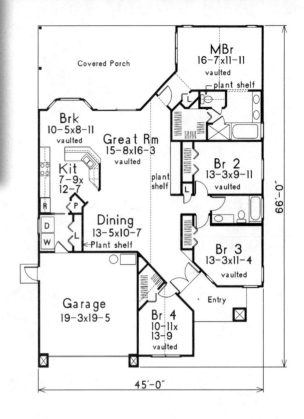

Plan #581-048D-0001

1,865 total square feet of living area

Special features

◆ Foyer opens into expansive dining area and great room

◆ Home features vaulted ceilings throughout

◆ Master bedroom has an angled entry, vaulted ceiling, plant shelf and bath with double vanity, tub and shower

◆ 4 bedrooms, 2 baths, 2-car garage

◆ Slab foundation, drawings also include crawl space foundation

Price Code D

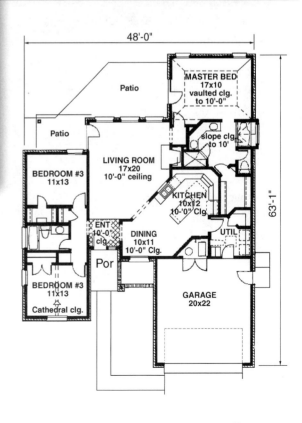

Plan #581-036D-0046

1,653 total square feet of living area

Special features

◆ Open kitchen accesses living room and backyard through sliding glass doors

◆ Master bedroom is separated from rest of the bedrooms for privacy

◆ Handy work island in kitchen

◆ 3 bedrooms, 2 baths, 2-car garage

◆ Slab foundation

Price Code B

Angles Add Interest

Plan #581-035D-0039

2,201 total square feet of living area

Special features

◆ Open floor plan makes home feel airy and bright

◆ Beautiful living room has cheerful bay window

◆ Master suite has two walk-in closets

◆ Family room, kitchen and breakfast area combine for added space

◆ 3 bedrooms, 2 1/2 baths, 2-car garage

◆ Walk-out basement, slab or crawl space foundation, please specify when ordering

Price Code D

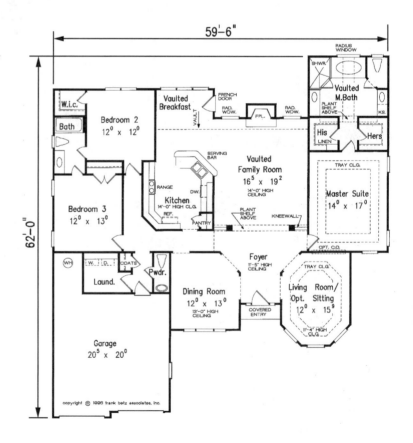

Plan #581-027D-0006

2,076 total square feet of living area

Special features

- ◆ Vaulted great room has fireplace flanked by windows and skylights that welcome the sun
- ◆ Kitchen leads to vaulted breakfast room and rear deck
- ◆ Study located off foyer is a great location for home office
- ◆ Large bay windows grace master bedroom and bath
- ◆ 3 bedrooms, 2 baths, 2-car garage
- ◆ Basement foundation

Price Code C

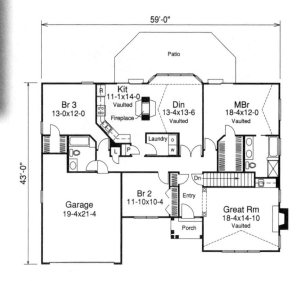

Plan #581-007D-0090

1,826 total square feet of living area

Special features

- ◆ An arched opening with columns invites you into a beautiful great room with fireplace, wet bar and vaulted ceiling
- ◆ Double entry doors leads into a large vaulted dining room with fireplace, plant shelves and a great view of the rear patio through a sweeping bay window
- ◆ 3 bedrooms, 2 baths, 2-car garage
- ◆ Basement foundation

Price Code C

Plan #581-049D-0005

1,389 total square feet of living area

Special features

◆ Formal living room has warming fire-place and a delightful bay window

◆ U-shaped kitchen shares a snack bar with the bayed family room

◆ Lovely master bedroom has its own private bath

◆ 3 bedrooms, 2 baths, 2-car garage

◆ Slab foundation

Price Code A

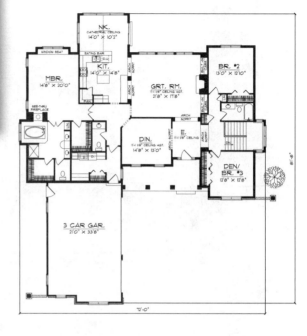

Plan #581-051D-0049

2,730 total square feet of living area

Special features

◆ See-through fireplace is a focal point shared by the master bedroom and master bath

◆ Great room has a window wall flooding the entire room with sunlight

◆ Arched soffits add a stunning element to the interior

◆ 3 bedrooms, 2 1/2 baths, 3-car side entry garage

◆ Basement foundation

Price Code E

Plan #581-052D-0080

2,542 total square feet of living area

Special features

◆ Formal entry opens to living and dining rooms

◆ Private master bedroom features double closets and access to the outdoors

◆ Extra storage can be found throughout

◆ 4 bedrooms, 2 1/2 baths, 2-car garage

◆ Basement, crawl space or slab foundation, please specify when ordering

Price Code D

Plan #581-001D-0058

1,720 total square feet of living area

Special features

- ◆ Lower level includes large family room with laundry area and half bath
- ◆ L-shaped kitchen has a convenient serving bar and pass-through to dining area
- ◆ Private half bath in master bedroom
- ◆ 3 bedrooms, 1 full bath, 2 half baths, 2-car drive under garage
- ◆ Basement foundation

Price Code B

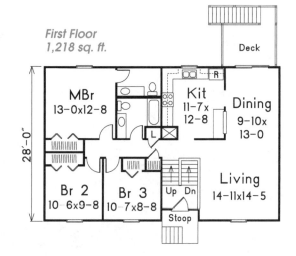

First Floor
1,218 sq. ft.

Deck

MBr
13-0x12-8

Kit
11-7x
12-8

Dining
9-10x
13-0

28'-0"

L

Br 2
10 6x9-8

Br 3
10 7x8-8

Up Dn

Living
14-11x14-5

Stoop

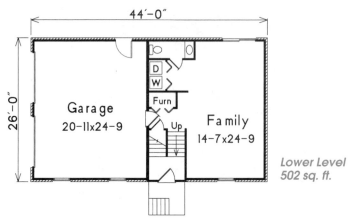

44'-0"

26'-0"

Garage
20-11x24-9

D
W

Furn

Up

Family
14-7x24-9

*Lower Level
502 sq. ft.*

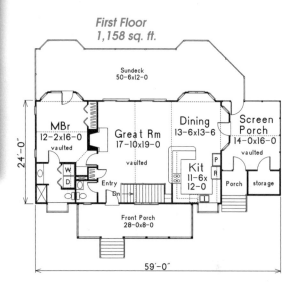

First Floor
1,158 sq. ft.

Sundeck
50-6x12-0

MBr
12-2x16-0
vaulted

Great Rm
17-10x19-0
vaulted

Dining
13-6x13-6

Screen
Porch
14-0x16-0
vaulted

Kit
11-6x
12-0

Entry
Dn

Front Porch
28-0x8-0

24'-0"

59'-0"

Lower Level
574 sq. ft.

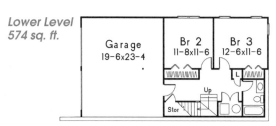

Garage
19-6x23-4

Br 2
11-8x11-6

Br 3
12-6x11-6

Up

Stor

Plan #581-053D-0043

1,732 total square feet of living area

Special features

- ◆ Vaulted great room with fireplace overlooks large sundeck
- ◆ Dining room boasts extensive windows and angled walls
- ◆ Vaulted master bedroom includes private bath with laundry area and accesses sundeck
- ◆ Second entrance leads to screened porch and dining area
- ◆ 3 bedrooms, 2 1/2 baths, 2-car drive under garage
- ◆ Basement foundation

Price Code B

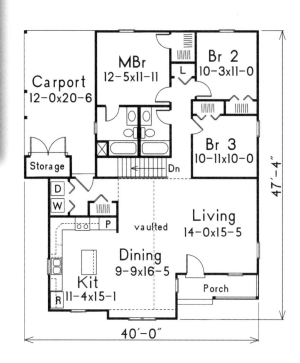

Carport
12-0x20-6

MBr
12-5x11-11

Br 2
10-3x11-0

Storage

Br 3
10-11x10-0

Dn

D
W
P

Kit
11-4x15-1

Dining
9-9x16-5

vaulted

Living
14-0x15-5

Porch

47'-4"

40'-0"

Plan #581-001D-0035

1,396 total square feet of living area

Special features

- ◆ Gabled front adds interest to facade
- ◆ Living and dining rooms share a vaulted ceiling
- ◆ Master bedroom has a walk-in closet and private bath
- ◆ Functional kitchen with a center work island and convenient pantry
- ◆ 3 bedrooms, 2 baths, 1-car carport
- ◆ Basement foundation, drawings also include crawl space foundation

Price Code A

Plan #581-021D-0014

1,856 total square feet of living area

Special features

- Living room features include fireplace, 12' ceiling and skylights
- Energy efficient home with 2" x 6" exterior walls
- Common vaulted ceiling creates an open atmosphere in kitchen and breakfast room
- Garage with storage areas conveniently accesses home through handy utility room
- Private hall separates secondary bedrooms from living areas
- 3 bedrooms, 2 baths, 2-car side entry garage
- Slab foundation, drawings also include crawl space foundation

Price Code C

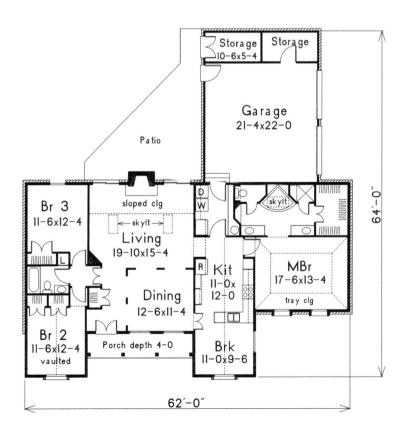

Fireplaces Are Unique

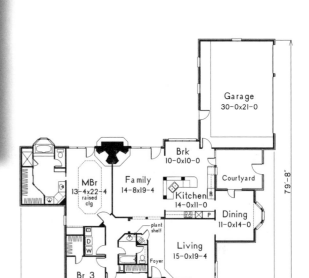

Plan #581-037D-0025

2,481 total square feet of living area

Special features

- Varied ceiling heights throughout this home
- Master bedroom features built-in desk and pocket door entrance into large master bath
- Master bath includes corner vanity and garden tub
- Breakfast area accesses courtyard
- 3 bedrooms, 2 baths, 3-car side entry garage
- Slab foundation

Price Code D

Inviting Arched Entry

Plan #581-018D-0008

2,109 total square feet of living area

Special features

- 12' ceilings in living and dining rooms
- Kitchen designed as an integral part of the family and breakfast rooms
- Secluded and spacious master bedroom has a plant shelf, walk-in closet and private bath
- 3 bedrooms, 2 baths, 2-car side entry garage
- Slab foundation, drawings also include crawl space foundation

Price Code C

*P*lan #581-039D-0001

1,253 total square feet of living area

Special features

◆ Sloped ceiling and fireplace in family room add drama

◆ U-shaped kitchen is efficiently designed

◆ Large walk-in closets are found in all the bedrooms

◆ 3 bedrooms, 2 baths, 2-car garage

◆ Crawl space or slab foundation, please specify when ordering

Price Code A

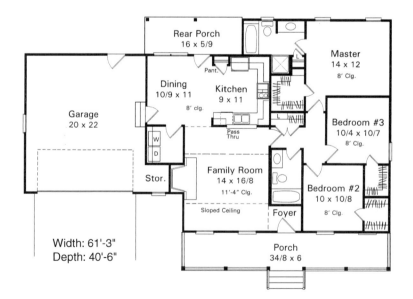

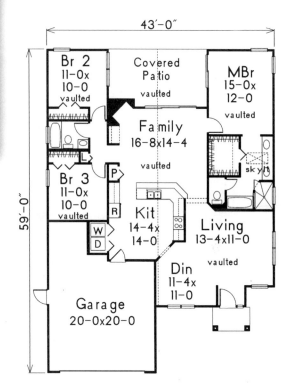

Plan #581-048D-0011

1,550 total square feet of living area

Special features

- Cozy corner fireplace provides focal point in family room
- Master bedroom features large walk-in closet, skylight and separate tub and shower
- Kitchen and breakfast bar connects to family room
- Family room and master bedroom access covered patio
- 3 bedrooms, 2 baths, 2-car garage
- Slab foundation

Price Code B

Columns Accent Room

Plan #581-018D-0005

2,598 total square feet of living area

Special features

- Varied ceiling heights throughout home
- Stylish see-through fireplace shared by great room and family room
- Walk-in pantry and laundry room located near kitchen
- Windows in abundance provide natural light
- 4 bedrooms, 2 1/2 baths, 2-car side entry garage
- Slab foundation, drawings also include crawl space foundation

Price Code D

Plan #581-051D-0063

1,801 total square feet of living area

Special features

- Stair access to the lower level from the garage
- Living room has tray ceiling, fireplace, built-in cabinets and French doors which open to the outdoors
- Kitchen has snack bar/island for extra seating
- 3 bedrooms, 2 1/2 baths, 3-car side entry garage
- Basement foundation

Price Code C

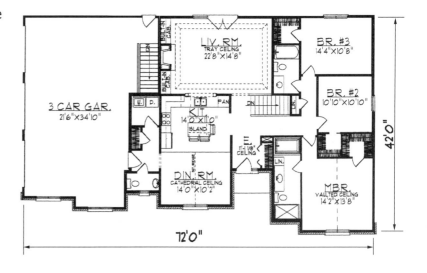

Plan #581-058D-0023

1,883 total square feet of living area

Special features

- ◆ Large laundry room located off the garage has coat closet and half bath
- ◆ Large family room with fireplace and access to covered porch is a great central gathering room
- ◆ U-shaped kitchen has breakfast bar, large pantry and swing door to dining room for convenient serving
- ◆ 3 bedrooms, 2 1/2 baths, 2-car side entry garage
- ◆ Basement foundation

Price Code C

Windows Enhance Entry

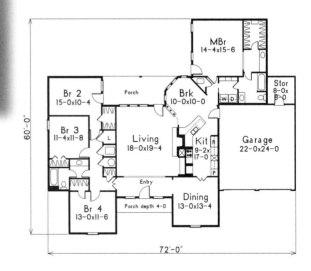

Plan #581-021D-0009

2,252 total square feet of living area

Special features

- ◆ Energy efficient home with 2" x 6" exterior walls
- ◆ Master bath has a nice dressing area
- ◆ Secondary bedrooms are in a suite arrangement with plenty of closet space
- ◆ Sunny breakfast room looks out over the porch and patio
- ◆ 4 bedrooms, 2 baths, 2-car garage
- ◆ Slab foundation, drawings also include basement and crawl space foundations

Price Code D

Plan #581-030D-0001

1,374 total square feet of living area

Special features

◆ Garage has extra storage space

◆ Spacious living room has fireplace

◆ Well-designed kitchen with adjacent breakfast nook

◆ Separated master suite maintains privacy

◆ 3 bedrooms, 2 baths, 2-car garage

◆ Slab or crawl space foundation, please specify when ordering

Price Code A

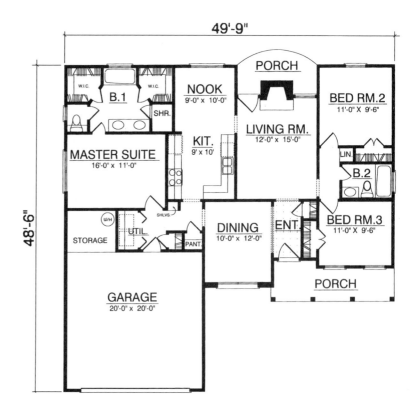

Plan #581-037D-0022

1,539 total square feet of living area

Special features

- Standard 9' ceilings
- Master bedroom features 10' tray ceiling, access to porch, ample closet space and full bath
- Serving counter separates kitchen and dining room
- Foyer has handy coat closet
- 3 bedrooms, 2 baths, 2-car garage
- Slab foundation

Price Code B

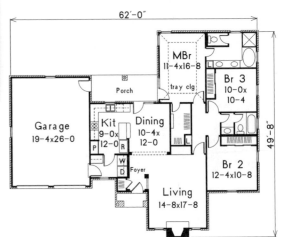

Spacious And Open

Plan #581-001D-0030

1,416 total square feet of living area

Special features

- Family room includes fireplace, elevated plant shelf and vaulted ceiling
- Patio is accessible from dining area and garage
- Centrally located laundry area
- Oversized walk-in pantry
- 3 bedrooms, 2 baths, 2-car garage
- Basement foundation, drawings also include crawl space and slab foundations

Price Code A

© Copyright MCMXCVIII – Ralph Jones

Plan #581-060D-0008

2,281 total square feet of living area

Special features

- ◆ Formal dining room features coffered ceilings
- ◆ Great room with fireplace and coffered ceiling overlooks covered back porch
- ◆ Kitchen with angled eating bar adjoins an angled morning room with bay window
- ◆ Salon bath has double walk-in closets and vanities, step-up tub and separate shower
- ◆ 3 bedrooms, 2 baths, 2-car side entry garage
- ◆ Slab or crawl space foundation, please specify when ordering

Price Code D

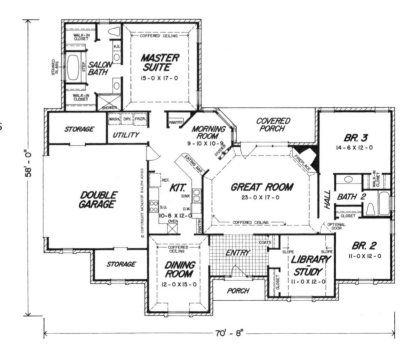

Plan #581-043D-0008

1,496 total square feet of living area

Special features

◆ Large utility room with sink and extra counterspace

◆ Covered patio off breakfast nook extends dining to the outdoors

◆ Eating counter in kitchen overlooks vaulted family room

◆ 3 bedrooms, 2 baths, 2-car side entry garage

◆ Crawl space foundation

Price Code A

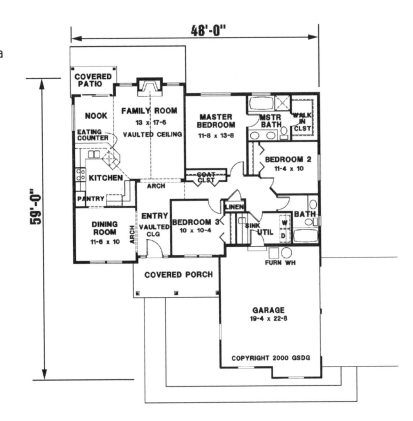

Distinctive Gabled Ranch

Plan #581-052D-0043

1,854 total square feet of living area

Special features

- ◆ Well-designed secondary bedrooms share a bath with double vanities
- ◆ Secluded master bedroom has an oversized walk-in closet and a private bath with all the amenities
- ◆ Large kitchen includes a center island perfect for food preparation
- ◆ 3 bedrooms, 2 1/2 baths, 2-car side entry garage
- ◆ Basement foundation

Price Code C

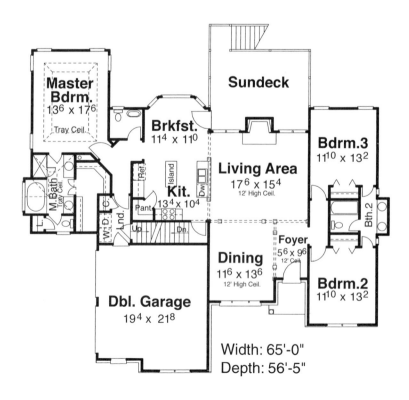

Width: 65'-0"
Depth: 56'-5"

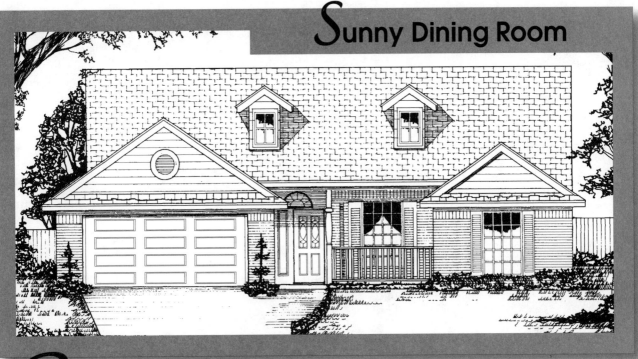

Plan #581-031D-0005

1,735 total square feet of living area

Special features

◆ Luxurious master bath has spa tub, shower, double vanity and large walk-in closet

◆ Peninsula in kitchen has sink and dishwasher

◆ Massive master bedroom has step-up ceiling and private location

◆ 3 bedrooms, 2 baths, 2-car garage

◆ Slab foundation

Price Code B

Width: 50'-0"
Depth: 55'-0"

*P*erfect For Entertaining

*P*lan #581-053D-0046

1,862 total square feet of living area

Special features

- ◆ Master bedroom includes tray ceiling, bay window, access to patio and a private bath with oversized tub and generous closet space
- ◆ Corner sink and breakfast bar faces into breakfast area and great room
- ◆ Spacious great room features vaulted ceiling, fireplace and access to rear patio
- ◆ 3 bedrooms, 2 baths, 2-car garage
- ◆ Slab foundation, drawings also include crawl space foundation

Price Code C

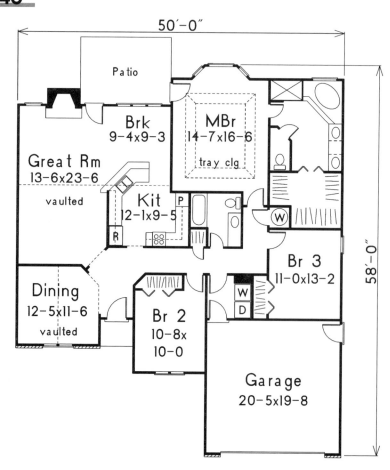

Grand Living Room

Plan #581-021D-0013

2,648 total square feet of living area

Special features

- ◆ Private study with access to master bedroom and porch
- ◆ Grand-sized living room with sloped ceiling, fireplace and entry to porches
- ◆ Energy efficient home with 2" x 6" exterior walls
- ◆ Master bedroom boasts an expansive bath with separate vanities, large walk-in closet and separate tub and shower units
- ◆ Large kitchen with eating area and breakfast bar
- ◆ Large utility room includes extra counterspace and storage closet
- ◆ 3 bedrooms, 2 baths, 2-car carport
- ◆ Crawl space foundation, drawings also include slab foundation

Price Code E

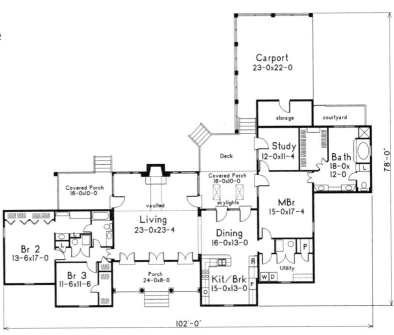

Plan #581-037D-0006

1,772 total square feet of living area

Special features

- Extended porches in front and rear provide a charming touch
- Large bay windows lend distinction to dining room and bedroom #3
- Efficient U-shaped kitchen
- Master bedroom includes two walk-in closets
- Full corner fireplace in family room
- 3 bedrooms, 2 baths, 2-car detached garage
- Slab foundation, drawings also include crawl space foundation

Price Code C

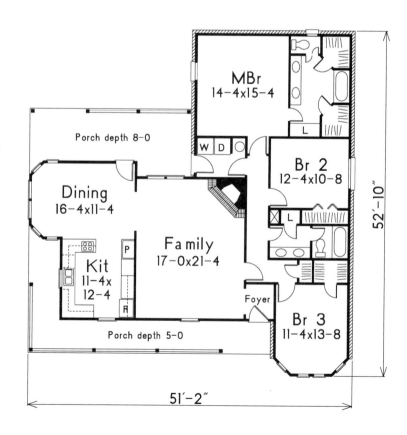

Plan #581-040D-0013

1,304 total square feet of living area

Special features

- ◆ Covered entrance leads into the family room with a cozy fireplace
- ◆ 10' ceilings in kitchen, dining and family rooms
- ◆ Master bedroom features a coffered ceiling, walk-in closet and private bath
- ◆ Efficient kitchen includes large window over the sink
- ◆ 3 bedrooms, 2 baths, 2-car garage
- ◆ Slab foundation

Price Code A

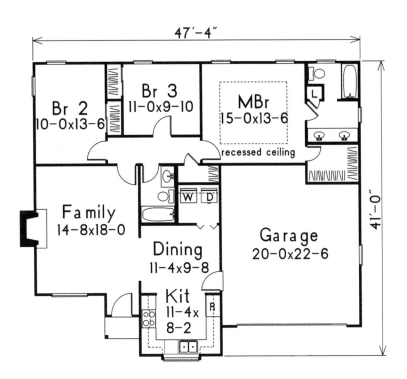

Ceilings Create Openness

Plan #581-058D-0027

2,516 total square feet of living area

Special features

- ◆ 12' ceiling in living areas
- ◆ Plenty of closet space in this open ranch plan
- ◆ Large kitchen/breakfast area joins great room via see-through fireplace creating large entering space
- ◆ Large three-car garage has extra storage area
- ◆ Master bedroom has eye-catching bay window
- ◆ 3 bedrooms, 2 1/2 baths, 3-car garage
- ◆ Basement foundation

Price Code D

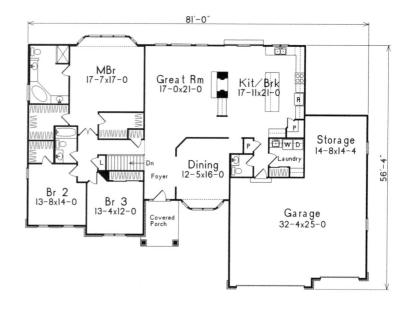

Plan #581-014D-0002

2,070 total square feet of living area

Special features

- Access to rear deck through nook area
- Energy efficient home with 2" x 6" exterior walls
- Master bedroom features arched entrance into bath with separate shower and tub, dressing area and walk-in closet
- Sunken family room with fireplace
- 3 bedrooms, 2 baths, 2-car garage
- Basement foundation, drawings also include slab and crawl space foundations

Price Code C

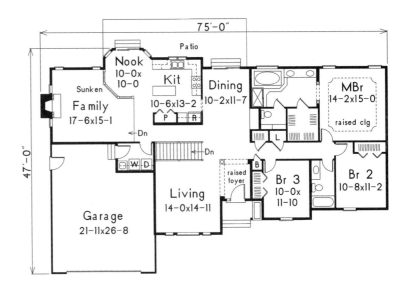

A Design For Privacy

Plan #581-007D-0120

1,914 total square feet of living area

Special features

◆ Great room features a vaulted ceiling, dining area, entry foyer, corner fireplace and 9' wide sliding doors to rear patio

◆ The secluded secondary bedrooms offer walk-in closets and share a Jack and Jill bath

◆ A multi-purpose room has laundry alcove and can easily be used as a hobby room, sewing room or small office

◆ Bedroom #4 can be open to the master bedroom suite and utilized as a private study or nursery

◆ 4 bedrooms, 3 baths, 2-car garage

◆ Basement foundation

Price Code C

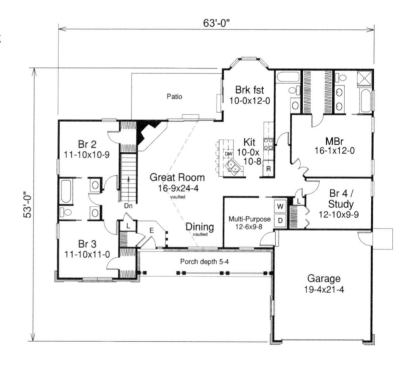

Plan #581-001D-0079

2,080 total square feet of living area

Special features

- ◆ Combined design elements create a unique facade
- ◆ Foyer leads into large living room and direct view to patio
- ◆ Master bedroom includes spacious bath with garden tub, separate shower, walk-in closet and dressing area
- ◆ 4 bedrooms, 2 baths, 2-car side entry garage
- ◆ Crawl space foundation, drawings also include basement and slab foundations

Price Code C

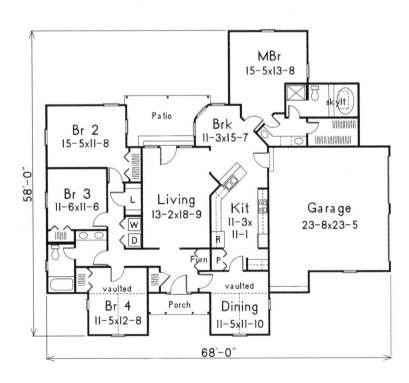

Unique Three-Way Fireplace

Plan #581-026D-0166

2,126 total square feet of living area

Special Features

- Elegant bay windows in master bed-room welcome the sun
- Double vanities in master bath are separated by a large whirlpool tub
- Secondary bedrooms each include a walk-in closet
- Nook has access to the outdoors onto the rear porch
- 3 bedrooms, 2 baths, 2-car side entry garage
- Slab foundation

Price Code C

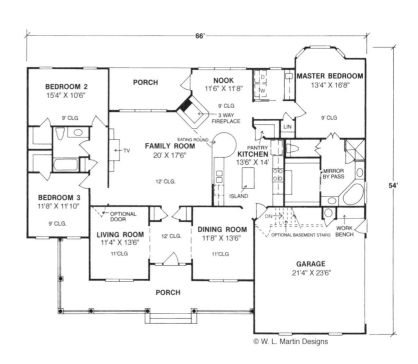

© W. L. Martin Designs

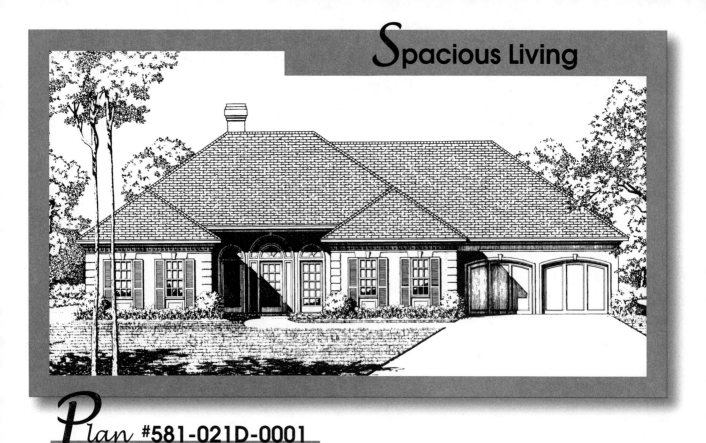

Plan #581-021D-0001

2,396 total square feet of living area

Special features

◆ Generously wide entry welcomes guests

◆ Central living area with a 12' ceiling and large fireplace serves as a convenient traffic hub

◆ Kitchen is secluded, yet has easy access to the living, dining and breakfast areas

◆ Deluxe master bath has a walk-in closet, oversized tub, shower and other amenities

◆ Energy efficient home with 2" x 6" exterior walls

◆ 4 bedrooms, 2 baths, 2-car garage

◆ Slab foundation, drawings also include basement and crawl space foundations

Price Code D

Plan #581-058D-0004

962 total square feet of living area

Special features

- Both the kitchen and family room share warmth from the fireplace
- Charming facade features covered porch on one side, screened porch on the other and attractive planter boxes
- L-shaped kitchen boasts convenient pantry
- 2 bedrooms, 1 bath
- Crawl space foundation

Price Code AA

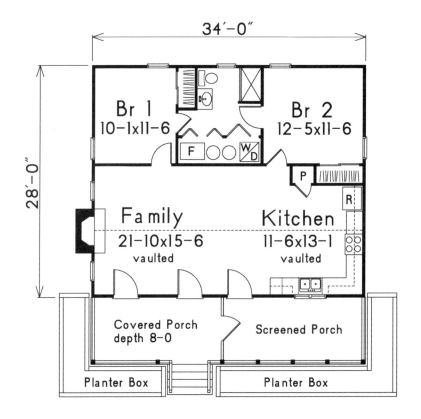

34'-0"

28'-0"

Br 1
10-1x11-6

Br 2
12-5x11-6

F

W
D

Family
21-10x15-6
vaulted

Kitchen
11-6x13-1
vaulted

P

R

Covered Porch
depth 8-0

Screened Porch

Planter Box

Planter Box

Plan #581-027D-0009

3,808 total square feet of living area

Special features

◆ Cozy hearth room shares fireplace with great room

◆ See-through fireplace connecting gathering areas

◆ Master bath features stylish angled glass block walls that frame private toilet and large shower

◆ 3 bedrooms, 3 baths, 2-car garage

◆ Basement foundation

Price Code F

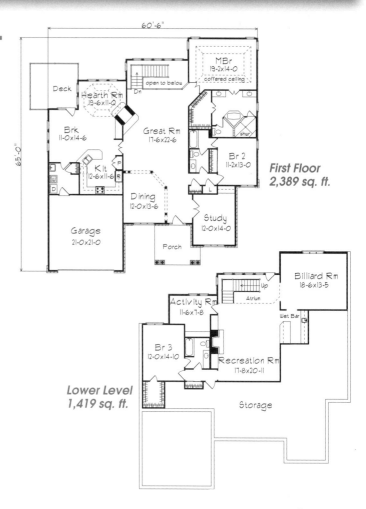

First Floor
2,389 sq. ft.

Lower Level
1,419 sq. ft.

Plan #581-068D-0011

2,532 total square feet of living area

Special features

- ◆ Covered patio surrounds rear of home
- ◆ Living and dining rooms feature tray ceiling
- ◆ Bedroom #3 has direct access to bath and plenty of closet space making it an ideal guest room
- ◆ 3 bedrooms, 4 baths, 2-car side entry garage
- ◆ Basement foundation, drawings also include crawl space and slab foundations

Price Code D

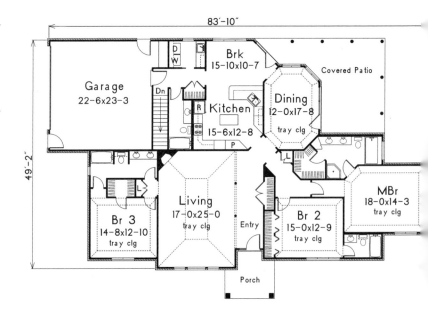

*P*lan #581-019D-0010

1,890 total square feet of living area

Special features

- ◆ 10' ceilings give this home a spacious feel
- ◆ Efficient kitchen has breakfast bar which overlooks living room
- ◆ Master bedroom has a private bath with walk-in closet
- ◆ 3 bedrooms, 2 baths, 2-car side entry garage
- ◆ Crawl space foundation, drawings also include slab foundation

Price Code C

WIDTH 65-10

*P*lan #581-007D-0078

2,514 total square feet of living area

Special features

◆ An expansive porch welcomes you to the foyer, spacious dining area with bay and a gallery-sized hall with plant shelf above

◆ A highly functional U-shaped kitchen is open to a bayed breakfast room, study and family room with a 46' vista

◆ Vaulted rear sunroom has fireplace

◆ 1,509 square feet of optional living area on the lower level with recreation room, bedroom #4 with bath and an office with storage closet

◆ 3 bedrooms, 2 baths, 3-car oversized side entry garage with workshop/storage area

◆ Walk-out basement foundation

Price Code D

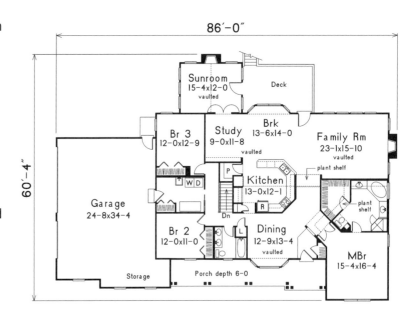

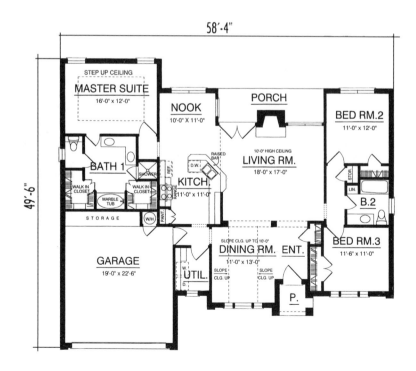

Plan #581-030D-0004

1,791 total square feet of living area

Special features

- ◆ Dining area has 10' high sloped ceiling
- ◆ Kitchen opens to large living room with fireplace and has access to a covered porch
- ◆ Master suite features private bath, double walk-in closets and whirlpool tub
- ◆ 3 bedrooms, 2 baths, 2-car garage
- ◆ Slab or crawl space foundation, please specify when ordering

Price Code B

L-Shaped Kitchen

Plan #581-001D-0089

1,000 total square feet of living area

Special features

- Master bedroom has double closets and an adjacent bath
- L-shaped kitchen includes side entrance, closet and convenient laundry area
- Living room features handy coat closet
- 3 bedrooms, 1 bath
- Crawl space foundation, drawings also include basement and slab foundations

Price Code AA

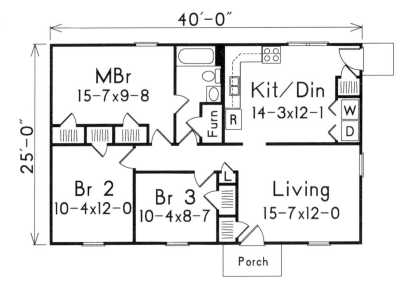

*L*arge Front Porch

*P*lan #581-037D-0017

829 total square feet of living area

Special features

- ◆ U-shaped kitchen opens into living area by a 42" high counter
- ◆ Oversized bay window and French door accent dining room
- ◆ Gathering space is created by the large living room
- ◆ Convenient utility room and linen closet
- ◆ 1 bedroom, 1 bath
- ◆ Slab foundation

Price Code AAA

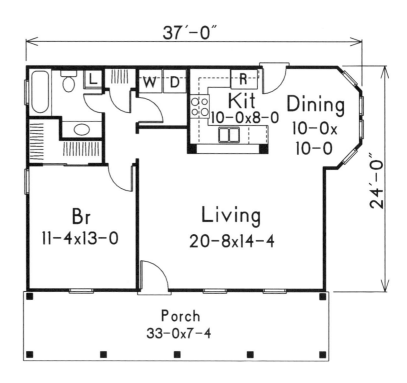

Plan #581-022D-0022

1,270 total square feet of living area

Special features

♦ Spacious living area features angled stairs, vaulted ceiling, exciting fireplace and deck access

♦ Master bedroom includes a walk-in closet and private bath

♦ Dining and living rooms join to create an open atmosphere

♦ Eat-in kitchen with convenient pass-through to dining room

♦ 3 bedrooms, 2 baths, 2-car garage

♦ Basement foundation

Price Code A

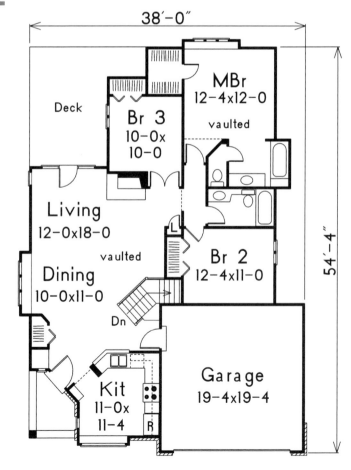

Plan #581-035D-0050

1,342 total square feet of living area

Special features

◆ 9' ceilings throughout home

◆ Master suite has tray ceiling and wall of windows that overlook backyard

◆ Dining room includes serving bar connecting it to the kitchen and sliding glass doors that lead outdoors

◆ 3 bedrooms, 2 baths, 2-car garage

◆ Slab, walk-out basement or crawl space foundation, please specify when ordering

Price Code A

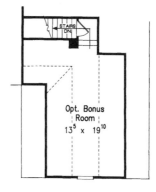

Optional Second Floor 350 sq. ft.

Opt. Bonus Room 13⁵ x 19¹⁰

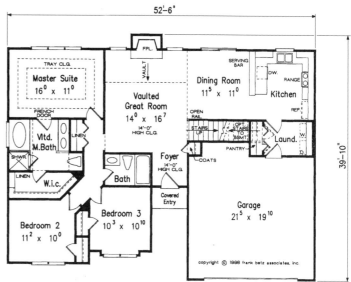

First Floor 1,342 sq. ft.

copyright © 1998 frank betz associates, inc.

Plan #581-028D-0006

1,700 total square feet of living area

Special features

- Oversized laundry room has large pantry and storage area as well as access to the outdoors
- Master bedroom is separated from other bedrooms for privacy
- Raised snack bar in kitchen allows extra seating for dining
- 3 bedrooms, 2 baths
- Crawl space foundation

Price Code B

50-0 WIDE X 42-0 DEEP
(INCLUDING COVERED PORCH)

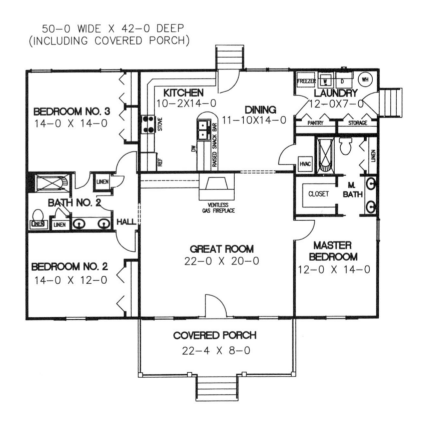

Lovely, Spacious Floor Plan

Plan #581-058D-0016

1,558 total square feet of living area

Special features

◆ Spacious utility room located conveniently between garage and kitchen/dining area

◆ Bedrooms are separated from living area by hallway

◆ Enormous living area with fireplace and vaulted ceiling opens to kitchen and dining area

◆ Master bedroom is enhanced with large bay window, walk-in closet and private bath

◆ 3 bedrooms, 2 baths, 2-car garage

◆ Basement foundation

Price Code B

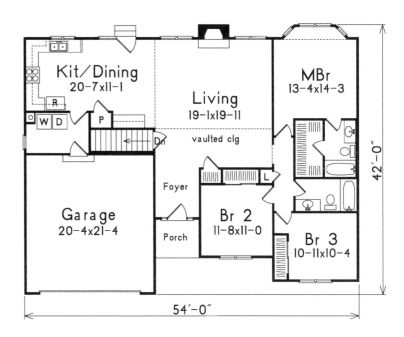

Kit/Dining
20-7x11-1

Living
19-1x19-11
vaulted clg

MBr
13-4x14-3

Foyer

Garage
20-4x21-4

Porch

Br 2
11-8x11-0

Br 3
10-11x10-4

54'-0"

42'-0"

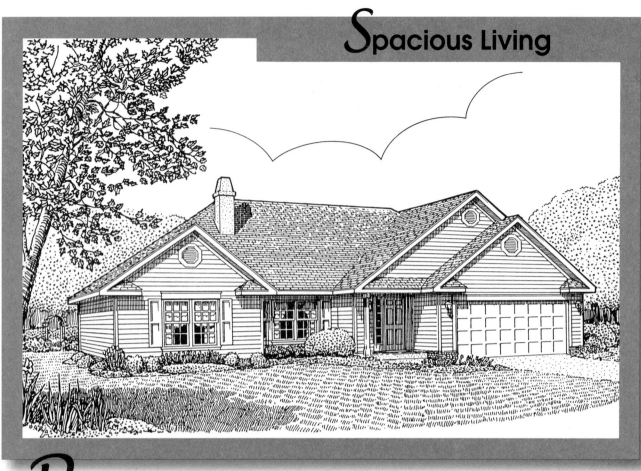

Plan #581-068D-0005

1,433 total square feet of living area

Special features

- ◆ Vaulted living room includes cozy fireplace and an oversized entertainment center
- ◆ Bedrooms #2 and #3 share a full bath
- ◆ Master bedroom has a full bath and large walk-in closet
- ◆ 3 bedrooms, 2 baths, 2-car garage
- ◆ Basement foundation, drawings also include crawl space and slab foundations

Price Code A

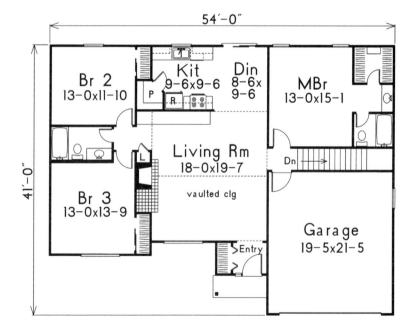

Plan #581-035D-0005

1,281 total square feet of living area

Special features

- ◆ Spacious master suite has a tray ceiling, double closets and private bath
- ◆ Vaulted family room has lots of sunlight from multiple windows and a fireplace
- ◆ Plant shelf above kitchen and dining room is a nice decorative touch
- ◆ 3 bedrooms, 2 baths, 2-car drive under garage
- ◆ Walk-out basement foundation

Price Code A

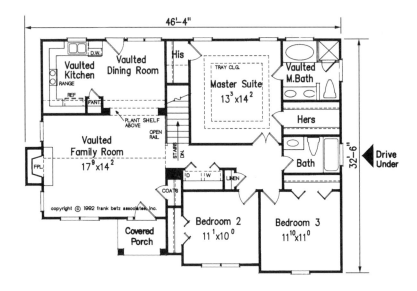

46'-4"

Vaulted Kitchen
RANGE
REF
D.W.

Vaulted Dining Room

His

TRAY CLG.
Master Suite
13³x14²

Vaulted M.Bath

Hers

PANT

PLANT SHELF ABOVE

OPEN RAIL

STAIRS DN.

Vaulted Family Room
17⁹x14²

FPL

Bath

32'-6"

Drive Under

D W LINEN

COATS

copyright © 1992 frank betz associates, inc.

Covered Porch

Bedroom 2
11¹x10⁰

Bedroom 3
11¹⁰x11⁰

Plan #581-053D-0032

1,404 total square feet of living area

Special features

- Split foyer entrance
- Bayed living area features unique vaulted ceiling and fireplace
- Wrap-around kitchen has corner windows for added sunlight and a bar that overlooks dining area
- Master bath features a garden tub with separate shower
- Rear deck provides handy access to dining room and kitchen
- 3 bedrooms, 2 baths, 2-car drive under garage
- Basement foundation, drawings also include partial crawl space foundation

Price Code A

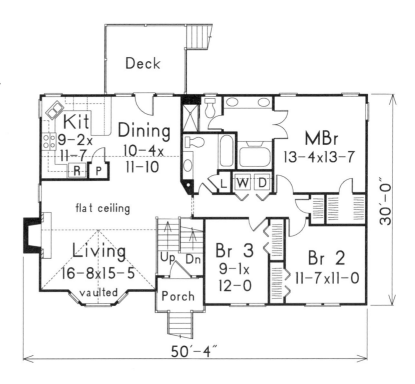

Plan #581-007D-0106

1,200 total square feet of living area

Special features

- Entry leads to a large dining area which opens to kitchen and sun-drenched living room
- An expansive window wall in the two-story atrium lends space and light to living room with fireplace
- The large kitchen features a break-fast bar, built-in pantry and storage galore
- 2 bedrooms, 1 bath
- Walk-out basement foundation

Price Code A

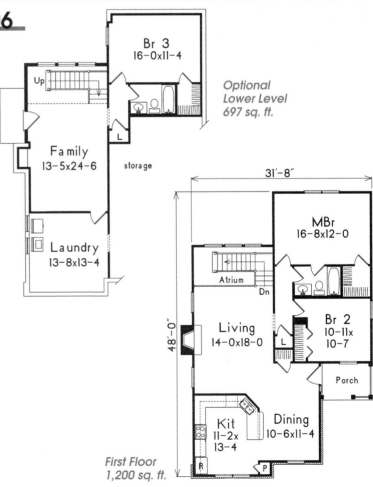

Optional Lower Level 697 sq. ft.

Br 3
16-0x11-4

Family
13-5x24-6

storage

Laundry
13-8x13-4

31'-8"

48'-0"

MBr
16-8x12-0

Atrium

Dn

Living
14-0x18-0

Br 2
10-11x 10-7

Porch

Kit
11-2x 13-4

Dining
10-6x11-4

First Floor 1,200 sq. ft.

Gabled Front Porch

Plan #581-052D-0013

1,379 total square feet of living area

Special features

- Living area has spacious feel with 11'-6" ceiling
- Kitchen has eat-in breakfast bar open to dining area
- Laundry closet is located near bedrooms
- Large cased opening with columns opens the living and dining areas
- 3 bedrooms, 2 baths, 2-car drive under garage
- Basement foundation

Price Code A

Family Room With Fireplace

Plan #581-040D-0008

1,631 total square feet of living area

Special features

◆ 9' ceilings throughout this home

◆ Utility room conveniently located near kitchen

◆ Roomy kitchen and dining area boast a breakfast bar and deck access

◆ Raised ceiling accents master bedroom

◆ 3 bedrooms, 2 baths, 2-car drive under garage

◆ Basement foundation

Price Code B

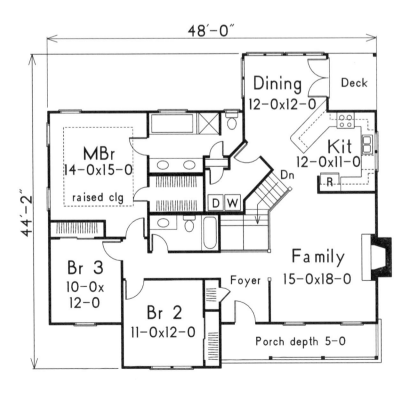

Gables Frame Front Porch

Plan #581-001D-0080

1,832 total square feet of living area

Special features

- Distinctive master bedroom enhanced by skylights, garden tub, separate shower and walk-in closet
- U-shaped kitchen features convenient pantry, laundry area and full view to breakfast room
- Foyer opens into spacious living room
- Large front porch creates enjoyable outdoor living
- 3 bedrooms, 2 baths, 2-car detached garage
- Crawl space foundation, drawings also include basement and slab foundations

Price Code C

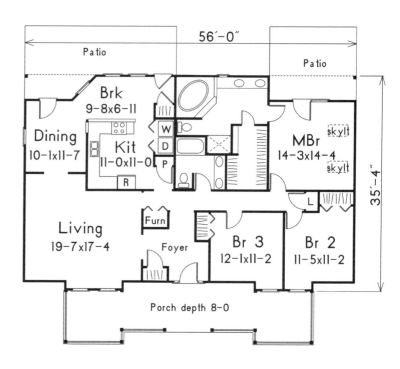

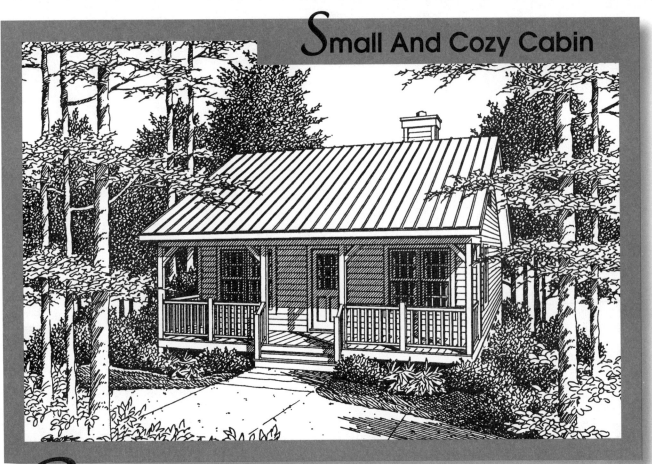

Small And Cozy Cabin

Plan #581-058D-0010

676 total square feet of living area

Special features

◆ See-through fireplace between bedroom and living area adds character

◆ Combined dining and living areas create an open feeling

◆ Full-length front covered porch is perfect for enjoying the outdoors

◆ Additional storage available in utility room

◆ 1 bedroom, 1 bath

◆ Crawl space foundation

Price Code AAA

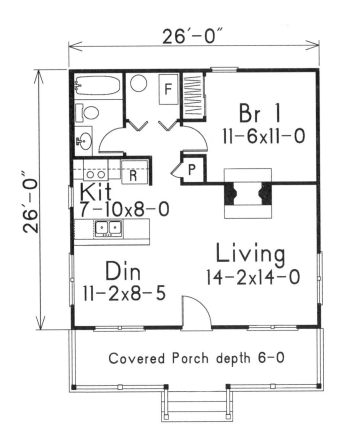

26'-0"

26'-0"

Br 1
11-6x11-0

Kit
7-10x8-0

Din
11-2x8-5

Living
14-2x14-0

Covered Porch depth 6-0

*P*lan #581-015D-0030

1,588 total square feet of living area

Special features

- ◆ Workshop in garage is ideal for storage and projects
- ◆ 12' vaulted master suite has double closets as well as a lovely bath with bayed soaking tub and compartmentalized shower and toilet area
- ◆ Lovely arched entry to 14' vaulted great room flows into the dining room and sky-lit kitchen
- ◆ 3 bedrooms, 2 baths, 2-car garage
- ◆ Basement foundation

Price Code B

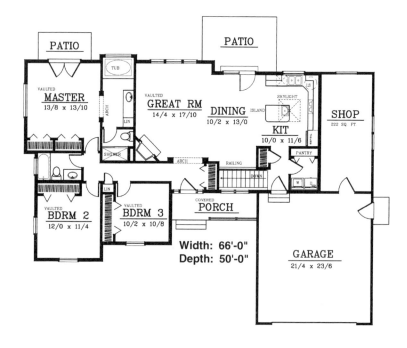

Width: 66'-0"
Depth: 50'-0"

Enchanting One-Level Home

Plan #581-065D-0010

1,508 total square feet of living area

Special features

- Grand opening between rooms creates a spacious effect
- Additional room for quick meals or serving a larger crowd is provided at the breakfast bar
- Sunny dining area accesses the outdoors as well
- 3 bedrooms, 2 baths, 2-car garage
- Basement or crawl space foundation, please specify when ordering

Price Code B

*P*lan #581-001D-0029

1,260 total square feet of living area

Special features

◆ Spacious kitchen and dining area feature a large pantry, storage area, easy access to garage and laundry room

◆ Pleasant covered front porch adds a practical touch

◆ Master bedroom with a private bath adjoins two other bedrooms, all with plenty of closet space

◆ 3 bedrooms, 2 baths, 2-car garage

◆ Basement foundation, drawings also include crawl space and slab foundations

Price Code A

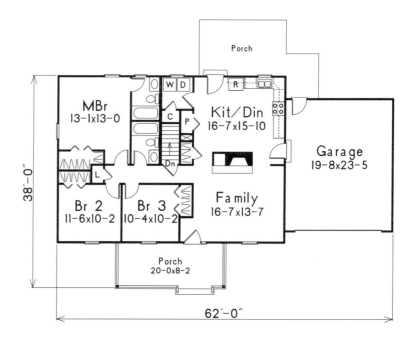

© COPYRIGHT MCMXC RALPH JONES

ARTIST'S CONCEPTION, ACTUAL CONSTRUCTION MAY VARY.

*P*lan #581-060D-0005

1,742 total square feet of living area

Special features

- ◆ Open formal entry with columns access dining area and great room
- ◆ Kitchen has eating bar overlooking the bayed breakfast room with separate laundry room and half bath
- ◆ Master bath has step-up tub with windows on two sides, separate shower and huge walk-in closet
- ◆ Large master suite has a coffered ceiling
- ◆ 3 bedrooms, 2 1/2 baths, 2-car side entry garage with storage
- ◆ Slab or crawl space foundation, please specify when ordering

Price Code B

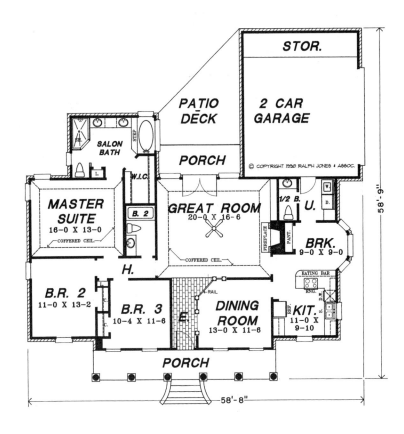

STOR.

PATIO DECK

2 CAR GARAGE

© COPYRIGHT 1990 RALPH JONES & ASSOC.

PORCH

SALON BATH

W.I.C.

MASTER SUITE
16-0 X 13-0
COFFERED CEIL.

B. 2

GREAT ROOM
20-0 X 16-6

1/2 B.

U.

PANT.

FIREPLACE

BRK.
9-0 X 9-0

EATING BAR

H.

COFFERED CEIL.

B.R. 2
11-0 X 13-2

B.R. 3
10-4 X 11-6

RAIL

DINING ROOM
13-0 X 11-6

KIT.
11-0 X 9-10

REF.

RNG.

D.W.

PORCH

58'-9"

58'-8"

Plan #581-007D-0116

2,100 total square feet of living area

Special features

- A large courtyard with stone walls, lantern columns and covered porch welcomes you into awesome open spaces

- The great room features a stone fireplace, built-in shelves, vaulted ceilings and atrium with dramatic staircase and a two and a half story window wall

- Two walk-in closets, vaulted ceiling with plant shelf and a luxury bath adorn the master bedroom suite

- 2 bedrooms, 2 baths, 3-car side entry garage

- Walk-out basement foundation

Price Code C

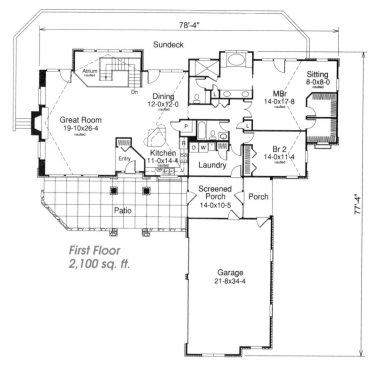

*First Floor
2,100 sq. ft.*

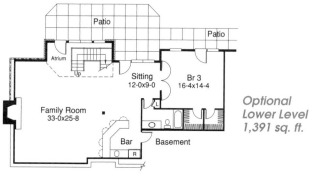

*Optional
Lower Level
1,391 sq. ft.*

Plan #581-053D-0052

2,513 total square feet of living area

Special features

- ◆ Coffered ceilings in master bedroom, living and dining rooms
- ◆ Kitchen features island cooktop and built-in desk
- ◆ Dramatic vaulted ceiling in breakfast room is framed by plenty of windows
- ◆ Covered entry porch leads into spacious foyer
- ◆ Family room features an impressive fireplace and vaulted ceiling that joins the breakfast room creating spacious entertainment area
- ◆ 4 bedrooms, 2 full baths, 2 half baths, 2-car side entry garage
- ◆ Basement foundation

Price Code D

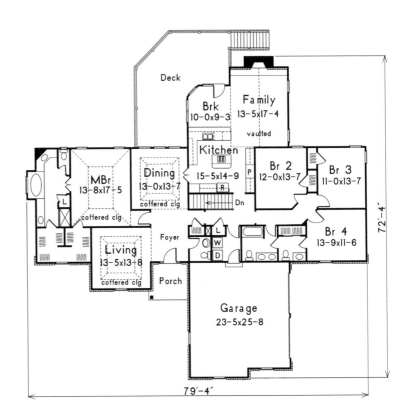

Plan #581-043D-0004

2,086 total square feet of living area

Special features

◆ Family room has desk and built-in bookshelves

◆ Master bath has corner tub and spacious walk-in closet

◆ Master bedroom has double-door entry, vaulted ceiling and access to patio outdoors

◆ Three-car garage plan option also included

◆ 3 bedrooms, 2 1/2 baths, 2-car garage with 3-car garage option

◆ Crawl space foundation

Price Code C

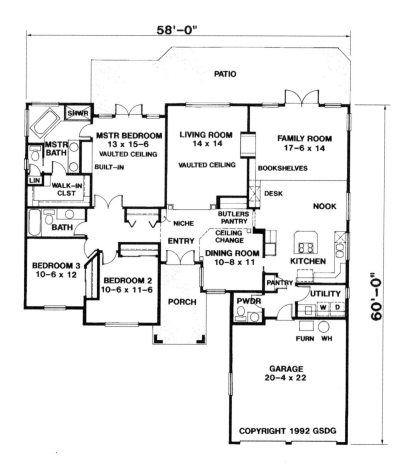

Plan #581-007D-0137

1,568 total square feet of living area

Special features

- Multiple entrances from three porches help to bring the outdoors in
- The lodge-like great room features a vaulted ceiling, stone fireplace, step-up entrance foyer and opens to a huge screened porch
- The kitchen has an island and peninsula, a convenient laundry room and adjoins a spacious dining area which leads to a screened porch and rear patio
- The master bedroom has two walk-in closets, a luxury bath and access to the screened porch and patio
- 2 bedrooms, 2 baths, 3-car side entry garage
- Crawl space foundation

Price Code B

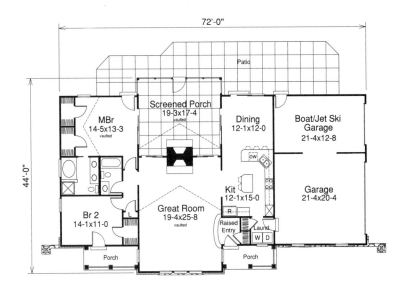

Rustic Charm

Plan #581-001D-0053

1,344 total square feet of living area

Special features

- Family/dining room has sliding glass doors to the outdoors
- Master bedroom has a private bath with shower
- Hall bath includes double vanity for added convenience
- U-shaped kitchen features large pantry and laundry area
- 3 bedrooms, 2 baths, 2-car garage
- Crawl space foundation, drawings also include basement and slab foundations

Price Code A

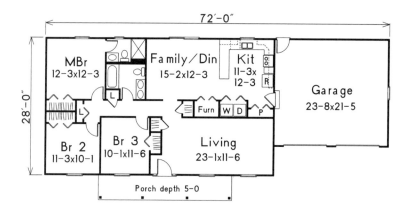

Plan #581-035D-0042

2,311 total square feet of living area

Special features

- ◆ Fireplaces warm master suite and family room
- ◆ Vaulted breakfast room near kitchen
- ◆ Formal living room near dining room
- ◆ 3 bedrooms, 2 1/2 baths, 2-car side entry garage
- ◆ Walk-out basement, slab or crawl space foundation, please specify when ordering

Price Code D

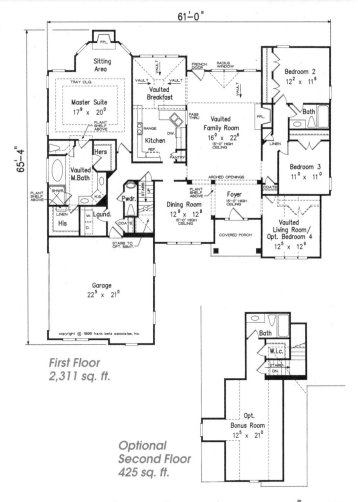

First Floor
2,311 sq. ft.

Optional
Second Floor
425 sq. ft.

*P*lan #581-069D-0010

1,458 total square feet of living area

Special features

◆ Divider wall allows for some privacy in the formal dining area while maintaining openness

◆ Two secondary bedrooms share a full bath

◆ Covered front and rear porches create enjoyable outdoor living spaces

◆ 3 bedrooms, 2 baths, 2-car garage

◆ Slab or crawl space foundation, please specify when ordering

Price Code A

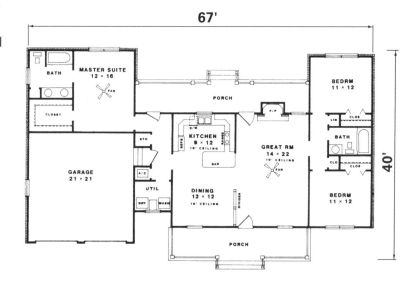

Plan #581-052D-0005

1,268 total square feet of living area

Special features

◆ Raised gable porch is a focal point creating a dramatic look

◆ 10' ceilings throughout living and dining areas

◆ Open kitchen is well-designed

◆ Master bedroom offers tray ceiling and private bath with both a garden tub and a 4' shower

◆ 3 bedrooms, 2 baths, 2-car drive under garage

◆ Basement foundation

Price Code A

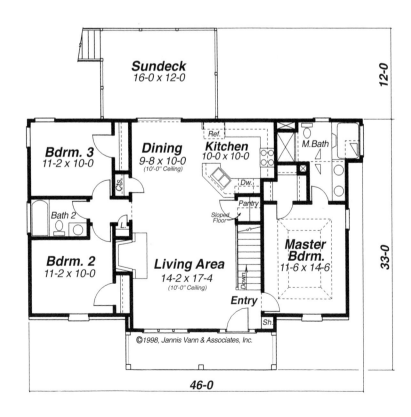

*G*raciously Designed

*P*lan #581-058D-0021

1,477 total square feet of living area

Special features

◆ Oversized porch provides protection from the elements

◆ Innovative kitchen employs step-saving design

◆ Kitchen has snack bar which opens to the breakfast room with bay window

◆ 3 bedrooms, 2 baths, 2-car side entry garage with storage area

◆ Basement foundation

Price Code A

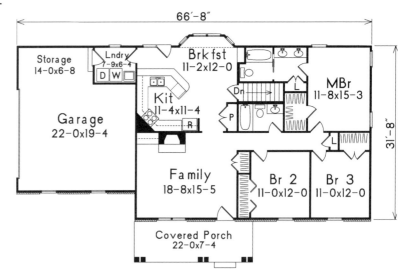

*P*lan #581-022D-0019

1,283 total square feet of living area

Special features

- ◆ Vaulted breakfast room has sliding doors that open onto deck
- ◆ Kitchen features convenient corner sink and pass-through to dining room
- ◆ Open living atmosphere in dining area and great room
- ◆ Vaulted great room features a fire-place
- ◆ 3 bedrooms, 2 baths, 2-car garage
- ◆ Basement foundation

Price Code A

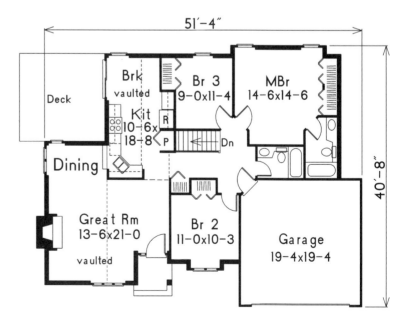

*P*lan #581-037D-0029

1,736 total square feet of living area

Special features

- ◆ Vaulted master bedroom with double-door entry and private bath
- ◆ Garage apartment comes complete with adjacent terrace and porch
- ◆ Windows surround the cozy dining room for added sunshine
- ◆ 3 bedrooms, 3 baths, 2-car garage
- ◆ Slab foundation

Price Code B

Rear View

Main House
1,268 sq. ft.

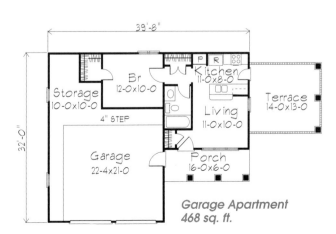

Garage Apartment
468 sq. ft.

Stonework Entry

Plan #581-010D-0005

1,358 total square feet of living area

Special features

◆ Vaulted master bath has walk-in closet, double-bowl vanity, large tub, shower and toilet area

◆ Galley kitchen opens to both the living room and the breakfast area

◆ Vaulted ceiling joins dining and living rooms

◆ Breakfast room with full wall of windows

◆ 3 bedrooms, 2 baths, 2-car garage

◆ Slab foundation

Price Code A

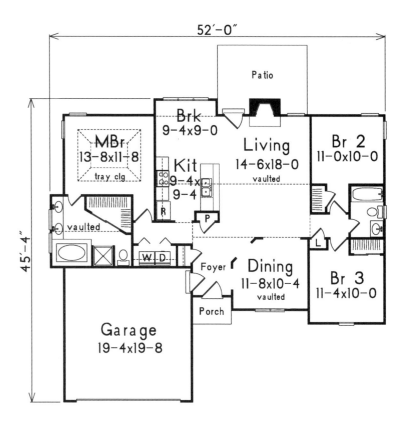

Plan #581-021D-0007

1,868 total square feet of living area

Special features

◆ Luxurious master bath is impressive with an angled quarter-circle tub, separate vanities and large walk-in closet

◆ Energy efficient home with 2" x 6" exterior walls

◆ Dining room is surrounded by a series of arched openings which complement the open feeling of this design

◆ Living room has a 12' ceiling accented by skylights and a large fireplace flanked by sliding doors

◆ Large storage areas

◆ 3 bedrooms, 2 baths, 2-car side entry garage

◆ Slab foundation, drawings also include crawl space foundation

Price Code D

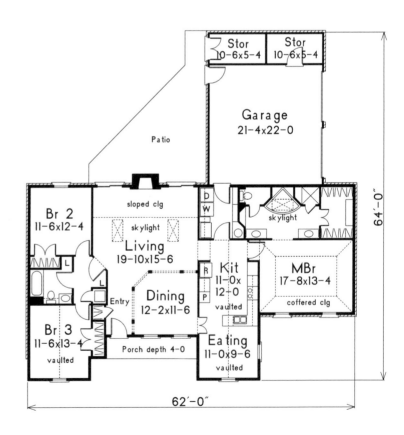

Kitchen Is A Chef's Dream

Plan #581-035D-0036

2,193 total square feet of living area

Special features

◆ Master suite includes a sitting room

◆ Dining room has decorative columns and overlooks family room

◆ Kitchen has lots of storage

◆ 3 bedrooms, 3 baths, 2-car side entry garage

◆ Walk-out basement, crawl space or slab foundation, please specify when ordering

Price Code C

Optional Second Floor 400 sq. ft.

First Floor 2,193 sq. ft.

Ranch With Style

Plan #581-051D-0060

1,591 total square feet of living area

Special features

- Fireplace in great room is accented by windows on both sides
- Practical kitchen is splendidly designed for organization
- Large screened porch for three-season entertaining
- 3 bedrooms, 2 baths, 3-car garage
- Basement foundation

Price Code B

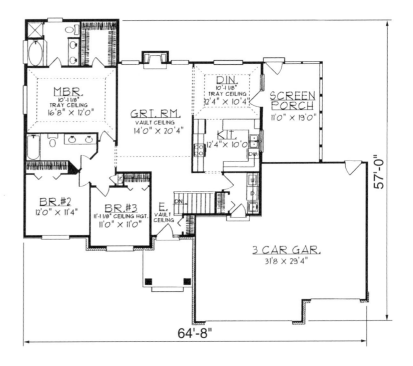

Sunny Eating Area

Plan #581-020D-0008

1,925 total square feet of living area

Special features

◆ Energy efficient home with 2" x 6" exterior walls

◆ Balcony off eating area adds character

◆ Master bedroom has dressing room, bath, walk-in closet and access to utility room

◆ 3 bedrooms, 2 baths, 2-car side entry garage

◆ Crawl space foundation, drawings also include slab foundation

Price Code C

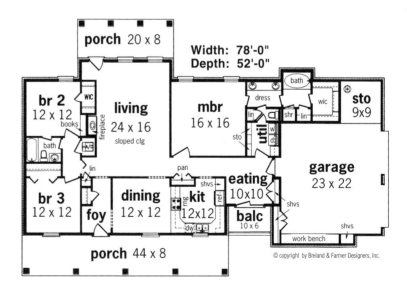

Width: 78'-0"
Depth: 52'-0"

porch 20 x 8

br 2
12 x 12

living
24 x 16
sloped clg

mbr
16 x 16

util

sto
9x9

dress

wic

bath

garage
23 x 22

br 3
12 x 12

foy

dining
12 x 12

kit
12x12

eating
10x10

balc
10 x 6

work bench

porch 44 x 8

© copyright by Breland & Farmer Designers, Inc.

$\mathcal{E}$legant Entrance

$\mathcal{P}lan$ #581-014D-0010

2,563 total square feet of living area

Special features

- ◆ Energy efficient home with 2" x 6" exterior walls
- ◆ Remote master bedroom features bath with double sinks, spa tub and separate room with toilet
- ◆ Arched columns separate foyer from great room which includes a fireplace and accesses the nook
- ◆ Well-designed kitchen provides plenty of workspace and storage plus room for extra cooks
- ◆ 4 bedrooms, 2 baths, 2-car garage
- ◆ Basement foundation

Price Code D

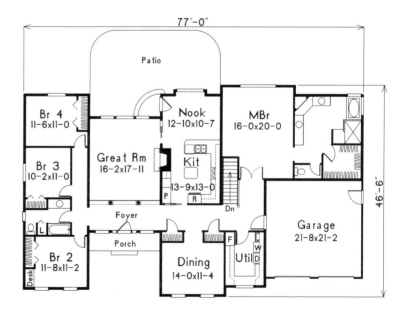

Plan #581-058D-0026

1,819 total square feet of living area

Special features

- Master bedroom features access to the outdoors, large walk-in closet and private bath
- 9' ceilings throughout
- Formal foyer with coat closet opens into vaulted great room with fireplace and formal dining room
- Kitchen and breakfast room create a cozy and casual area
- 3 bedrooms, 2 baths, 2-car side entry garage
- Basement foundation

Price Code C

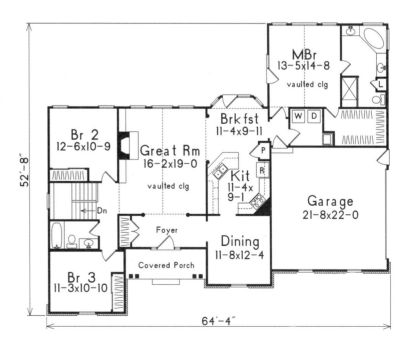

*P*lan #581-013D-0030

2,288 total square feet of living area

Special features

- ◆ Truly sumptuous master bedroom includes 12' ceiling, two walk-in closets, sitting area and full bath
- ◆ Family room features 14' ceiling and a rear window wall with French doors leading to an enormous deck
- ◆ Cozy hearth room includes a T.V. niche
- ◆ 3 bedrooms, 2 1/2 baths, 2-car side entry garage
- ◆ Basement or crawl space foundation, please specify when ordering

Price Code D

Plan #581-007D-0108

983 total square feet of living area

Special features

◆ Spacious front porch leads you into living and dining areas open to a pass-through kitchen

◆ A small patio with privacy fence creates exterior access from living room

◆ The master bedroom includes a large walk-in closet and its own private full bath

◆ 3 bedrooms, 2 baths, 2-car garage

◆ Crawl space foundation, drawings also include slab foundation

Price Code AA

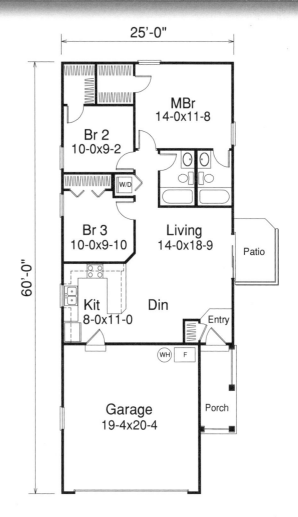

25'-0"

60'-0"

MBr
14-0x11-8

Br 2
10-0x9-2

W/D

Br 3
10-0x9-10

Living
14-0x18-9

Patio

Kit
8-0x11-0

Din

Entry

WH F

Porch

Garage
19-4x20-4

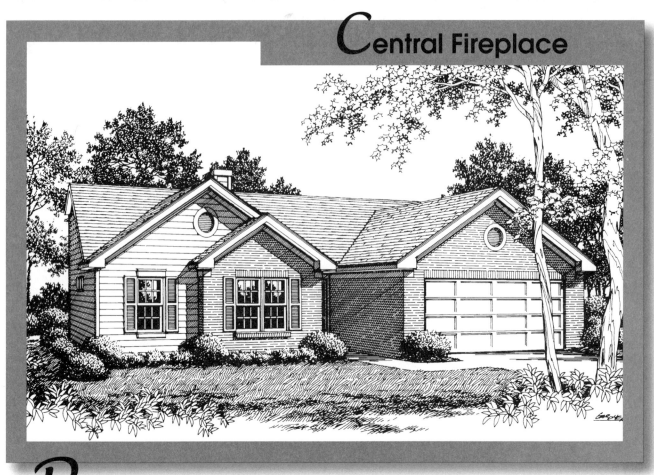

Plan #581-053D-0037

1,408 total square feet of living area

Special features

- Handsome see-through fireplace offers a gathering point for the family room, breakfast area and kitchen
- Vaulted ceiling and large bay window in the master bedroom add charm to this room
- A dramatic angular wall and large windows add brightness to the kitchen and breakfast area
- Kitchen, breakfast and family rooms have vaulted ceilings, adding to this central living area
- 3 bedrooms, 2 baths, 2-car garage
- Crawl space foundation, drawings also include slab foundation

Price Code A

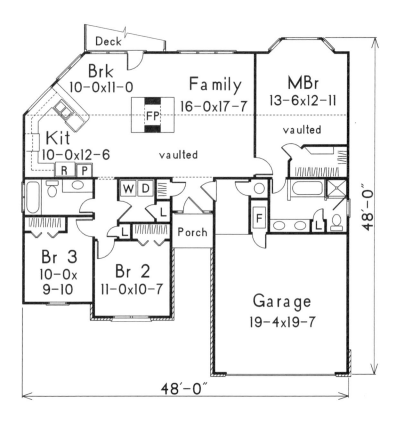

Convenient Ranch

Plan #581-001D-0093

1,120 total square feet of living area

Special features

◆ Master bedroom includes a half bath with laundry area, linen closet and kitchen access

◆ Kitchen has charming double-door entry, breakfast bar and a convenient walk-in pantry

◆ Welcoming front porch opens to large living room with coat closet

◆ 3 bedrooms, 1 1/2 baths

◆ Crawl space foundation, drawings also include basement and slab foundations

Price Code AA

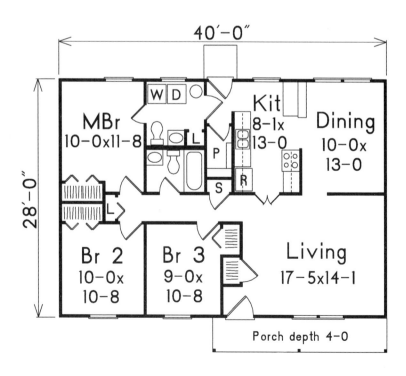

40'-0"

28'-0"

MBr 10-0x11-8

W D

L

P

S

L

Kit 8-1x 13-0

R

Dining 10-0x 13-0

Br 2 10-0x 10-8

Br 3 9-0x 10-8

Living 17-5x14-1

Porch depth 4-0

Endless Possibilities

Plan #581-051D-0050

1,763 total square feet of living area

Special features

- Spacious laundry room counterspace and a closet
- Skylights enhance the great room with sunlight
- Large windows provide a sunny eating area directly off kitchen with center island
- 3 bedrooms, 2 baths, 2-car garage
- Basement foundation

Price Code B

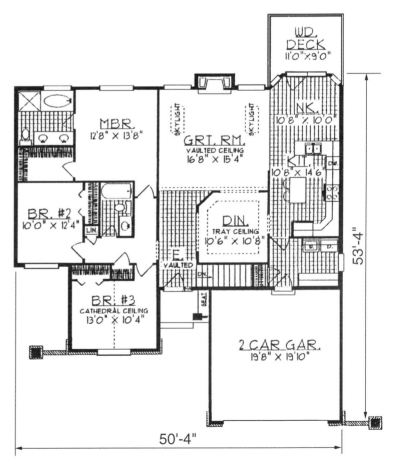

Plan #581-047D-0019

1,783 total square feet of living area

Special features

◆ Grand foyer leads to family room

◆ Walk-in pantry in kitchen

◆ Master bath has a step-down door-less shower, huge vanity and a large walk-in closet

◆ 3 bedrooms, 2 baths, 2-car garage

◆ Slab foundation

Price Code B

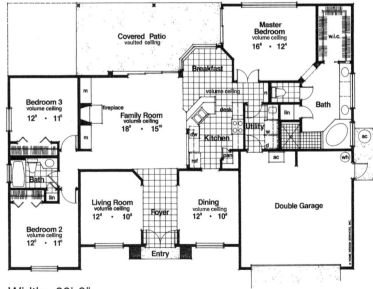

Width: 60'-0"
Depth: 45'-0"

Elegant European Styling

Plan #581-060D-0010

2,600 total square feet of living area

Special features

◆ Formal entry has large openings to dining and great rooms both with coffered ceilings

◆ Great room has corner fireplace and atrium doors leading to rear covered porch

◆ Morning room with rear view and an angled eating bar is sunny and bright

◆ Exercise room could easily serve as an office or computer room

◆ 4 bedrooms, 2 1/2 baths, 3-car side entry garage

◆ Slab or crawl space foundation, please specify when ordering

Price Code E

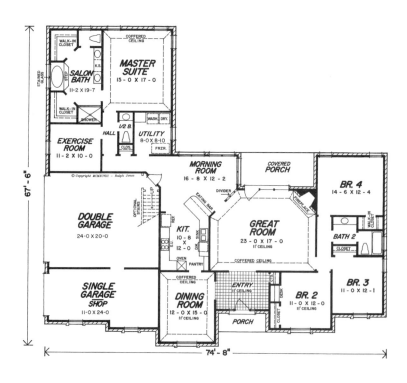

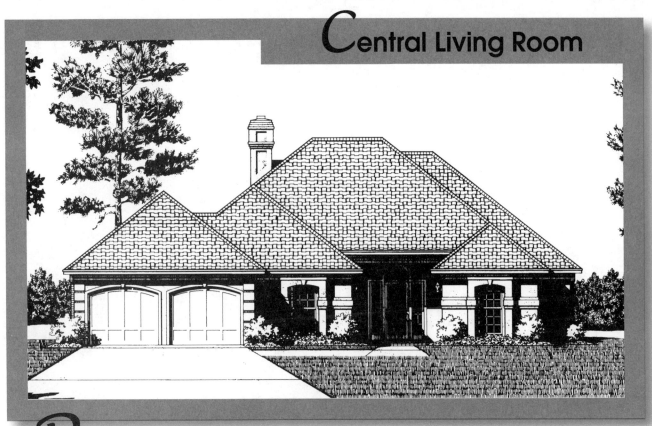

Plan #581-021D-0005

2,177 total square feet of living area

Special features

- Master bedroom features a sitting area and double-door entry to an elegant master bath
- Secondary bedrooms are spacious with walk-in closets and a shared bath
- Breakfast room with full windows opens to the rear porch
- Exterior window treatments create a unique style
- Kitchen features an island cooktop, eating bar and wet bar that is accessible to the living room
- 3 bedrooms, 2 baths, 2-car garage
- Slab foundation, drawings also include basement and crawl space foundations

Price Code C

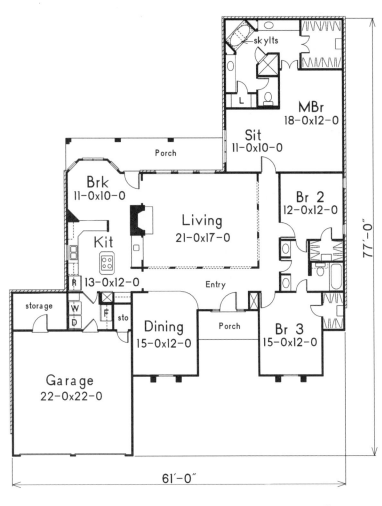

Plan #581-052D-0026

1,675 total square feet of living area

Special features

- ◆ Country accents give this home curb appeal
- ◆ Spacious laundry room is located off master bedroom
- ◆ Cathedral ceiling in living area
- ◆ Alternate floor plan design includes handicap accessibility that is 100% ADA compliant
- ◆ 3 bedrooms, 2 baths, 2-car side entry garage
- ◆ Crawl space or slab foundation, please specify when ordering

Price Code B

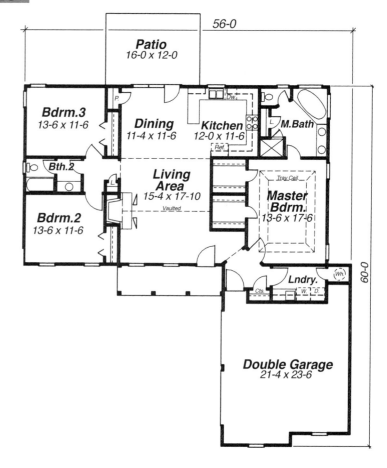

Plan #581-040D-0014

1,595 total square feet of living area

Special features

- ◆ Dining room has convenient built-in desk and provides access to the outdoors
- ◆ L-shaped kitchen area features island cooktop
- ◆ Family room has high ceiling and a fireplace
- ◆ Private master bedroom includes large walk-in closet and bath with separate tub and shower units
- ◆ 3 bedrooms, 2 baths, 2-car side entry garage
- ◆ Slab foundation, drawings also include crawl space foundation

Price Code B

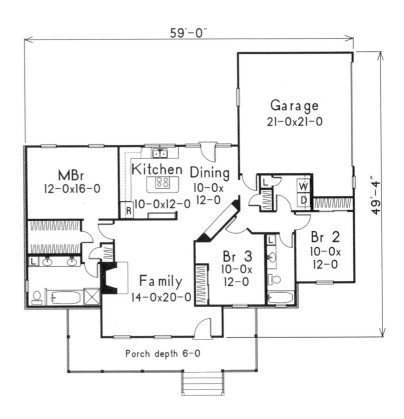

$\mathcal{B}$right And Airy

$\mathcal{P}$lan #581-007D-0140

1,591 total square feet of living area

Special features

- Spacious porch and patio provided for outdoor enjoyment
- Large entry foyer leads to a cheery kitchen and breakfast room which welcomes the sun through a wide array of windows
- The great room features a vaulted ceiling, corner fireplace, wet bar and access to the rear patio
- Double walk-in closets, private porch and a luxury bath are special highlights of the vaulted master bedroom suite
- 3 bedrooms, 2 baths, 2-car side entry garage
- Basement foundation

Price Code B

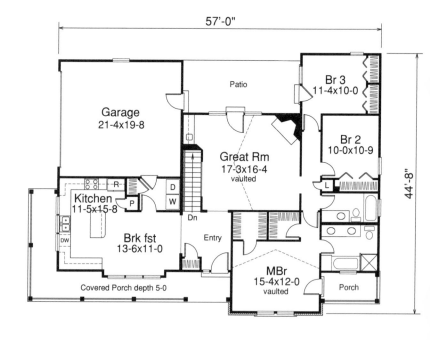

Plan #581-001D-0041

1,000 total square feet of living area

Special features

- Bath includes convenient closeted laundry area
- Master bedroom includes double closets and private access to bath
- Foyer features handy coat closet
- L-shaped kitchen provides easy access outdoors
- 3 bedrooms, 1 bath
- Crawl space foundation, drawings also include basement and slab foundations

Price Code AA

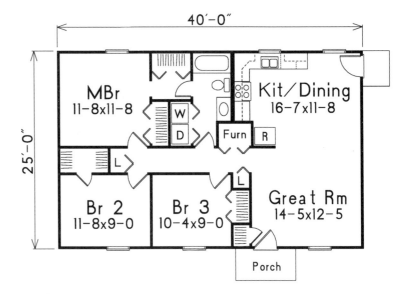

Plan #581-069D-0017

1,926 total square feet of living area

Special features

- ◆ Large covered rear porch is spacious enough for entertaining
- ◆ L-shaped kitchen is compact yet efficient and includes a snack bar for extra dining space
- ◆ Oversized utility room has counterspace, extra shelves and space for a second refrigerator
- ◆ Secluded master suite has a private bath and a large walk-in closet
- ◆ 3 bedrooms, 2 baths, 2-car side entry garage
- ◆ Slab or crawl space foundation, please specify when ordering

Price Code C

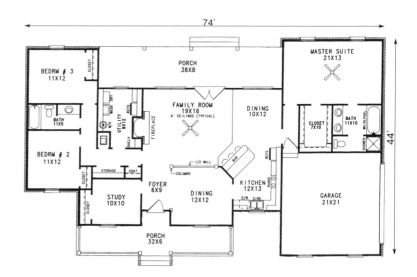

Plan #581-035D-0014

2,236 total square feet of living area

Special features

- Luxurious master suite has enormous sitting room with fireplace and vaulted private bath
- Cozy family room off breakfast area
- Two secondary bedrooms share a bath
- 3 bedrooms, 2 1/2 baths, 2-car side entry garage
- Walk-out basement or crawl space foundation, please specify when ordering

Price Code D

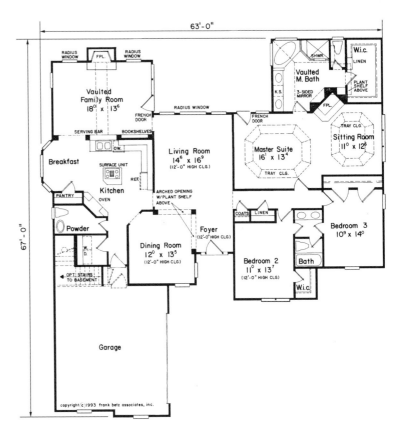

*P*lan #581-068D-0004

1,969 total square feet of living area

Special features

- ◆ Master bedroom boasts luxurious bath with double sinks, two walk-in closets and an oversized tub
- ◆ Corner fireplace warms a conveniently located family area
- ◆ Formal living and dining areas in the front of the home lend a touch of privacy when entertaining
- ◆ Spacious utility room has counter space and a sink
- ◆ 3 bedrooms, 2 baths, 2-car garage
- ◆ Crawl space foundation, drawings also include slab foundation

Price Code C

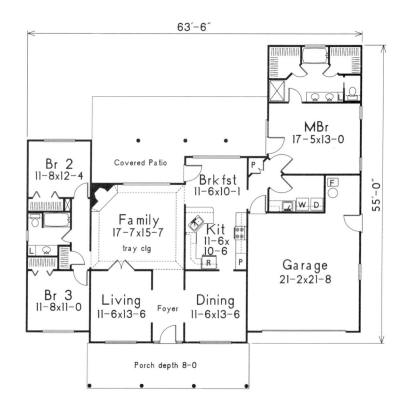

Plan #581-045D-0003

1,958 total square feet of living area

Special features

- ◆ Large wrap-around kitchen opens to a bright and cheerful breakfast area with access to large covered deck and open stairway to basement
- ◆ Kitchen is nestled between the dining and breakfast rooms
- ◆ Master bedroom includes a large walk-in closet, double-bowl vanity, garden tub and separate shower
- ◆ Foyer features attractive plant shelves and opens into living room that includes an attractive central fireplace
- ◆ 3 bedrooms, 2 baths, 2-car garage
- ◆ Basement foundation

Price Code C

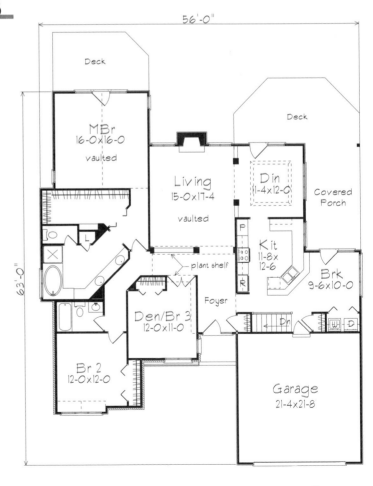

Quaint And Cozy

Plan #581-020D-0015

1,191 total square feet of living area

Special features

◆ Energy efficient home with 2" x 6" exterior walls

◆ Master bedroom is located near living areas for maximum convenience

◆ Living room has cathedral ceiling and stone fireplace

◆ 3 bedrooms, 2 baths, 2-car side entry garage

◆ Slab foundation, drawings also include crawl space foundation

Price Code AA

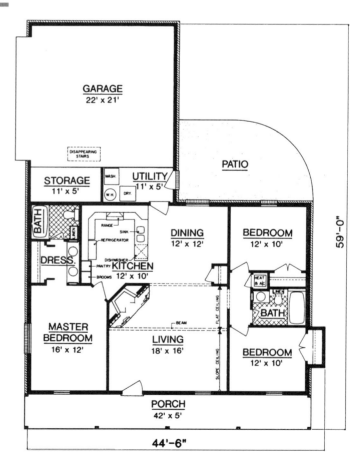

*P*lan #581-026D-0138

1,853 total square feet of living area

Special features

◆ Bedrooms have plenty of closet space

◆ A snack bar separates the kitchen and well-lit dining area

◆ 3 bedrooms, 3 baths, 2-car side entry garage

◆ Basement foundation

Price Code C

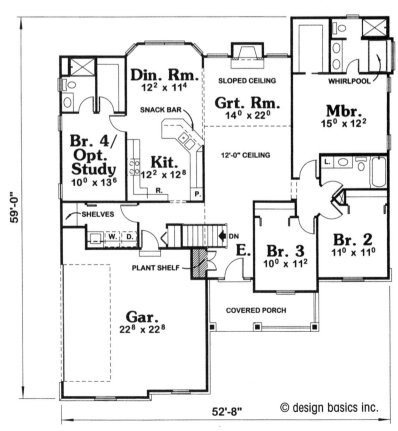

Bays Accent Facade

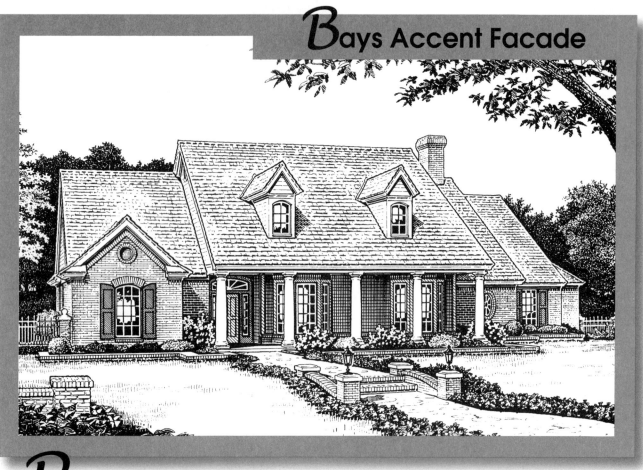

Plan #581-036D-0058

2,529 total square feet of living area

Special features

- Kitchen and breakfast area are located between the family and living rooms for easy access
- Master bedroom includes sitting area, private bath and access to covered patio
- 4 bedrooms, 3 baths, 3-car side entry garage
- Slab foundation

Price Code D

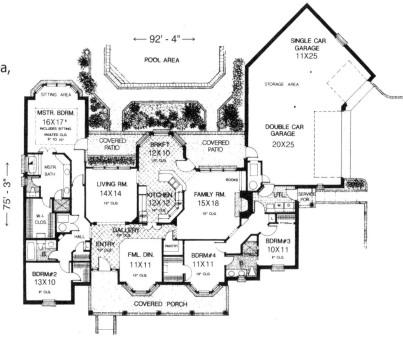

Plan #581-015D-0003

2,255 total square feet of living area

Special features

◆ Well-lit foyer with transom overlooks sunken formal living room with 12' ceiling

◆ Family room and kitchen are situated separately for more casual living

◆ Breakfast room nook offers access to deck and overlooks family room with a fireplace surrounded by built-in shelves

◆ Master suite has vaulted ceiling and a huge walk-in closet

◆ 3 bedrooms, 2 baths, 2-car garage

◆ Crawl space foundation

Price Code D

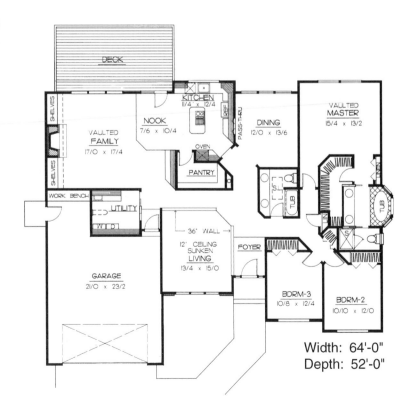

Width: 64'-0"
Depth: 52'-0"

*G*racious Atrium Ranch

*P*lan #581-007D-0065

2,218 total square feet of living area

Special features

- ◆ Vaulted great room has an arched colonnade entry, bay windowed atrium with staircase and a fireplace
- ◆ Vaulted kitchen enjoys bay doors to deck, pass-through breakfast bar and walk-in pantry
- ◆ Breakfast room offers bay window and snack bar open to kitchen with laundry nearby
- ◆ 4 bedrooms, 2 baths, 2-car garage
- ◆ Walk-out basement foundation

Price Code D

Rear View

First Floor 2,218 sq. ft.

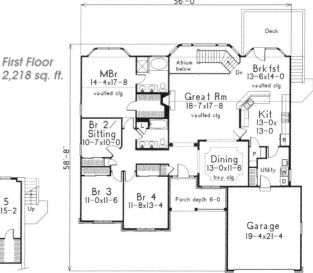

Optional Lower Level 1,217 sq. ft.

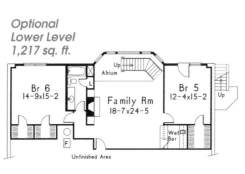

Plan #581-016D-0049

1,793 total square feet of living area

Special features

◆ Beautiful foyer leads into the great room that has a fireplace flanked by two sets of beautifully transomed doors both leading to a large covered porch

◆ Dramatic eat-in kitchen includes an abundance of cabinets and work-space in an exciting angled shape

◆ Delightful master bedroom has many amenities

◆ Optional bonus room above the garage has an additional 779 square feet of living area

◆ 3 bedrooms, 2 baths, 2-car side entry garage

◆ Basement, crawl space or slab foun-dation, please specify when ordering

Price Code B

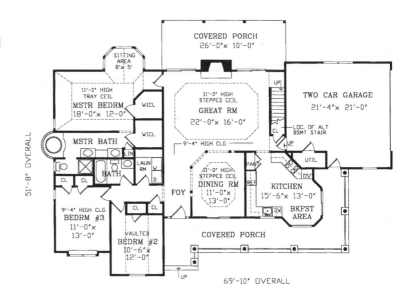

Plan #581-020D-0005

1,770 total square feet of living area

Special features

- Open floor plan makes this home feel spacious
- 12' ceilings in kitchen, living, breakfast and dining areas
- Kitchen is the center of activity with views into all gathering places
- 3 bedrooms, 2 baths, 2-car side entry garage
- Slab foundation, drawings also include crawl space foundation

Price Code B

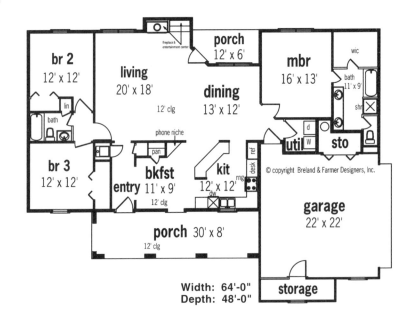

br 2
12' x 12'

living
20' x 18'
12' clg

porch
12' x 6'

fireplace & entertainment center

dining
13' x 12'

mbr
16' x 13'

wic

bath
11' x 9'

shr

lin

bath

phone niche

pan

bkfst
11' x 9'
12' clg

kit
12' x 12'

desk

ref

util

d

W

sto

br 3
12' x 12'

entry

© copyright Breland & Farmer Designers, Inc.

garage
22' x 22'

porch 30' x 8'
12' clg

storage

Width: 64'-0"
Depth: 48'-0"

Plan #581-047D-0036

2,140 total square feet of living area

Special features

◆ Living and dining areas traditionally separated by foyer

◆ Media wall and fireplace are located in cozy family room

◆ Generous master bedroom has sliding glass doors onto patio, walk-in closet and a private bath

◆ 4 bedrooms, 3 baths, 2-car side entry garage

◆ Slab foundation

Price Code C

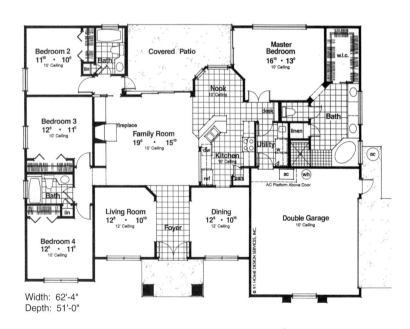

Width: 62'-4"
Depth: 51'-0"

Plan #581-043D-0006

2,355 total square feet of living area

Special features

- ◆ Double-doors lead into a private den perfect for a home office
- ◆ Vaulted ceilings and a fireplace make the family room a terrific gathering spot
- ◆ Cheerful nook off kitchen makes an ideal breakfast area
- ◆ 9' ceilings throughout home
- ◆ 3 bedrooms, 3 baths, 3-car side entry garage
- ◆ Crawl space foundation

Price Code D

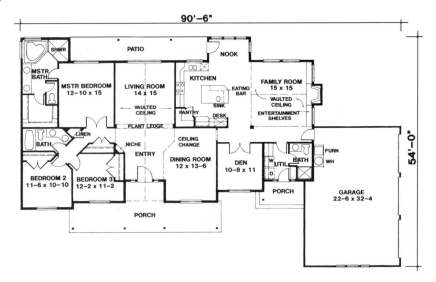

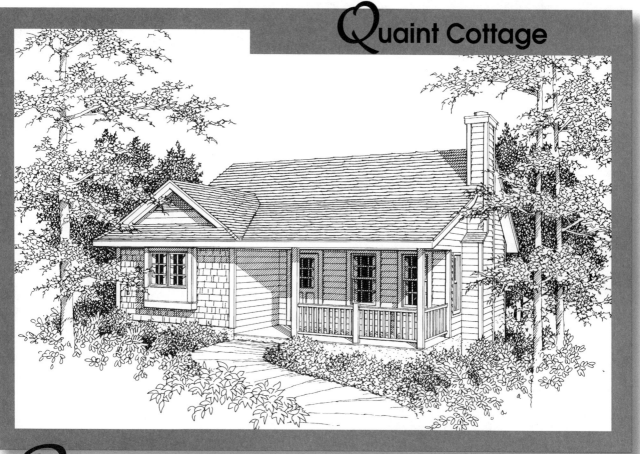

Quaint Cottage

Plan #581-058D-0003

1,020 total square feet of living area

Special features

◆ Living room is warmed by a fireplace

◆ Dining and living rooms are enhanced by vaulted ceilings and plant shelves

◆ U-shaped kitchen with large window over the sink

◆ 2 bedrooms, 1 bath

◆ Slab foundation

Price Code AA

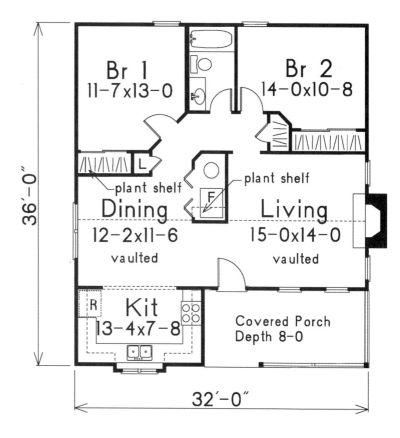

Br 1
11-7x13-0

Br 2
14-0x10-8

plant shelf

plant shelf

Dining
12-2x11-6
vaulted

Living
15-0x14-0
vaulted

Kit
13-4x7-8

Covered Porch
Depth 8-0

36'-0"

32'-0"

Terrific Master Bedroom

Plan #581-018D-0003

2,517 total square feet of living area

Special features

◆ Energy efficient home with 2" x 6" exterior walls

◆ Central living room features large windows and attractive transoms

◆ Varied ceiling heights throughout home

◆ Secluded master bedroom enjoys a double-door entry, luxurious bath with separate shower, step-up whirlpool tub, double vanities and walk-in closets

◆ Kitchen with walk-in pantry overlooks large family room with fireplace and unique octagon-shaped breakfast room

◆ 4 bedrooms, 2 1/2 baths, 2-car garage

◆ Slab foundation, drawings also include crawl space foundation

Price Code D

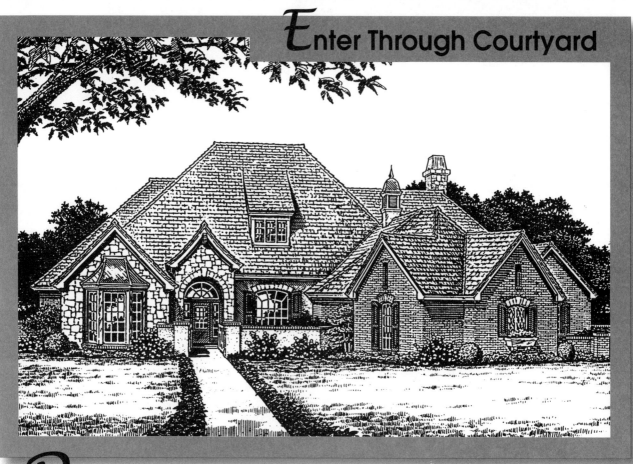

*P*lan #581-036D-0051

2,911 total square feet of living area

Special features

- ◆ Well-designed plan with great room and adjacent gallery area
- ◆ Master bedroom has access to covered patio, a private bath and walk-in closet
- ◆ Enter study through double-doors to find built-in bookshelves
- ◆ 4 bedrooms, 3 1/2 baths, 3-car side entry garage
- ◆ Basement or slab foundation, please specify when ordering

Price Code E

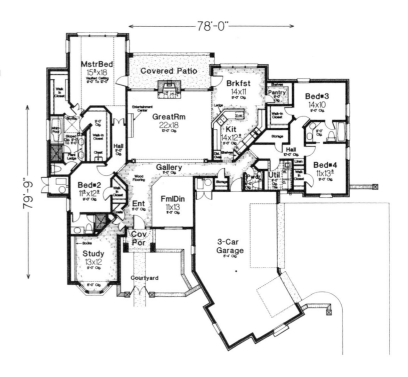

Plan #581-065D-0025

1,755 total square feet of living area

Special features

- The spacious kitchen with bar seating, dining area with angled bay and delightful rear porch complement this splendid floor plan
- The master bedroom has a lavishly equipped bath and large walk-in closet
- A warm and inviting fireplace is flanked by French doors creating a grand first impression in the great room
- 3 bedrooms, 2 baths, 3-car garage
- Walk-out basement or basement foundation, please specify when ordering

Price Code B

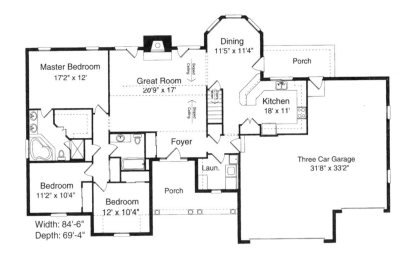

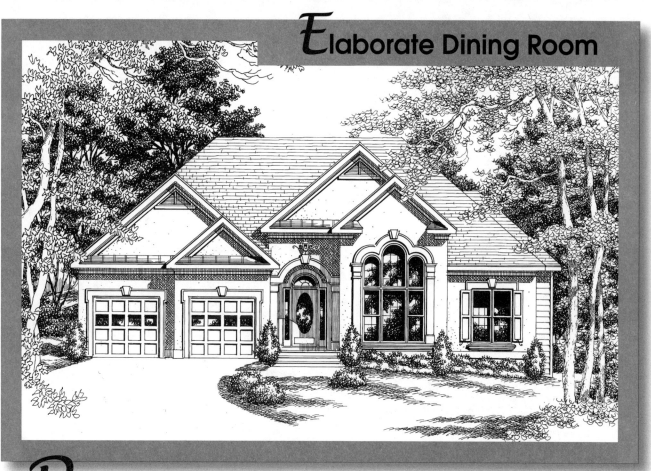

*P*lan #581-035D-0028

1,779 total square feet of living area

Special features

◆ Well-designed floor plan has vaulted family room with fireplace and access to the outdoors

◆ Decorative columns separate dining area from foyer

◆ A vaulted ceiling adds spaciousness in master bath with walk-in closet

◆ 3 bedrooms, 2 baths, 2-car garage

◆ Walk-out basement, slab or crawl space foundation, please specify when ordering

Price Code B

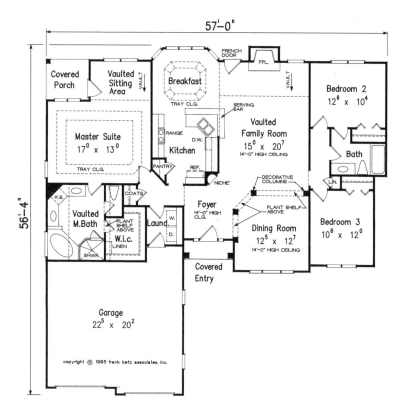

Gabled Front Facade

Plan #581-058D-0017

2,412 total square feet of living area

Special features

- ◆ Coffered ceiling in dining room adds character and spaciousness
- ◆ Great room enhanced by a vaulted ceiling and an atrium window wall
- ◆ Spacious well-planned kitchen includes counterspace dining and overlooks breakfast room and beyond to deck
- ◆ Luxurious master bedroom features enormous walk-in closet, private bath and easy access to laundry area
- ◆ 4 bedrooms, 2 baths, 3-car side entry garage
- ◆ Walk-out basement foundation

Price Code D

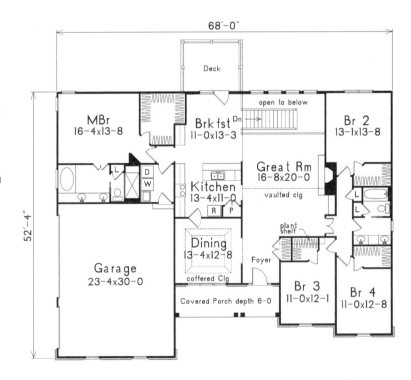

Great Views At Rear

*P*lan #581-011D-0010

2,197 total square feet of living area

Special features

◆ Centrally located great room opens to kitchen, breakfast nook and private backyard

◆ Den located off entry ideal for home office

◆ Vaulted master bath has spa tub, shower and double vanity

◆ 3 bedrooms, 2 1/2 baths, 3-car garage

◆ Crawl space foundation

Price Code C

Handsome Accents

*P*lan #581-001D-0013

1,882 total square feet of living area

Special features

- ◆ Wide, handsome entrance opens to the vaulted great room with fireplace
- ◆ Living and dining areas are conveniently joined but still allow privacy
- ◆ Private covered porch extends breakfast area
- ◆ Practical passageway runs through laundry and mud room from garage to kitchen
- ◆ Vaulted ceiling in master bedroom
- ◆ 3 bedrooms, 2 baths, 2-car garage
- ◆ Basement foundation

Price Code D

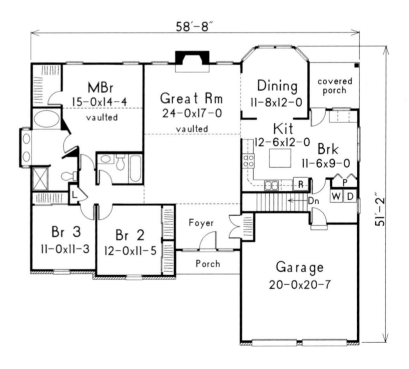

Perfect For A Growing Family

$\mathcal{P}$lan #581-065D-0039

1,794 total square feet of living area

Special features

- The great room with sloped ceiling and a fireplace connects with the kitchen and dining area for an open atmosphere
- Seating at the snack bar, angled walls and French doors to a covered porch from the dining area create spectacular surroundings
- 3 bedrooms, 2 baths, 2-car side entry garage
- Basement foundation

Price Code B

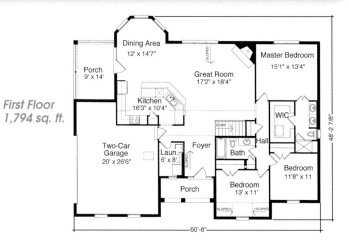

First Floor
1,794 sq. ft.

Dining Area 12' x 14'7"
Porch 9' x 14'
Great Room 17'2" x 18'4"
Master Bedroom 15'1" x 13'4"
Kitchen 16'3" x 10'4"
WIC
Two-Car Garage 20' x 26'6"
Laun. 6' x 8'
Foyer
Bath
Hall
Bedroom 11'8" x 11
Porch
Bedroom 13' x 11'
60'-8"
48'-2 7/8"

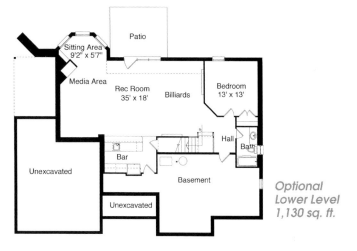

Optional
Lower Level
1,130 sq. ft.

Patio
Sitting Area 9'2" x 5'7"
Media Area
Rec Room 35' x 18'
Billiards
Bedroom 13' x 13'
Hall
Bath
Bar
Basement
Unexcavated
Unexcavated

Plan #581-025D-0009

1,680 total square feet of living area

Special features

◆ Vaulted great room has a wet bar making it an ideal space for entertaining

◆ Spacious dining area features an eating bar for additional seating

◆ Fourth bedroom could easily be converted to a study

◆ 4 bedrooms, 2 baths, 2-car garage

◆ Slab foundation

Price Code B

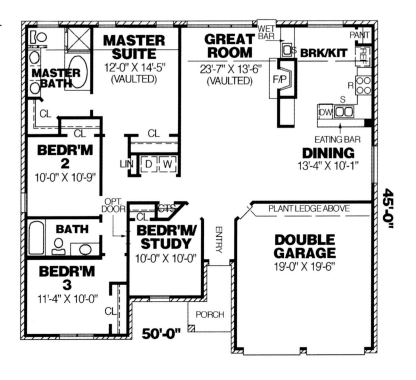

Country Charm

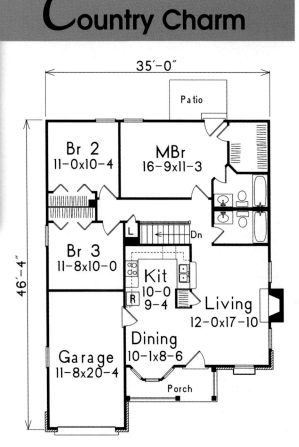

Plan #581-007D-0110

1,169 total square feet of living area

Special features

- Living room has a wood-burning fireplace
- A stylish U-shaped kitchen offers an abundance of cabinet and counterspace with view to living room
- A large walk-in closet, access to rear patio and private bath are many features of the master bedroom
- 3 bedrooms, 2 baths, 1-car garage
- Basement foundation

Price Code AA

Victorian Ranch

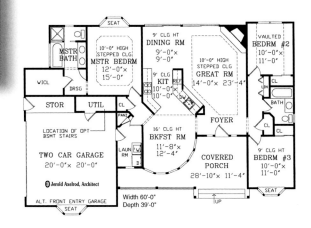

Plan #581-016D-0053

1,466 total square feet of living area

Special features

- Sliding French doors open to the backyard from both the great room and adjoining formal dining room
- A turreted breakfast room overlooks the spacious front porch
- 3 bedrooms, 2 baths, 2-car side entry garage
- Basement, crawl space or slab foundation, please specify when ordering

Price Code B

*B*onus Game Room

*P*lan #581-055D-0053

1,957 total square feet of living area

Special features

◆ Breakfast room with bay window opens to kitchen with bar

◆ 9' ceilings throughout this home

◆ Master suite has 10' boxed ceiling and atrium doors to rear porch

◆ 3 bedrooms, 2 baths, 2-car garage

◆ Basement, walk-out basement, slab or crawl space foundation, please specify when ordering

Price Code C

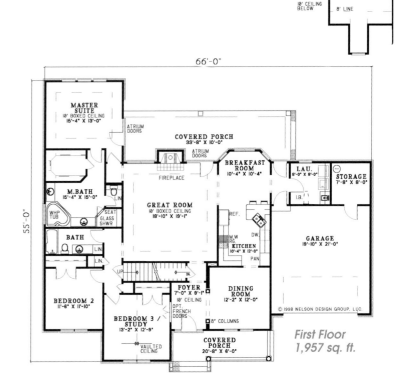

Optional Second Floor 479 sq. ft.

First Floor 1,957 sq. ft.

First Floor
1,297 sq. ft.

Lower Level
1,234 sq. ft.

*P*lan #581-007D-0004

2,531 total square feet of living area

Special features

- ◆ Charming porch with dormers leads into vaulted great room with atrium
- ◆ Well-designed kitchen and breakfast bar adjoin extra large laundry/mud room
- ◆ Double sinks, tub with window above and plant shelf complete vaulted master bath
- ◆ 4 bedrooms, 2 1/2 baths, 2-car side entry garage
- ◆ Walk-out basement foundation

Price Code D

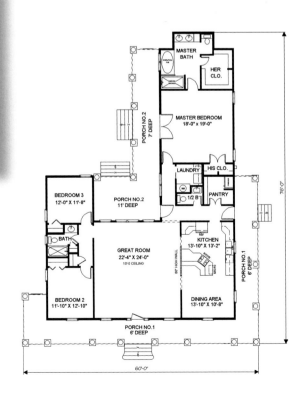

*P*lan #581-028D-0011

2,123 total square feet of living area

Special features

- ◆ L-shaped porch extends the entire length of this home creating lots of extra space for outdoor living
- ◆ Master bedroom is secluded for privacy and has two closets, double vanity in bath and a double-door entry onto covered porch
- ◆ Efficiently designed kitchen
- ◆ 3 bedrooms, 2 1/2 baths
- ◆ Crawl space foundation

Price Code C

Warm And Inviting

Plan #581-065D-0040

1,874 total square feet of living area

Special features

◆ The bayed dining area, kitchen and great room with a fireplace combine for an open living area

◆ The master bedroom pampers with a corner whirlpool tub, double vanity and walk-in closet

◆ 9' ceilings throughout home add to the spaciousness

◆ 3 bedrooms, 2 baths, 3-car side entry garage

◆ Basement or walk-out basement foundation, please specify when ordering

Price Code C

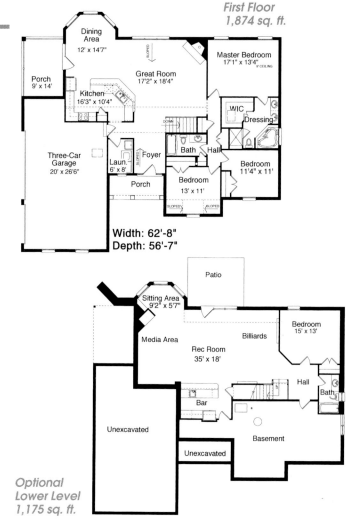

First Floor
1,874 sq. ft.

Dining Area
12' x 14'7"

Porch
9' x 14'

Great Room
17'2" x 18'4"

Kitchen
16'3" x 10'4"

Master Bedroom
17'1" x 13'4"

WIC

Dressing

Three-Car Garage
20' x 26'6"

Laun.
6' x 8'

Foyer

Bath

Hall

Bedroom
11'4" x 11'

Porch

Bedroom
13' x 11'

Width: 62'-8"
Depth: 56'-7"

Patio

Sitting Area
9'2" x 5'7"

Media Area

Billiards

Bedroom
15' x 13'

Rec Room
35' x 18'

Hall

Bath

Bar

Unexcavated

Basement

Unexcavated

*Optional
Lower Level
1,175 sq. ft.*

First Floor
1,231 sq. ft.

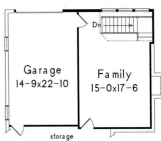

Optional
Lower Level
380 sq. ft.

Plan #581-007D-0103

1,231 total square feet of living area

Special features

- Dutch gables and stone accents provide an enchanting appearance
- Living room offers a masonry fireplace, atrium with window wall and is open to a dining area with bay window
- Kitchen has a breakfast counter, lots of cabinet space and glass sliding doors to a balcony
- 2 bedrooms, 2 baths, 1-car drive-under garage
- Walk-out basement foundation

Price Code A

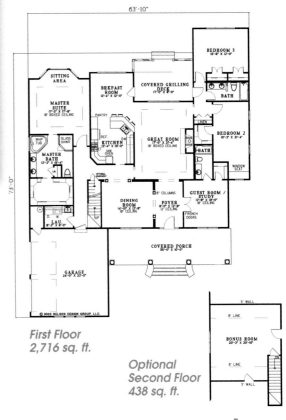

First Floor
2,716 sq. ft.

Optional
Second Floor
438 sq. ft.

Plan #581-055D-0103

2,716 total square feet of living area

Special features

- Master suite has lots of privacy from other bedrooms
- 10' ceiling in formal dining room makes an impression
- 4 bedrooms, 4 baths, 2-car side entry garage
- Crawl space or slab foundation, please specify when ordering

Price Code E

Plan #581-028D-0003

1,716 total square feet of living area

Special features

- ◆ Great room boasts a fireplace and access to the kitchen/breakfast area through a large arched opening
- ◆ Master bedroom includes a huge walk-in closet and French doors that lead onto an L-shaped porch
- ◆ Bedrooms #2 and #3 share a bath and linen closet
- ◆ 3 bedrooms, 2 baths, 2-car detached garage
- ◆ Crawl space or slab foundation, please specify when ordering

Price Code B

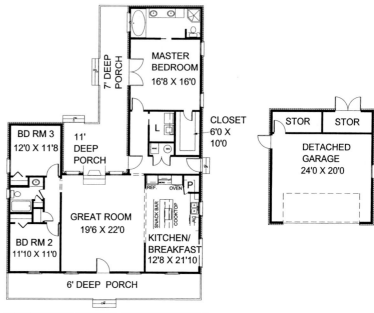

44'-0" WIDE X 65'-0" DEEP - WITHOUT GARAGE

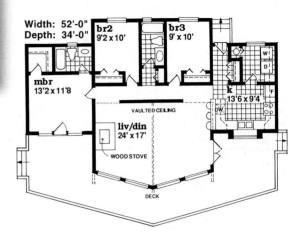

Plan #581-062D-0049

1,292 total square feet of living area

Special features

◆ Master bedroom features a walk-in closet, private bath and access to the outdoors onto an expansive deck

◆ Prominent woodstove enhances vaulted living/dining area

◆ Two secondary bedrooms share a bath

◆ Kitchen has a convenient snack counter

◆ 3 bedrooms, 2 baths

◆ Crawl space foundation

Price Code A

Plan #581-011D-0001

1,275 total square feet of living area

Special features

◆ Center island expands the kitchen into the dining area

◆ Decorative columns keep the living area open to other areas

◆ Covered front porch adds charm to the entry

◆ 3 bedrooms, 2 baths, 2-car garage

◆ Crawl space foundation

Price Code C

*P*lan #581-021D-0011

1,800 total square feet of living area

Special features

- ◆ Energy efficient home with 2" x 6" exterior walls
- ◆ Covered front and rear porches add outdoor living area
- ◆ 12' ceilings in kitchen, eating area, dining and living rooms
- ◆ Private master bedroom features an expansive bath
- ◆ Side entry garage has two storage areas
- ◆ Pillared styling with brick and stucco exterior finish
- ◆ 3 bedrooms, 2 baths, 2-car side entry garage
- ◆ Crawl space foundation, drawings also include slab foundation

Price Code D

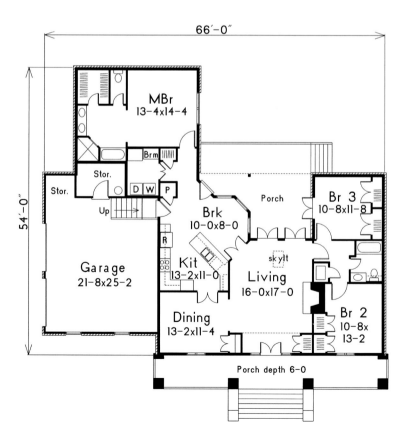

Optional Second Floor 231 sq. ft.

FUTURE PLAYROOM

First Floor 2,095 sq. ft.

*P*lan #581-025D-0020

2,095 total square feet of living area

Special features

- ◆ Decorative columns add interest to foyer and separate it from the dining and great rooms
- ◆ Built-in bookshelves flank a large fireplace
- ◆ Stunning U-shaped kitchen has a large amount of space
- ◆ 3 bedrooms, 2 baths, 2-car side entry garage
- ◆ Basement or slab foundation, please specify when ordering

Price Code C

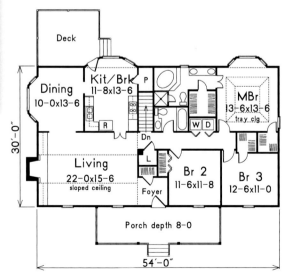

*P*lan #581-053D-0002

1,668 total square feet of living area

Special features

- ◆ Large bay windows in breakfast area, master bedroom and dining room
- ◆ Extensive walk-in closets and storage spaces throughout
- ◆ Handy covered entry porch
- ◆ Large living room has fireplace, built-in bookshelves and sloped ceiling
- ◆ 3 bedrooms, 2 baths, 2-car drive under garage
- ◆ Basement foundation

Price Code C

Plan #581-003D-0002

1,676 total square feet of living area

Special features

- ◆ The living area skylights and large breakfast room with bay window provide plenty of sunlight
- ◆ The master bedroom has a walk-in closet and both the secondary bedrooms have large closets
- ◆ Vaulted ceilings, plant shelving and a fireplace provide a quality living area
- ◆ 3 bedrooms, 2 baths, 2-car garage
- ◆ Basement foundation, drawings also include crawl space and slab foundations

Price Code B

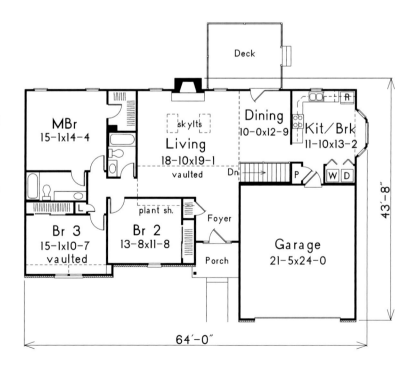

Width: 59'-10"
Depth: 60'-10"

Plan #581-024D-0017

2,697 total square feet of living area

Special features

◆ Secluded study with full bath nearby is an ideal guest room or office

◆ Master bedroom has access to outdoor patio

◆ 351 square feet of additional unfinished living space available in the attic

◆ 3 bedrooms, 3 baths, 2-car side entry garage

◆ Slab foundation

Price Code E

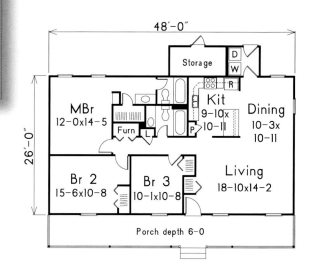

Plan #581-001D-0067

1,285 total square feet of living area

Special features

◆ Accommodating home with ranch-style porch

◆ Large storage area on back of home

◆ Master bedroom includes dressing area, private bath and built-in bookcase

◆ Kitchen has a pantry and a breakfast bar

◆ 3 bedrooms, 2 baths

◆ Crawl space foundation, drawings also include basement and slab foundations

Price Code B

Luxury Home With Extras

Plan #581-047D-0056

3,426 total square feet of living area

Special features

- Enormous master bath features double walk-in closets and an enormous whirlpool tub under a bay window
- Angled walls throughout add interest to every room
- Open and airy kitchen looks into a cozy breakfast nook as well as the casual family room
- 5 bedrooms, 4 baths, 3-car side entry garage
- Slab foundation

Price Code F

First Floor
3,426 sq. ft.

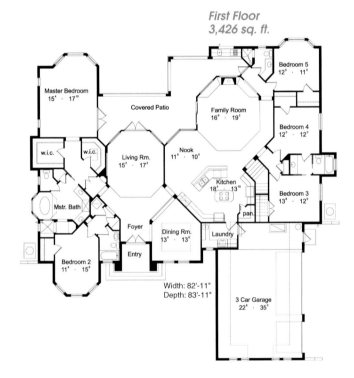

Optional
Second Floor
515 sq. ft.

Plan #581-065D-0013

2,041 total square feet of living area

Special features

- Great room accesses directly onto covered rear deck with ceiling fan above
- Private master bedroom has a beautiful octagon-shaped sitting area that opens and brightens the space
- Two secondary bedrooms share a full bath
- 3 bedrooms, 2 baths, 2-car side entry garage
- Basement or walk-out basement foundation, please specify when ordering

Price Code C

Plan #581-053D-0005

1,833 total square feet of living area

Special features

- Master bedroom suite comes with a garden tub, walk-in closet and bay window
- Walk-through kitchen and breakfast room
- Front bay windows offer a deluxe touch
- Foyer with convenient coat closet opens into large vaulted living room with an attractive fireplace
- 3 bedrooms, 2 baths, 2-car drive under garage
- Basement foundation

Price Code C

*P*lan #581-016D-0011

1,815 total square feet of living area

Special features

- ◆ A true great room features a 10' ceiling, built-in fireplace and a bright, airy feeling from several windows
- ◆ The kitchen and breakfast area are visually connected and the formal dining room is nearby for convenience
- ◆ 3 bedrooms, 2 baths, 2-car side entry garage
- ◆ Basement, crawl space or slab foundation, please specify when ordering

Price Code D

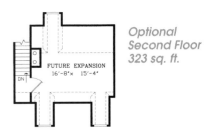

Optional Second Floor 323 sq. ft.

Width 75'-0"
Depth 43'-0"

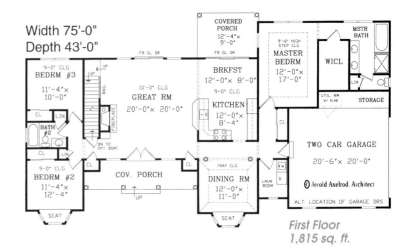

First Floor 1,815 sq. ft.

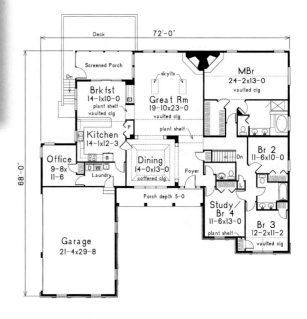

Plan #581-007D-0048

2,758 total square feet of living area

Special features

- ◆ Vaulted great room excels with fireplace, wet bar, plant shelves and skylights
- ◆ Fabulous master bedroom enjoys a fireplace, large bath, walk-in closet and vaulted ceiling
- ◆ Trendsetting kitchen and breakfast rooms adjoin spacious screened porch
- ◆ 4 bedrooms, 2 1/2 baths, 3-car side entry garage
- ◆ Basement foundation

Price Code E

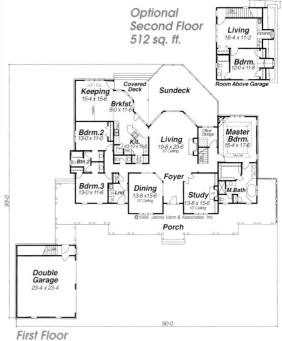

Optional Second Floor 512 sq. ft.

First Floor 2,911 sq. ft.

Plan #581-052D-0089

2,911 total square feet of living area

Special features

- ◆ Wrap-around porch with double columns
- ◆ Beautiful master bath with corner tub, separate shower and large walk-in closet
- ◆ Large sundeck offers a great area to relax
- ◆ 3 bedrooms, 2 1/2 baths, 2-car side entry garage
- ◆ Basement foundation

Price Code E

Plan #581-55D-0105

1,023 total square feet of living area

Special features

- ◆ Kitchen includes a snack bar and is open to the great room and breakfast room
- ◆ Master suite features a private bath
- ◆ Centrally located laundry area
- ◆ 3 bedrooms, 2 baths, 2-car garage
- ◆ Crawl space or slab foundation, please specify when ordering

Price Code A

45'-0"

47'-0"

BEDROOM 3
9'-6" X 10'-0"

MASTER SUITE
11'-0" X 12'-6"

BATH

BEDROOM 2
9'-6" X 10'-6"

STORAGE
10'-0" X 2'-8"

BATH

KITCHEN
11'-0" X 9'-0"

GARAGE
19'-8" X 22'-8"

GREAT RM.
13'-4" X 16'-4"

BREAKFAST ROOM
11'-0" X 7'-4"

COVERED PORCH
16'-0" X 6'-0"

© 1991 NELSON DESIGN GROUP, LLC.

Plan #581-007D-0008

2,452 total square feet of living area

Special features

◆ Spacious home office room with private entrance and bath, two closets, vaulted ceiling and transomed window perfect shown as a home office or a fourth bedroom

◆ Vaulted great room features a fireplace, extra storage closets and patio doors to sundeck

◆ Vaulted master bedroom has walk-in closet and bath

◆ 4 bedrooms, 2 1/2 baths, 3-car garage

◆ Basement foundation

Price Code D

Country Home

First Floor 1,744 sq. ft.

Lower Level 1,096 sq. ft.

Plan #581-011D-0009

2,840 total square feet of living area

Special features

◆ Secluded den has a half bath perfect for a home office

◆ Corner columns separate formal dining room while maintaining openness

◆ Built-in bookshelves flank each side of the fireplace in the great room

◆ 3 bedrooms, 2 1/2 baths, 2-car garage

◆ Crawl space foundation

Price Code F

Plan #581-055D-0024

1,680 total square feet of living area

Special features

- ◆ Enormous and luxurious master suite
- ◆ Kitchen and dining room have vaulted ceilings creating an open feeling
- ◆ Double sinks grace second bath
- ◆ 3 bedrooms, 2 baths, 2-car garage
- ◆ Walk-out basement, basement, crawl space or slab foundation, please specify when ordering

Price Code B

Bayed Dining Room

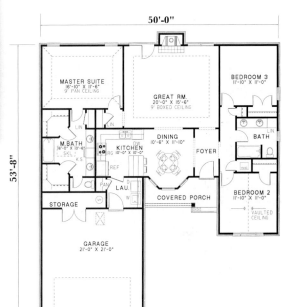

Plan #581-055D-0026

1,538 total square feet of living area

Special features

- Dining and great rooms highlighted in this design
- Master suite has many amenities
- Kitchen and laundry are accessible from any room in the house
- 3 bedrooms, 2 baths, 2-car garage
- Walk-out basement, basement, crawl space or slab foundation, please specify when ordering

Price Code B

Floridian Architecture

First Floor
2,408 sq. ft.

Plan #581-007D-0066

2,408 total square feet of living area

Special features

- Great room overlooks atrium and window wall, adjoins dining room, spacious breakfast room with bay and pass-through kitchen
- Private bedroom with bath, separate from other bedrooms, is perfect for mother-in-law suite or children home from college
- 4 bedrooms, 3 baths, 3-car side entry garage
- Walk-out basement foundation

Price Code D

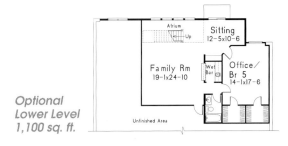

Optional
Lower Level
1,100 sq. ft.

*P*lan #581-040D-0003

1,475 total square feet of living area

Special features

- ◆ Family room features a high ceiling and prominent corner fireplace
- ◆ Kitchen with island counter and garden window makes a convenient connection between the family and dining rooms
- ◆ Hallway leads to three bedrooms all with large walk-in closets
- ◆ Covered breezeway joins main house and garage
- ◆ Full-width covered porch entry lends a country touch
- ◆ 3 bedrooms, 2 baths, 2-car side entry garage
- ◆ Slab foundation, drawings also include crawl space foundation

Price Code B

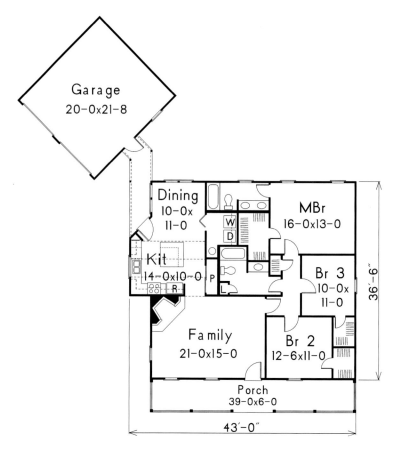

Plan #581-007D-0010

1,721 total square feet of living area

Special features

◆ Roof dormers add great curb appeal

◆ Vaulted dining and great rooms immersed in light from atrium window wall

◆ 3 bedrooms, 2 baths, 3-car garage

◆ Walk-out basement foundation, drawings also include crawl space and slab foundations

◆ 1,604 square feet on the first floor and 117 square feet on the lower level

Price Code C

Plan #581-065D-0026

2,269 total square feet of living area

Special features

◆ An open atmosphere encourages an easy flow of activities

◆ Grand windows and a covered porch offer a cozy atmosphere

◆ The master bedroom boasts a double vanity, whirlpool tub and spacious walk-in closet

◆ 3 bedrooms, 2 baths, 2-car garage

◆ Basement foundation

Price Code D

A Traditional Feel

Plan #581-038D-0012

1,575 total square feet of living area

Special features

◆ Two secondary bedrooms share a full bath

◆ Formal dining room features column accents

◆ Breakfast room has sliding glass doors leading to an outdoor deck

◆ 3 bedrooms, 2 baths, 2-car garage

◆ Basement foundation

Price Code B

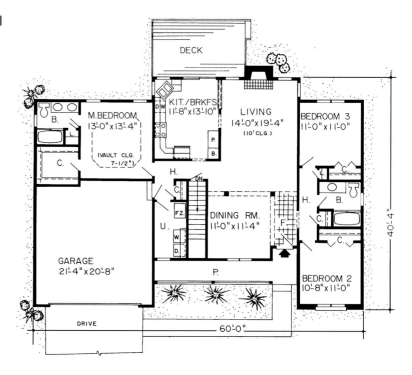

A Home For Views

55'-8"

46'-4"

Balcony

MBr 18-4x13-0

Kit 10-2x 11-9

Dining   Dn

Great Rm 16-0x21-4 vaulted

W D

Entry

Br 2 12-8x14-0

Br 3 11-4x12-6

Porch depth 6-0

First Floor
1,684 sq. ft.

Plan #581-007D-0075

1,684 total square feet of living area

Special features

- ◆ Delightful wrap-around porch anchored by a full masonry fireplace
- ◆ Great room includes a large bay window, fireplace, dining balcony and atrium window wall
- ◆ Double walk-in closets, large bath and sliding doors to balcony are a few features of the master bedroom
- ◆ 3 bedrooms, 2 baths, 2-car drive under garage
- ◆ Walk-out basement foundation

Price Code B

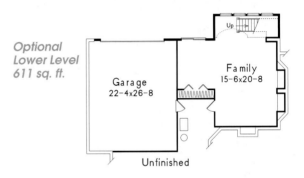

Optional Lower Level 611 sq. ft.

Garage 22-4x26-8

Family 15-6x20-8

Up

Unfinished

Contemporary Feel

Optional Second Floor 849 sq. ft.

Bonus Rm. 18' · 15'

Bath

Office 11' · 13'

Study Niche 9' 7'

Mech.

78'-0"

75'-4"

Lanai

Stor

Bedroom 12' · 11'

Family Room 17' · 15'

Lanai

First Floor 3,098 sq. ft.

Bath

Breakfast 12' · 9'

Lanai

Sitting

Bedroom 11' · 12'

Kitchen 15' · 13'

Living 14' · 13'

Bath

Master Bedroom 15' · 14'

Utility

W.I.C.

Dining 12' · 14'

Foyer

Study 10' · 12'

Master Bath

3 Car Garage 20' · 31'

Entry

W.I.C.

Plan #581-047D-0052

3,098 total square feet of living area

Special features

- ◆ Master bedroom is ultra luxurious with private bath, enormous walk-in closet and sitting area leading to the lanai
- ◆ Vaulted family room has lots of windows and a corner fireplace
- ◆ Secluded study has double closets and built-ins
- ◆ Framing - only concrete block available
- ◆ 4 bedrooms, 4 baths, 3-car side entry garage
- ◆ Slab foundation

Price Code F

*E*nchanting Country Cottage

*P*lan #581-007D-0030

1,140 total square feet of living area

Special features

- ◆ Open and spacious living and dining areas for family gatherings
- ◆ Well-organized kitchen with an abundance of cabinetry and a built-in pantry
- ◆ Roomy master bath features double-bowl vanity
- ◆ 3 bedrooms, 2 baths, 2-car drive under garage
- ◆ Basement foundation

Price Code AA

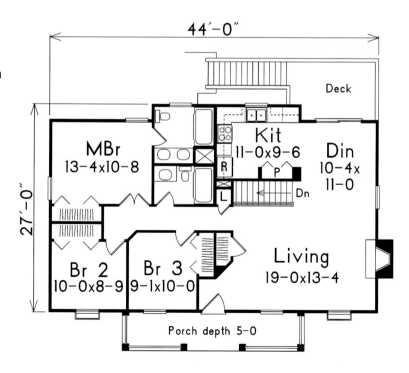

44'-0"

27'-0"

Deck

MBr
13-4x10-8

Kit
11-0x9-6

Din
10-4x
11-0

R

P

Dn

L

Br 2
10-0x8-9

Br 3
9-1x10-0

Living
19-0x13-4

Porch depth 5-0

Plan #581-013D-0001

1,050 total square feet of living area

Special features

- Master bedroom has its own private bath and access to the outdoors onto a private patio
- Vaulted ceilings in the living and dining areas create a feeling of spaciousness
- Laundry closet is convenient to all bedrooms
- Efficient U-shaped kitchen
- 3 bedrooms, 2 baths, 1-car garage
- Basement or slab foundation, please specify when ordering

Price Code AA

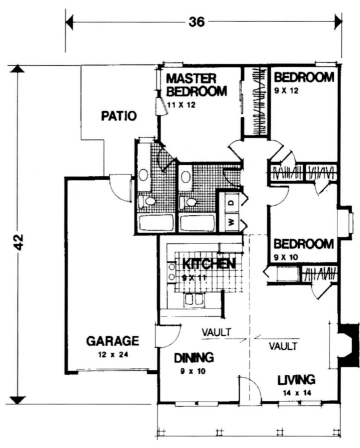

*P*lan #581-016D-0005

2,347 total square feet of living area

Special features

◆ Angled floor plan provides enhanced flexibility in site placement

◆ The fourth bedroom could easily double as a home office or study

◆ A spacious rear-facing great room is the focal point of the living area with high stepped ceiling, fireplace and space for built-ins

◆ 4 bedrooms, 2 1/2 baths, 2-car side entry garage

◆ Basement, crawl space or slab foundation, please specify when ordering

Price Code E

Optional Second Floor 823 sq. ft.

First Floor 2,347 sq. ft.

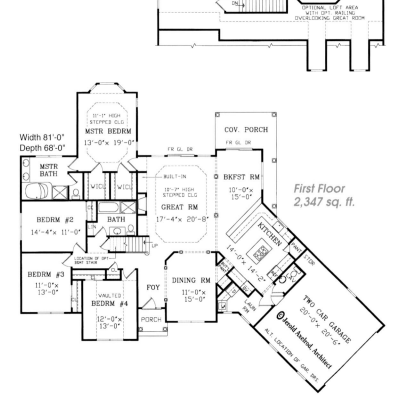

Plan #581-038D-0039

1,771 total square feet of living area

Special features

- Den has a sloped ceiling and charming window seat
- Private master bedroom has access to the outdoors
- Central kitchen allows for convenient access when entertaining
- 2 bedrooms, 2 baths, 2-car garage
- Basement, crawl space or slab foundation, please specify when ordering

Price Code B

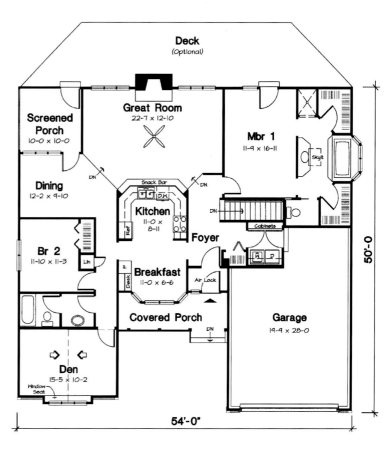

Outdoor Covered Deck

Plan #581-065D-0041

3,171 total square feet of living area

Special features

◆ An enormous walk-in closet is located in the master bath and dressing area

◆ The great room, breakfast area and kitchen combine with 12' ceilings to create an open feel

◆ The optional lower level has an additional 1,897 square feet of living area and is designed for entertaining featuring a wet bar with seating, a billiards room, large media room, two bedrooms and a full bath

◆ 3 bedrooms, 2 1/2 baths, 3-car side entry garage

◆ Basement or walk-out basement foundation, please specify when ordering

Price Code E

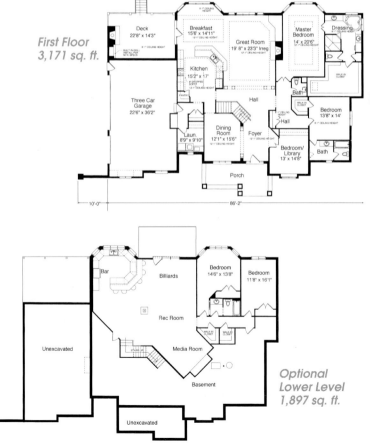

First Floor
3,171 sq. ft.

Optional
Lower Level
1,897 sq. ft.

Shakes Accent Gables

Plan #581-038D-0043

1,539 total square feet of living area

Special features

- A tray ceiling tops the master bed-room
- The peninsula counter in the kitchen doubles as a breakfast bar
- A walk-in closet in the foyer has space for additional storage
- 3 bedrooms, 2 baths, 2-car garage
- Basement, crawl space or slab foundation, please specify when ordering

Price Code B

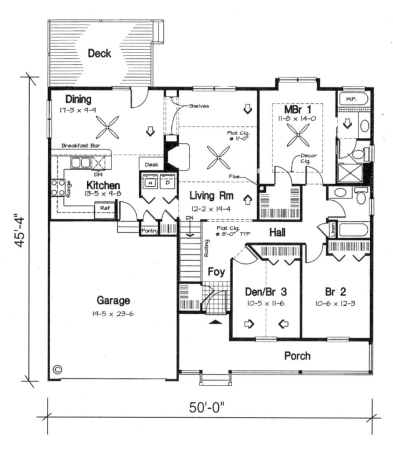

*P*lan #581-053D-0047

1,438 total square feet of living area

Special features

◆ Vaulted living and dining rooms unite to provide open space for entertaining

◆ Secondary bedrooms share full bath

◆ Compact, yet efficient kitchen

◆ Vaulted master bedroom includes private bath, large walk-in closet and access to patio

◆ 3 bedrooms, 2 baths, 2-car side entry garage

◆ Crawl space foundation, drawings also include slab foundation

Price Code A

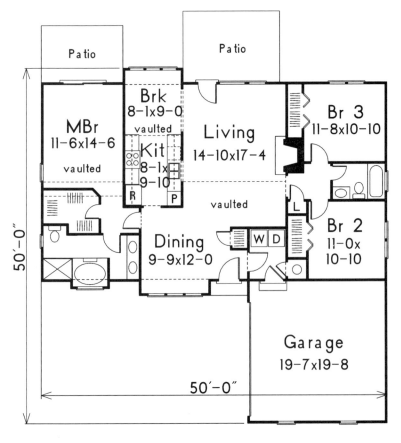

Plan #581-047D-0046

2,597 total square feet of living area

Special features

- ◆ Angled design creates unlimited views and spaces that appear larger
- ◆ Den/bedroom #4 makes a perfect home office or guest suite
- ◆ Island kitchen with view to nook and family room includes a walk-in pantry
- ◆ Pool bath is shared by outdoor and indoor areas
- ◆ 4 bedrooms, 3 baths, 3-car rear entry garage
- ◆ Slab foundation

Price Code D

Width: 98'-6"
Depth: 50'-0"

Stately Large Porch

© COPYRIGHT MCMXCIII RALPH JONES

Plan #581-060D-0020

1,389 total square feet of living area

Special features

- ◆ Great open space for entertaining with eating bar in kitchen overlooking breakfast and great rooms
- ◆ Private master suite has sloped ceiling and secluded bath
- ◆ Handy extra storage space in garage
- ◆ 3 bedrooms, 2 baths, 2-car garage
- ◆ Slab or crawl space foundation, please specify when ordering

Price Code A

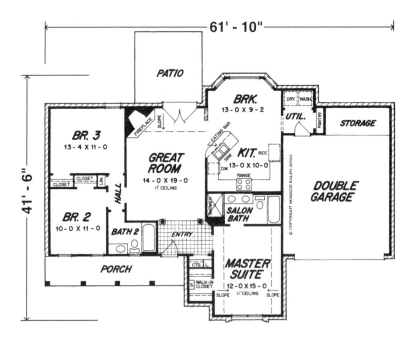

Plan #581-001D-0076

1,584 total square feet of living area

Special features

- ◆ Master bedroom includes dressing area, private bath and walk-in closet
- ◆ Secondary bedrooms feature large walk-in closets
- ◆ Large living room with patio door to outdoors
- ◆ U-shaped kitchen features pantry, outdoor access and convenient laundry closet
- ◆ 3 bedrooms, 2 baths
- ◆ Crawl space foundation, drawings also include basement and slab foundations

Price Code B

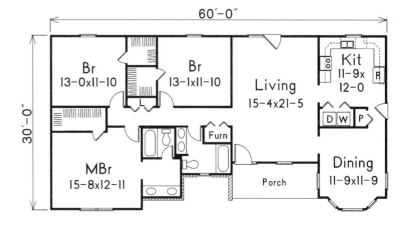

Lovely Arched Touches

Plan #581-069D-0012

1,594 total square feet of living area

Special features

- Corner fireplace in the great room creates a cozy feel
- Spacious kitchen combines with the dining room creating a terrific gathering place
- A handy family and guest entrance is a casual and convenient way to enter the home
- 3 bedrooms, 2 baths, 2-car garage
- Slab or crawl space foundation, please specify when ordering

Price Code B

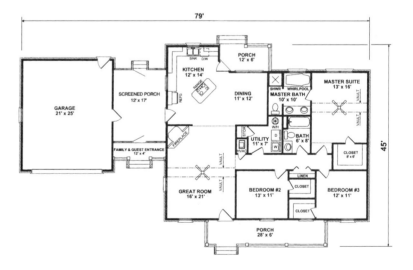

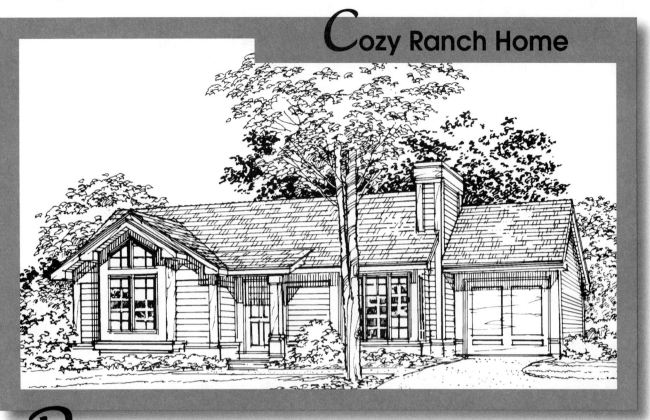

*C*ozy Ranch Home

*P*lan #581-022D-0023

950 total square feet of living area

Special features

- Deck adjacent to kitchen/breakfast area for outdoor dining
- Vaulted ceiling, open stairway and fireplace complement great room
- Bedroom #2 with sloped ceiling and box bay window can convert to a den
- Master bedroom with walk-in closet, plant shelf, separate dressing area and private access to bath
- Kitchen has garage access and opens to great room
- 2 bedrooms, 1 bath, 1-car garage
- Basement foundation

Price Code AA

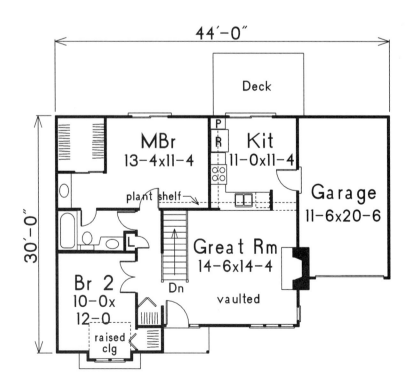

Plan #581-061D-0002

1,950 total square feet of living area

Special features

- Large corner kitchen with island cooktop opens to family room
- Master bedroom features double-door entry, raised ceiling, double-bowl vanity and walk-in closet
- Plant shelf accents hall
- 4 bedrooms, 2 baths, 3-car garage
- Crawl space foundation

Price Code C

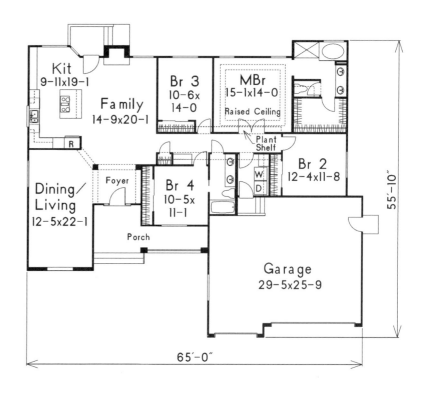

Plan #581-048D-0008

2,089 total square feet of living area

Special features

- Family room features fireplace, built-in bookshelves and triple sliders opening to covered patio
- Kitchen overlooks family room and features pantry and desk
- Separated from the three secondary bedrooms, the master bedroom becomes a quiet retreat with patio access
- Master bedroom features an oversized bath with walk-in closet and corner tub
- 4 bedrooms, 3 baths, 2-car garage
- Slab foundation

Price Code C

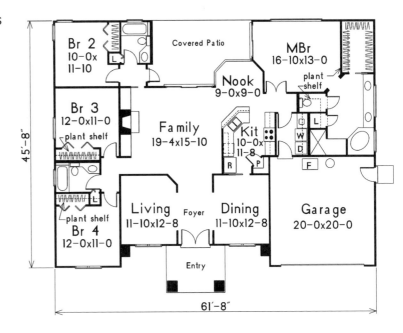

Br 2
10-0x 11-10

Covered Patio

MBr
16-10x13-0

plant shelf

Nook
9-0x9-0

Br 3
12-0x11-0

plant shelf

Family
19-4x15-10

Kit
10-0x 11-8

45'-8"

plant shelf

Living
11-10x12-8

Foyer

Dining
11-10x12-8

Garage
20-0x20-0

Br 4
12-0x11-0

Entry

61'-8"

Affordable Upscale Ranch

*P*lan #581-006D-0001

1,643 total square feet of living area

Special features

◆ Family room has vaulted ceiling, open staircase and arched windows allowing for plenty of light

◆ Kitchen captures full use of space, with pantry, storage, ample counter-space and work island

◆ Large closets and storage areas throughout

◆ Roomy master bath has a skylight for natural lighting plus separate tub and shower

◆ Rear of house provides ideal location for future screened-in porch

◆ 3 bedrooms, 2 baths, 2-car side entry garage

◆ Basement foundation, drawings also include slab and crawl space foundations

Price Code B

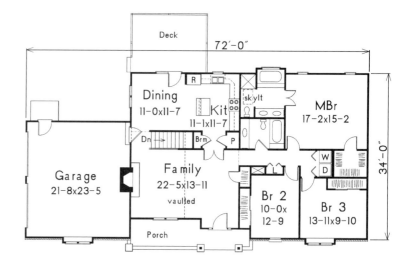

Impressive Corner Fireplace

Plan #581-053D-0042

1,458 total square feet of living area

Special features

◆ Convenient snack bar joins kitchen with breakfast room

◆ Large living room has fireplace, plenty of windows, vaulted ceiling and nearby plant shelf

◆ Master bedroom offers a private bath with vaulted ceiling, walk-in closet, plant shelf and coffered ceiling

◆ Corner windows provide abundant light in breakfast room

◆ 3 bedrooms, 2 baths, 2-car garage

◆ Crawl space foundation, drawings also include slab foundation

Price Code A

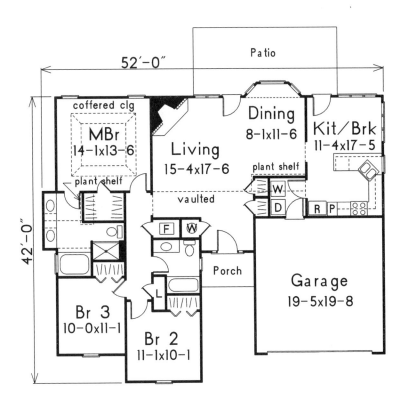

Fountain Graces Entry

Plan #581-048D-0004

2,397 total square feet of living area

Special features

- ◆ Covered entrance with fountain leads to double-door entry and foyer
- ◆ Kitchen features two pantries and opens into breakfast and family rooms
- ◆ Master bath features huge walk-in closet, electric clothes carousel, double-bowl vanity and corner tub
- ◆ 3 bedrooms, 2 1/2 baths, 2-car garage
- ◆ Slab foundation

Price Code E

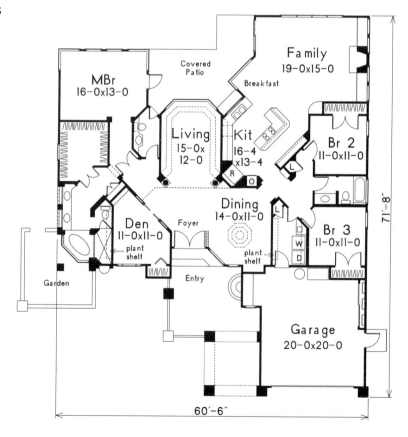

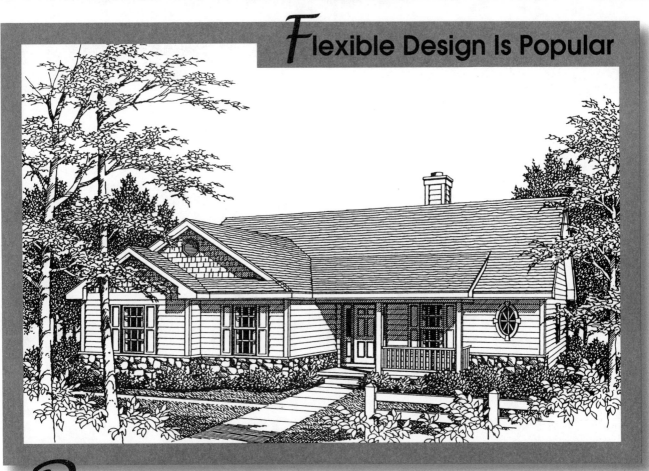

Plan #581-058D-0033

1,440 total square feet of living area

Special features

- ◆ Open floor plan with access to covered porches in front and back
- ◆ Lots of linen, pantry and closet space throughout
- ◆ Laundry/mud room between kitchen and garage is a convenient feature
- ◆ 2 bedrooms, 2 baths, 2-car side entry garage
- ◆ Basement foundation

Price Code A

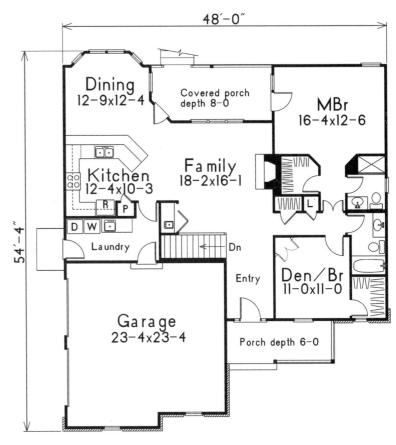

Home With Many Extras

Plan #581-049D-0012

1,295 total square feet of living area

Special features

- Wrap-around porch is a lovely place for dining

- A fireplace gives a stunning focal point to the great room that is heightened with a sloped ceiling

- The master suite is full of luxurious touches such as a walk-in closet and a lush private bath

- 2 bedrooms, 2 baths, 2-car garage

- Basement foundation

Price Code A

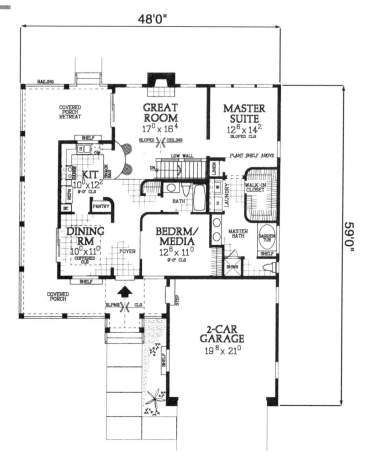

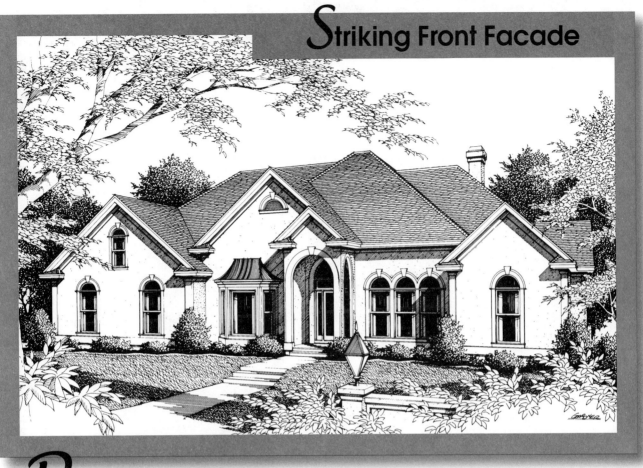

Plan #581-053D-0050

2,718 total square feet of living area

Special features

- ◆ Master bedroom has tray ceiling, access to the rear deck, walk-in closet and an impressive private bath
- ◆ Dining and living rooms flank the foyer and both feature tray ceilings
- ◆ Spacious family room features 12' ceiling, fireplace and access to the rear deck
- ◆ Kitchen has a 9' ceiling, large pantry and bar overlooking the breakfast room
- ◆ 4 bedrooms, 2 1/2 baths, 2-car side entry garage
- ◆ Basement foundation

Price Code E

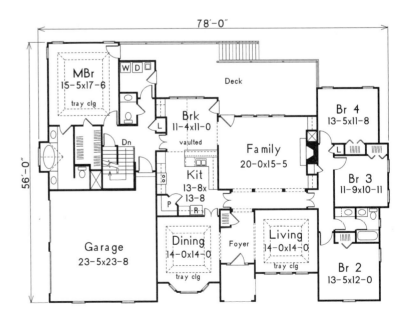

*P*lan #581-036D-0057

2,578 total square feet of living area

Special features

- ◆ Enormous entry has an airy feel with gallery nearby
- ◆ Living room with bay window is tucked away from traffic areas
- ◆ Large kitchen and breakfast area both access covered patio
- ◆ Great room has entertainment center, fireplace and cathedral ceiling
- ◆ 4 bedrooms, 3 1/2 baths, 3-car side entry garage
- ◆ Slab foundation

Price Code D

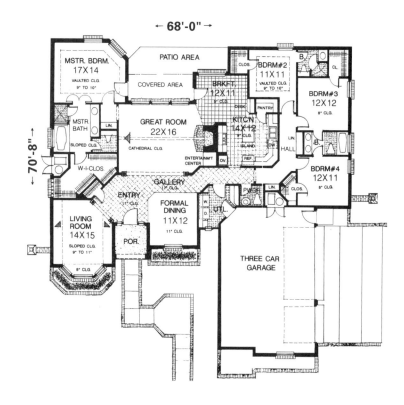

*P*lan #581-001D-0085

720 total square feet of living area

Special features

- ◆ Abundant windows in living and dining rooms provide generous sunlight
- ◆ Secluded laundry area with handy storage closet
- ◆ U-shaped kitchen with large breakfast bar opens into living area
- ◆ Large covered deck offers plenty of outdoor living space
- ◆ 2 bedrooms, 1 bath
- ◆ Crawl space foundation, drawings also include slab foundation

Price Code AAA

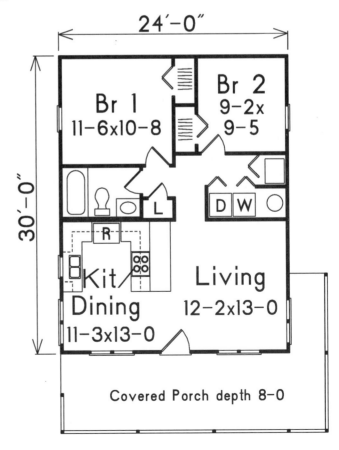

*P*lan #581-052D-0046

1,869 total square feet of living area

Special features

- ◆ Kitchen counter overlooks breakfast and living rooms creating a feeling of openness

- ◆ Dining room features columns separating it from the other spaces in a unique and formal way

- ◆ A sunny spa tub is featured in the master bath

- ◆ 3 bedrooms, 2 baths, 2-car side entry garage

- ◆ Basement, crawl space or slab foundation, please specify when ordering

Price Code C

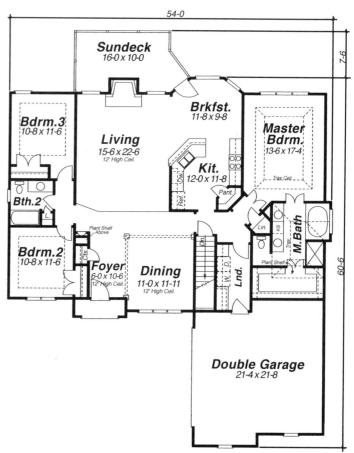

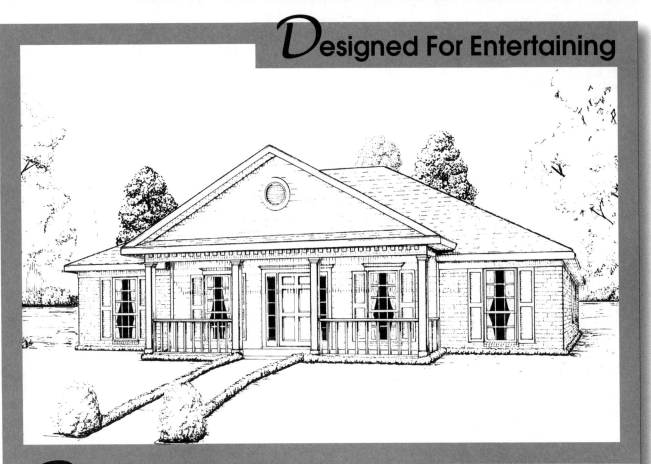

Plan #581-023D-0018

1,556 total square feet of living area

Special features

- ◆ Corner fireplace in living area warms surroundings
- ◆ Spacious master bedroom includes walk-in closet and private bath with double-bowl vanity
- ◆ Compact kitchen designed for efficiency
- ◆ Covered porches in both front and back of home add coziness
- ◆ 3 bedrooms, 2 baths, 2-car attached carport
- ◆ Slab foundation

Price Code B

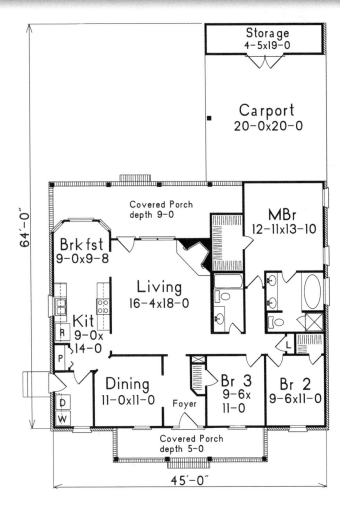

Well-Designed Ranch Style

Plan #581-004D-0002

1,823 total square feet of living area

Special Features

- ◆ Vaulted living room is spacious and easily accesses the dining area
- ◆ The master bedroom boasts a tray ceiling, large walk-in closet and a private bath with a corner whirlpool tub
- ◆ Cheerful dining area is convenient to the U-shaped kitchen and also enjoys patio access
- ◆ 3 bedrooms, 2 baths, 2-car garage
- ◆ Basement foundation

Price Code C

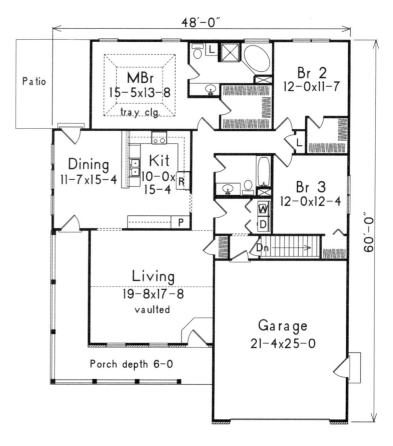

Patio

48'-0"

MBr
15-5x13-8
tray clg.

Br 2
12-0x11-7

Dining
11-7x15-4

Kit
10-0x
15-4

Br 3
12-0x12-4

60'-0"

Living
19-8x17-8
vaulted

Dn

W
D

P

Garage
21-4x25-0

Porch depth 6-0

Dramatic Roof Line

Plan #581-037D-0021

2,260 total square feet of living area

Special features

- Luxurious master bedroom includes a raised ceiling, bath with oversized tub, separate shower and large walk-in closet
- Convenient kitchen and breakfast area with ample pantry storage
- Formal foyer leads into large living room with warming fireplace
- Convenient secondary entrance for everyday traffic
- 3 bedrooms, 2 baths, 2-car garage
- Slab foundation

Price Code D

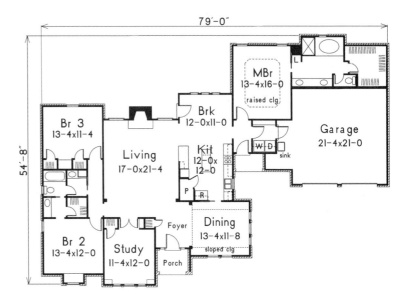

*S*ecluded Bedroom

*P*lan #581-001D-0090

1,300 total square feet of living area

Special features

- ◆ Combination kitchen/dining area creates an open atmosphere
- ◆ Isolated master bedroom has private bath
- ◆ Kitchen includes side entrance, pantry, closet and convenient laundry area
- ◆ 4 bedrooms, 2 baths
- ◆ Crawl space foundation, drawings also include basement and slab foundations

Price Code A

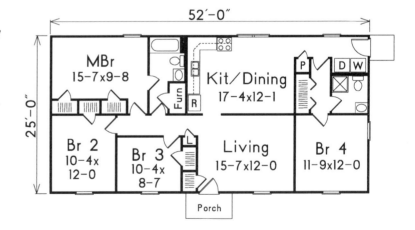

Plan #581-039D-0007

1,550 total square feet of living area

Special features

- ◆ Wrap-around front porch is an ideal gathering place
- ◆ Handy snack bar is positioned so kitchen flows into family room
- ◆ Master bedroom has many amenities
- ◆ 3 bedrooms, 2 baths, 2-car detached side entry garage
- ◆ Slab or crawl space foundation, please specify when ordering

Price Code B

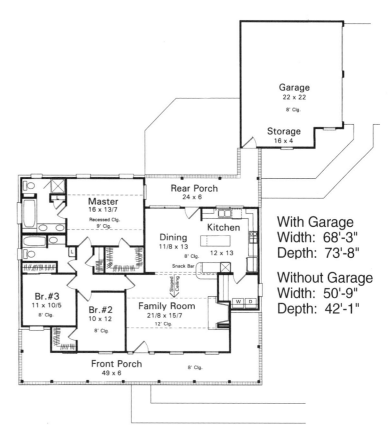

With Garage
Width: 68'-3"
Depth: 73'-8"

Without Garage
Width: 50'-9"
Depth: 42'-1"

Plan #581-053D-0049

1,261 total square feet of living area

Special features

- ◆ Great room, brightened by windows and doors, features vaulted ceiling, fireplace and access to deck
- ◆ Vaulted master bedroom enjoys a private bath
- ◆ Split level foyer leads to living space or basement
- ◆ Centrally located laundry area is near bedrooms
- ◆ 3 bedrooms, 2 baths, 2-car drive under garage
- ◆ Basement foundation

Price Code A

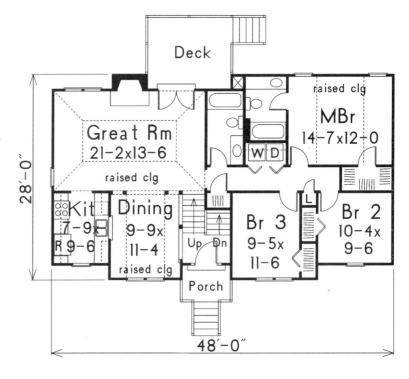

*P*lan #581-024D-0002

1,405 total square feet of living area

Special features

◆ Compact design has all the luxuries of a larger home

◆ Master bedroom has its privacy away from other bedrooms

◆ Living room has corner fireplace, access to the outdoors and easily reaches the dining area and kitchen

◆ Large utility room has access to the outdoors

◆ 3 bedrooms, 2 baths

◆ Slab foundation

Price Code A

Width: 42'
Depth: 51'

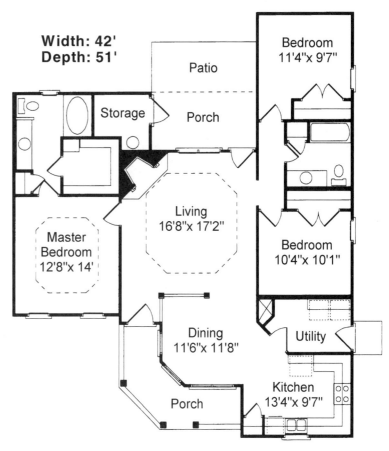

*W*ork Island In Kitchen

*P*lan #581-036D-0053

2,528 total square feet of living area

Special features

- ◆ Cozy family room is a great place to gather with bar ledge overlooking from kitchen, a fireplace and access to covered patio
- ◆ Kitchen has lots of cabinetry, plus walk-in pantry
- ◆ Elaborate master bath
- ◆ 4 bedrooms, 3 baths, 3-car garage
- ◆ Slab foundation

Price Code D

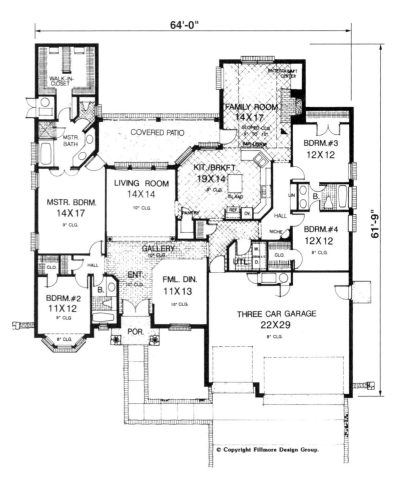

© Copyright Fillmore Design Group.

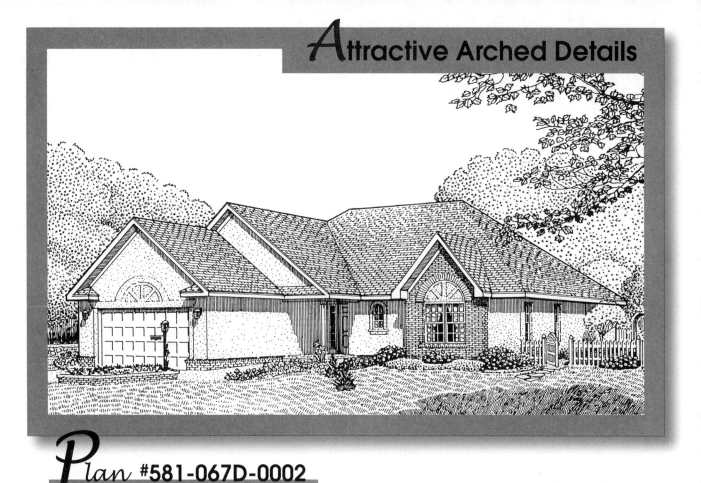

Plan #581-067D-0002

1,627 total square feet of living area

Special features

- Cathedral ceiling in living room adds drama to this space
- Cozy corner dining area just off the kitchen is convenient
- Large master bedroom is cheerful with many windows and includes its own bath and walk-in closet
- 3 bedrooms, 2 baths, 2-car garage
- Crawl space or slab foundation, please specify when ordering

Price Code B

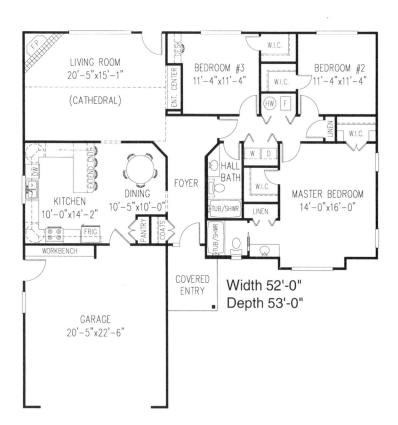

Width 52'-0"
Depth 53'-0"

Plan #581-060D-0007

2,079 total square feet of living area

Special features

◆ Large formal entry foyer with openings to formal dining and great rooms

◆ Great room has built-in bookshelves, a fireplace, and a coffered ceiling

◆ Unique angled morning room with bay windows overlooks covered deck

◆ Master bath with double walk-in closets, step-up tub, separate shower and a coffered ceiling

◆ 3 bedrooms, 2 baths, 2-car garage

◆ Slab or crawl space foundation, please specify when ordering

Price Code C

Plan #581-031D-0013

2,380 total square feet of living area

Special features

- Unique master bedroom walks out to back porch
- Well-designed kitchen has plenty of counterspace
- Open dining room is perfect for formal entertaining
- 4 bedrooms, 3 baths, 2-car side entry garage
- Slab foundation

Price Code D

Width: 64'-4"
Depth: 66'-0"

© David C. Lutz

Attractive Front Dormers

Plan #581-001D-0034

1,642 total square feet of living area

Special features

◆ Walk-through kitchen boasts vaulted ceiling and corner sink overlooking family room

◆ Vaulted family room features cozy fireplace and access to rear patio

◆ Master bedroom includes sloped ceiling, walk-in closet and private bath

◆ 3 bedrooms, 2 baths, 2-car garage

◆ Basement foundation, drawings also include slab and crawl space foundations

Price Code B

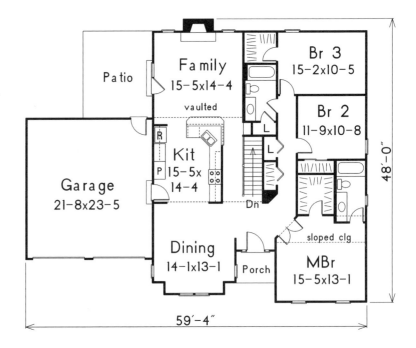

Patio

Family
15-5x14-4
vaulted

Br 3
15-2x10-5

Br 2
11-9x10-8

Garage
21-8x23-5

Kit
15-5x
14-4

R
P

Dn

48'-0"

Dining
14-1x13-1

Porch

sloped clg

MBr
15-5x13-1

59'-4"

Plan #581-035D-0046

1,080 total square feet of living area

Special features

- ◆ Secondary bedrooms are separate from master suite allowing privacy
- ◆ Compact kitchen is well-organized
- ◆ Conveniently located laundry closet
- ◆ 3 bedrooms, 2 baths, 2-car garage
- ◆ Walk-out basement or crawl space foundation, please specify when ordering

Price Code AA

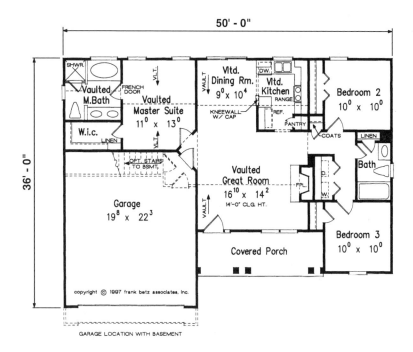

50' - 0"

36' - 0"

SHWR.

Vaulted M.Bath

FRENCH DOOR

Vaulted Master Suite 11⁰ x 13⁰

W.i.c.

LINEN

OPT. STAIRS TO BSMT.

Garage 19⁸ x 22³

Vltd. Dining Rm. 9⁰ x 10⁴

DW

Vltd. Kitchen

RANGE

KNEEWALL W/ CAP

REF.

PANTRY

COATS

Bedroom 2 10⁰ x 10⁰

LINEN

Bath

Vaulted Great Room 16¹⁰ x 14² 14'-0" CLG. HT.

FPL

D.

W.

Covered Porch

Bedroom 3 10⁰ x 10⁰

copyright © 1997 frank betz associates, inc.

GARAGE LOCATION WITH BASEMENT

Cozy With Spacious Features

Plan #581-007D-0125

1,302 total square feet of living area

Special features

- Triple gables, decorative porch and brickwork create a handsome exterior
- The U-shaped kitchen features a snack bar, built-in pantry, open woodcrafted stair to basement and adjacent laundry/mud room
- Sliding doors to the patio and a fireplace with flanking windows adorn the large vaulted family room
- The master bedroom accesses the patio through glass sliding doors and includes a private bath and walk-in closet
- 3 bedrooms, 2 baths, 2-car garage
- Basement foundation

Price Code A

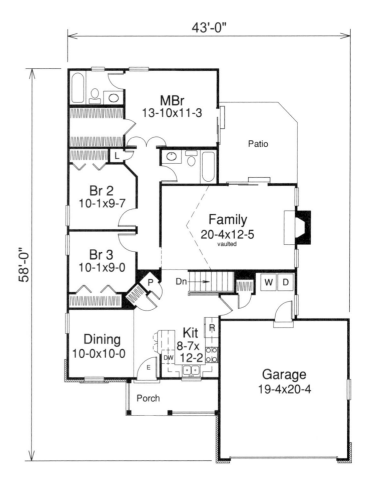

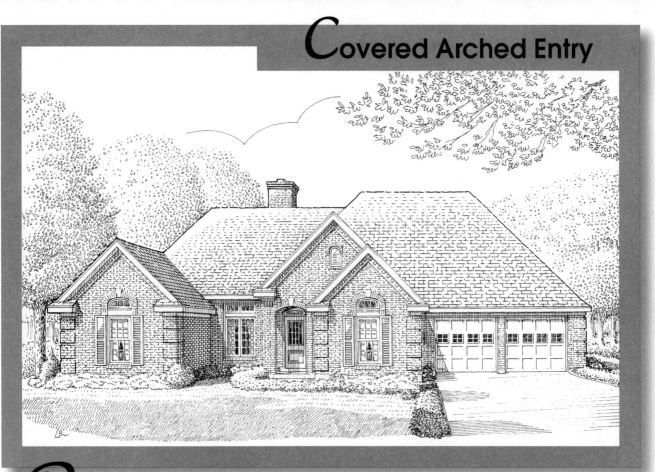

Covered Arched Entry

Plan #581-037D-0031

1,923 total square feet of living area

Special features

◆ Foyer opens into spacious living room with fireplace and splendid view of covered porch

◆ Kitchen has a walk-in pantry adjacent to laundry area and breakfast room

◆ All bedrooms feature walk-in closets

◆ Secluded master bedroom includes unique angled bath with spacious walk-in closet

◆ 3 bedrooms, 2 baths, 2-car garage

◆ Slab foundation

Price Code C

Rear View

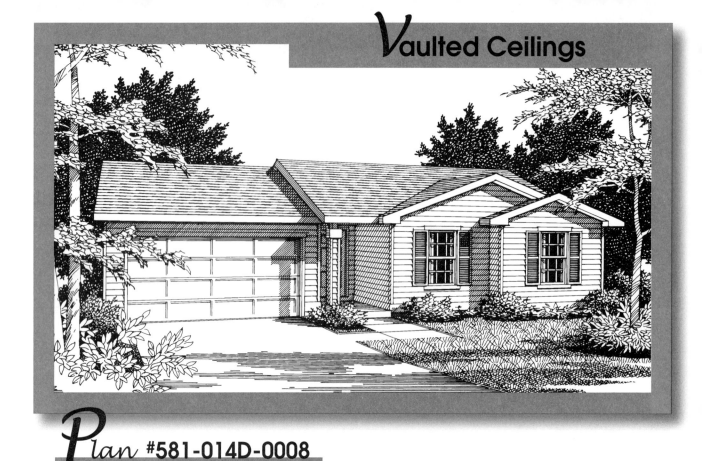

Plan #581-014D-0008

1,135 total square feet of living area

Special features

- ◆ Living and dining rooms feature vaulted ceilings and a corner fireplace
- ◆ Energy efficient home with 2" x 6" exterior walls
- ◆ Master bedroom offers a vaulted ceiling, private bath and generous closet space
- ◆ Compact but functional kitchen complete with pantry and adjacent utility room
- ◆ 3 bedrooms, 2 baths, 2-car garage
- ◆ Basement foundation, drawings also include crawl space foundation

Price Code AA

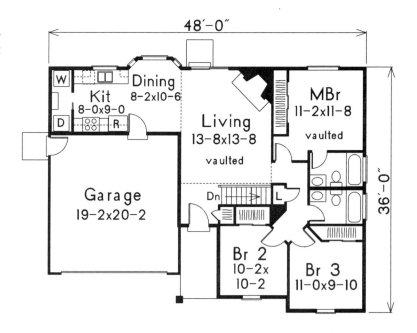

Plan #581-053D-0053

1,609 total square feet of living area

Special features

- ◆ Efficient kitchen with corner pantry and adjacent laundry room
- ◆ Breakfast room boasts plenty of windows and opens onto rear deck
- ◆ Master bedroom features tray ceiling and private deluxe bath
- ◆ Entry opens into large living area with fireplace
- ◆ 4 bedrooms, 2 baths, 2-car garage
- ◆ Basement foundation

Price Code B

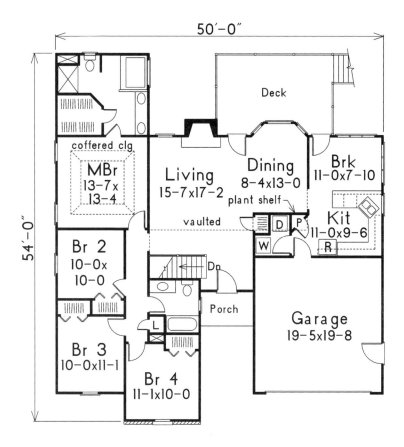

50'-0"

54'-0"

Deck

coffered clg.

MBr
13-7x
13-4

Living
15-7x17-2

vaulted

Dining
8-4x13-0

plant shelf

Brk
11-0x7-10

Kit
11-0x9-6

Br 2
10-0x
10-0

Dn

Porch

Garage
19-5x19-8

Br 3
10-0x11-1

Br 4
11-1x10-0

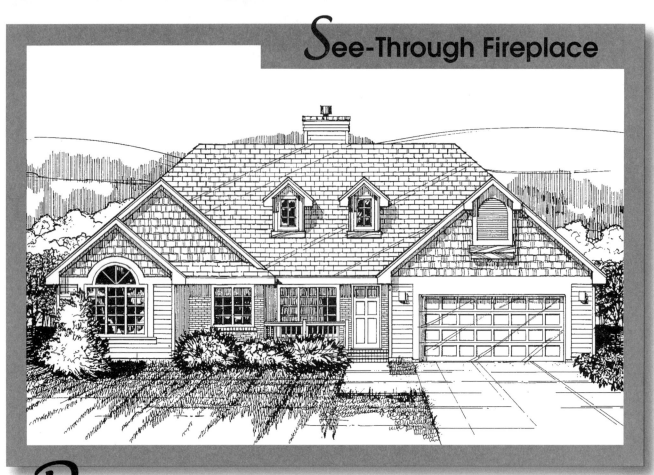

*P*lan #581-045D-0009

1,684 total square feet of living area

Special features

- Convenient double-doors in dining area provide access to a large deck
- Family room features several large windows for brightness
- Bedrooms are separate from living areas for privacy
- Master bedroom offers a bath with walk-in closet, double-bowl vanity and both a shower and a whirlpool tub
- 3 bedrooms, 2 1/2 baths, 2-car garage
- Basement foundation

Price Code B

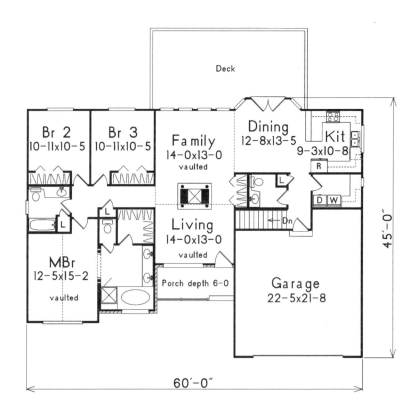

Plan #581-001D-0048

1,400 total square feet of living area

Special features

◆ Front porch offers warmth and welcome

◆ Large great room opens into dining
room creating an open living atmosphere

◆ Kitchen features convenient laundry
area, pantry and breakfast bar

◆ 3 bedrooms, 2 baths, 2-car garage

◆ Crawl space foundation, drawings
also include basement and slab foundations

Price Code A

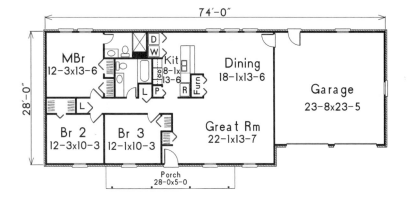

P*lan* #581-068D-0001

2,437 total square feet of living area

Special features

- ◆ Spacious breakfast area with access to the covered porch is adjacent to kitchen and great room
- ◆ Elegant dining area has columned entrance and built-in corner cabinets
- ◆ Cozy study has handsome double-door entrance off a large foyer
- ◆ Raised ceiling and lots of windows in master bedroom create a spacious, open feel
- ◆ 3 bedrooms, 2 baths, 2-car side entry garage
- ◆ Slab foundation, drawings also include crawl space foundation

Price Code D

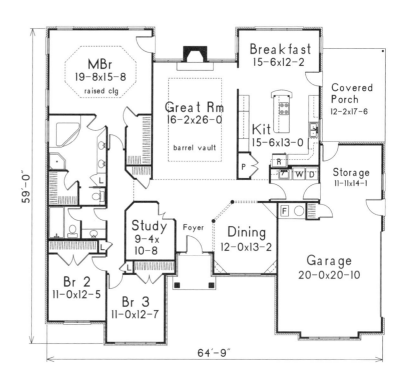

Cozy And Functional Design

Plan #581-058D-0008

1,285 total square feet of living area

Special features

- ◆ Dining nook creates warm feeling with sunny box bay window
- ◆ Second floor loft is perfect for a recreation space or office hideaway
- ◆ Bedrooms include walk-in closets allowing extra storage space
- ◆ Kitchen, dining and living areas combine making a perfect gathering place
- ◆ 2 bedrooms, 1 bath
- ◆ Crawl space foundation

Price Code A

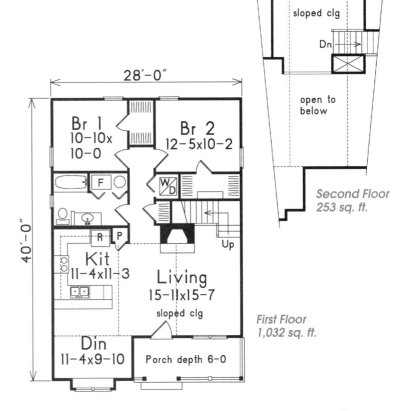

Loft
13-3x20-0
sloped clg

Dn

open to
below

Second Floor
253 sq. ft.

28'-0"

40'-0"

Br 1
10-10x
10-0

Br 2
12-5x10-2

W
D

F

R   P

Kit
11-4x11-3

Living
15-11x15-7
sloped clg

Up

Din
11-4x9-10

Porch depth 6-0

First Floor
1,032 sq. ft.

*P*lan #581-068D-0009

2,128 total square feet of living area

Special features

◆ Versatile kitchen has plenty of space for entertaining with large dining area and counter seating

◆ Luxurious master bedroom has double-door entry and private bath with jacuzzi tub, double sinks and large walk-in closet

◆ Secondary bedrooms include spacious walk-in closets

◆ Coat closet in front entry is a nice added feature

◆ 4 bedrooms, 2 baths, 2-car garage

◆ Slab foundation, drawings also include crawl space foundation

Price Code C

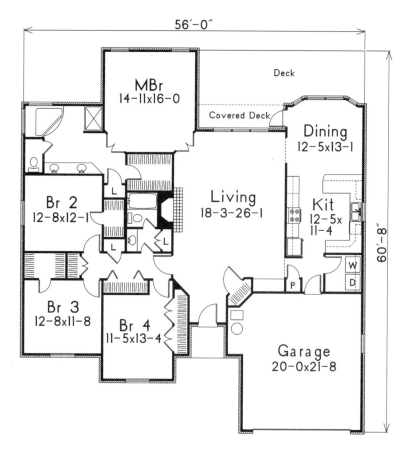

$\mathcal{Q}$uiet Retreat In Parlor

$\mathcal{P}$lan #581-047D-0058

3,106 total square feet of living area

Special features

- ◆ Unique angled rooms create an exciting feel
- ◆ Well-organized kitchen with island is adjacent to family room
- ◆ Beautiful sculptured ceilings in master suite
- ◆ The guest house would make an ideal in-law suite or secluded home office
- ◆ 4 bedrooms, 4 baths, 2-car and 1-car garage
- ◆ Slab foundation

Price Code E

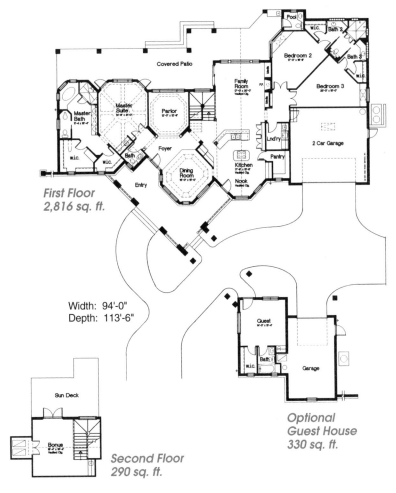

First Floor
2,816 sq. ft.

Width: 94'-0"
Depth: 113'-6"

Second Floor
290 sq. ft.

Optional
Guest House
330 sq. ft.

Southern Elegance

Plan #581-028D-0017

2,669 total square feet of living area

Special features

- Nice-sized corner pantry in kitchen
- Guest bedroom, located off the great room, has a full bath and would make an excellent office
- Master bath has double walk-in closets, whirlpool tub and a large shower
- 4 bedrooms, 3 1/2 baths, 2-car side entry garage
- Basement or slab foundation, please specify when ordering

Price Code E

80-0 WIDE X 63-0 DEEP

*C*ozy Traditional

*P*lan #581-019D-0003

1,310 total square feet of living area

Special features

◆ Family room features corner fireplace adding warmth

◆ Efficiently designed kitchen has a corner sink with windows

◆ Master bedroom includes large walk-in closet and private bath

◆ 3 bedrooms, 2 baths, 2-car garage

◆ Crawl space foundation, drawings also include slab foundation

Price Code A

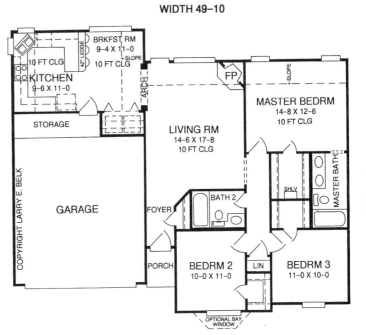

WIDTH 49–10

BRKFST RM
9-4 X 11-0

10 FT CLG

KITCHEN
9-6 X 11-0

STORAGE

COPYRIGHT LARRY E. BELK

GARAGE

FOYER

PORCH

LIVING RM
14-6 X 17-8
10 FT CLG

FP

MASTER BEDRM
14-8 X 12-6
10 FT CLG

SLOPE

ARCH

BATH 2

SHLV

MASTER BATH

BEDRM 2
10-0 X 11-0

LIN

BEDRM 3
11-0 X 10-0

OPTIONAL BAY
WINDOW

DEPTH 40–6

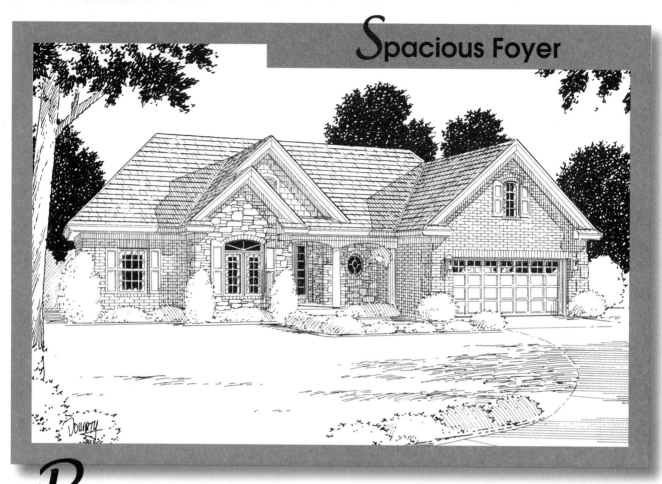

Plan #581-065D-0022

1,593 total square feet of living area

Special features

- ◆ The rear porch is a pleasant surprise and perfect for enjoying the outdoors
- ◆ Great room is filled with extras like a corner fireplace, sloping ceiling and view to the outdoors
- ◆ Separating the kitchen from the dining area is a large island with seating
- ◆ 3 bedrooms, 2 baths, 2-car garage
- ◆ Basement foundation

Price Code B

Open Feeling In This Ranch

Plan #581-034D-0008

1,875 total square feet of living area

Special features

- ◆ Peninsula separating kitchen and dining room has sink, dishwasher and eating area
- ◆ Tall ceilings throughout living area create spaciousness
- ◆ Columned foyer adds style
- ◆ 3 bedrooms, 2 1/2 baths, 2-car garage
- ◆ Basement foundation

Price Code C

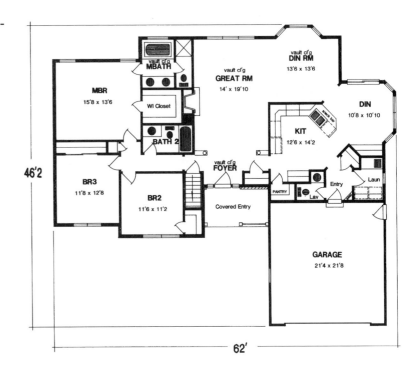

Plan #581-051D-0053

1,461 total square feet of living area

Special features

- ◆ Casual dining room
- ◆ Cathedral ceilings in great room and dining area give home a spacious feel
- ◆ Relaxing master bedroom boasts an expansive bath and large walk-in closet
- ◆ 3 bedrooms, 2 baths, 2-car garage
- ◆ Basement foundation

Price Code A

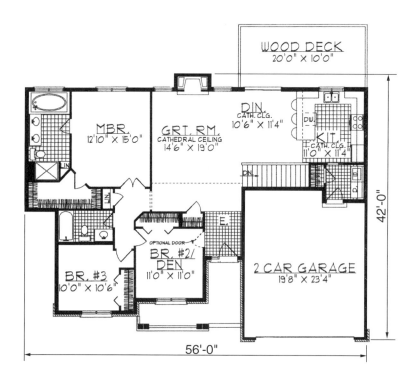

*P*lan #581-007D-0045

1,321 total square feet of living area

Special features

- Rear entry garage and elongated brick wall add to appealing facade
- Dramatic vaulted living room includes corner fireplace and towering feature windows
- Breakfast room is immersed in light from two large windows and glass sliding doors
- 3 bedrooms, 2 baths, 1-car rear entry garage
- Basement foundation

Price Code A

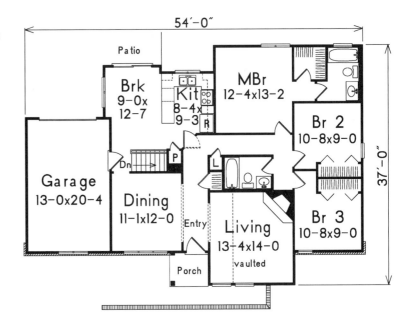

Many Decorative Touches

Plan #581-043D-0007

2,788 total square feet of living area

Special features

- ◆ Breakfast nook flooded with sunlight from skylights
- ◆ Fireplace in great room framed by media center and shelving
- ◆ Large game room is secluded for active children
- ◆ 3 bedrooms, 2 1/2 baths, 3-car side entry garage
- ◆ Crawl space foundation

Price Code E

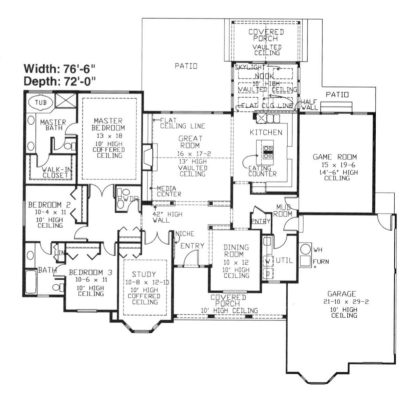

Width: 76'-6"
Depth: 72'-0"

Plan #581-069D-0011

1,558 total square feet of living area

Special Features

- ◆ Kitchen with a breakfast bar and walk-in pantry makes cooking a delight
- ◆ Roomy master suite features a private bath and walk-in closet
- ◆ Two secondary bedrooms share a centrally located full bath
- ◆ Spacious great room includes a built-in fireplace
- ◆ 3 bedrooms, 2 baths, 2-car garage
- ◆ Slab or crawl space foundation, please specify when ordering

Price Code B

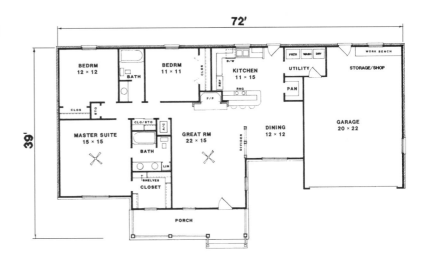

Stylish Central Kitchen

Plan #581-014D-0003

3,003 total square feet of living area

Special features

- ◆ Vaulted master bedroom features large walk-in closet, spa, separate shower room and access to rear patio
- ◆ Covered entrance opens into foyer with large greeting area
- ◆ Formal living room with 12' ceiling and 36" walls on two sides
- ◆ Island kitchen features large pantry and nook
- ◆ Cozy fireplace accents vaulted family room that opens onto a covered deck
- ◆ Utility room with generous space is adjacent to a half bath
- ◆ 3 bedrooms, 2 1/2 baths, 3-car garage
- ◆ Crawl space foundation

Price Code E

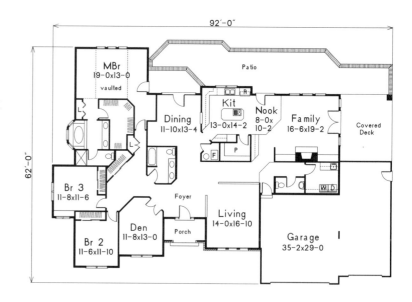

Plan #581-022D-0030

3,412 total square feet of living area

Special Features

◆ Large formal dining room with vaulted ceiling adjacent to entry foyer

◆ Expansive great room boasts dramatic fireplace and vaulted ceiling

◆ Master bedroom and library are secluded from other living areas

◆ Family-style kitchen includes pantry, island cooktop and large breakfast area

◆ Sunken master bedroom has patio access and luxurious private bath

◆ 3 bedrooms, 2 full baths, 2 half baths, 2-car side entry garage

◆ Basement foundation

Price Code F

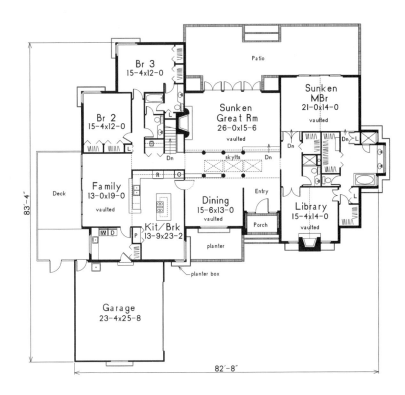

Elegant Barrier-Free Design

*P*lan #581-015D-0008

1,785 total square feet of living area

Special features

◆ Vaulted foyer opens to the living room which features a graceful archway framed by decorative columns and overhead plant shelves

◆ Bayed dining room also features an 11' ceiling and a French door that opens to a covered patio

◆ Open floor plan allows this home to be wheelchair accessible

◆ 3 bedrooms, 2 baths, 2-car garage

◆ Basement, crawl space or slab foundation, please specify when ordering

Price Code B

Width: 58'-0"
Depth: 57'-0"

*C*entral Living Space

*P*lan #581-053D-0041

1,364 total square feet of living area

Special features

- ◆ Master bedroom includes a full bath
- ◆ Pass-through kitchen opens into breakfast room with laundry closet and access to deck
- ◆ Adjoining dining and living rooms with vaulted ceilings and a fireplace create an open living area
- ◆ Dining room features large bay window
- ◆ 3 bedrooms, 2 baths, 2-car drive under garage
- ◆ Basement foundation

Price Code A

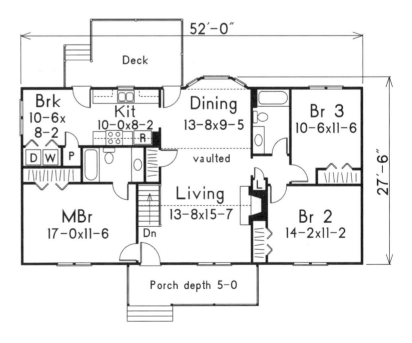

*P*lan #581-040D-0026

1,393 total square feet of living area

Special features

◆ L-shaped kitchen features walk-in pantry, island cooktop and is convenient to laundry room and dining area

◆ Master bedroom features large walk-in closet and private bath with separate tub and shower

◆ Convenient storage/coat closet in hall

◆ View to the patio from the dining area

◆ 3 bedrooms, 2 baths, 2-car detached garage

◆ Crawl space foundation, drawings also include slab foundation

Price Code B

*P*lan #581-052D-0030

1,716 total square feet of living area

Special features

◆ The combination of a stone and siding finish gives home a country feel

◆ Formal dining area has bay windows looking out to sundeck

◆ Master bedroom has a private bath with large walk-in closet, double vanity, large tub and shower

◆ 4 bedrooms, 2 baths, 2-car side entry garage

◆ Basement foundation

Price Code B

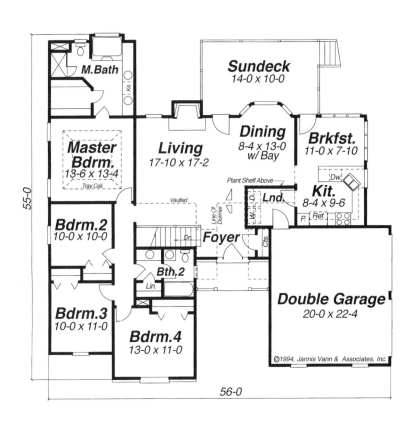

M. Bath

Sundeck
14-0 x 10-0

Master Bdrm.
13-6 x 13-4
Tray Ceil.

Living
17-10 x 17-2

Dining
8-4 x 13-0
w/ Bay

Brkfst.
11-0 x 7-10

Plant Shelf Above

Kit.
8-4 x 9-6

Dw.
P. Ref.

Bdrm.2
10-0 x 10-0

Vaulted

Line Of Dormer

Foyer

Lnd.

W. D.

Bth.2
Lin.

Bdrm.3
10-0 x 11-0

Bdrm.4
13-0 x 11-0

Double Garage
20-0 x 22-4

©1994, Jannis Vann & Associates, Inc.

55-0

56-0

Ranch With Hip Roof

Plan #581-017D-0004

1,315 total square feet of living area

Special features

- Dining room with a sliding door to the rear patio
- Large storage space in garage
- Cozy eating area in the kitchen
- Kitchen has easy access to the laundry/mud room
- Large living room with double closets for storage and coats
- 3 bedrooms, 2 baths, 2-car garage
- Basement foundation, drawings also include slab foundation

Price Code B

*P*lan #581-001D-0072

1,288 total square feet of living area

Special features

- ◆ Kitchen, dining area and great room join to create an open living space
- ◆ Master bedroom includes private bath
- ◆ Secondary bedrooms include ample closet space
- ◆ Hall bath features convenient laundry closet
- ◆ Dining room accesses the outdoors
- ◆ 3 bedrooms, 2 baths
- ◆ Crawl space foundation, drawings also include basement and slab foundations

Price Code A

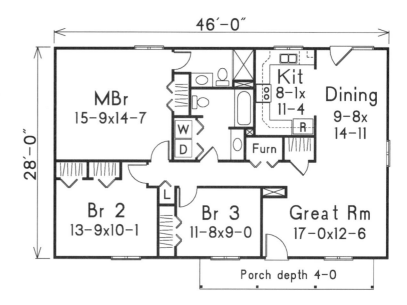

Plan #581-043D-0005

1,734 total square feet of living area

Special features

- ◆ Large entry with coffered ceiling and display niches
- ◆ Sunken great room has 10' ceiling
- ◆ Kitchen island includes eating counter
- ◆ 9' ceiling in master bedroom
- ◆ Master bath features corner tub and double sinks
- ◆ 3 bedrooms, 2 baths, 2-car garage
- ◆ Crawl space foundation

Price Code B

Plan #581-039D-0002

1,333 total square feet of living area

Special features

- Country charm with covered front porch
- Dining area looks into family room with fireplace
- Master suite has walk-in closet and private bath
- 3 bedrooms, 2 baths, 2-car attached carport
- Slab or crawl space foundation, please specify when ordering

Price Code A

Width: 55'-6"
Depth: 64'-3"

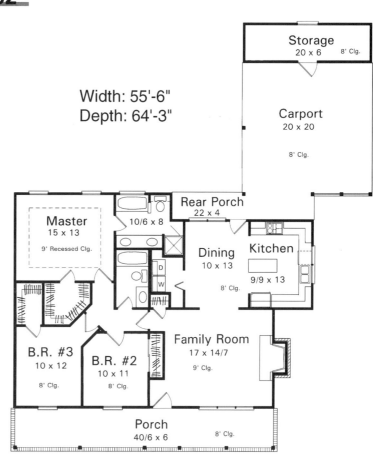

*E*xciting Atrium

*P*lan #581-007D-0069

2,070 total square feet of living area

Special features

- ◆ Great room has fireplace, wet bar and rear views through two-story vaulted atrium
- ◆ Dining area near U-shaped kitchen, walk-in pantry, computer center and breakfast balcony with atrium overlook
- ◆ Master bath has Roman whirlpool tub, TV alcove, separate shower/toilet area and linen closet
- ◆ Extra storage in garage
- ◆ 3 bedrooms, 2 baths, 2-car drive under garage with storage area
- ◆ Walk-out basement foundation

Price Code C

Rear View

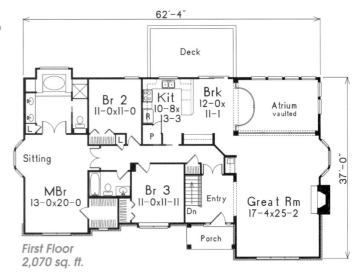

First Floor
2,070 sq. ft.

Optional
Lower Level
1,062 sq. ft.

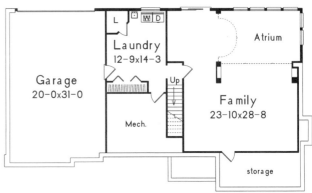

Plan #581-019D-0016

2,678 total square feet of living area

Special features

◆ Elegant arched opening graces entrance

◆ Kitchen has double ovens, walk-in pantry and an eating bar

◆ Master bedroom has beautiful bath spotlighting a step-up tub

◆ 4 bedrooms, 2 1/2 baths, 2-car side entry garage

◆ Crawl space foundation, drawings also include slab foundation

Price Code E

*P*lan #581-030D-0007

2,050 total square feet of living area

Special features

- ◆ Living room is immersed in sunlight from wall of windows
- ◆ Master suite features amenities such as double walk-in closets, private bath and view onto covered porch
- ◆ Cozy family room enjoys built-in shelves and a fireplace
- ◆ 3 bedrooms, 2 baths, 2-car side entry garage
- ◆ Slab or crawl space foundation, please specify when ordering

Price Code C

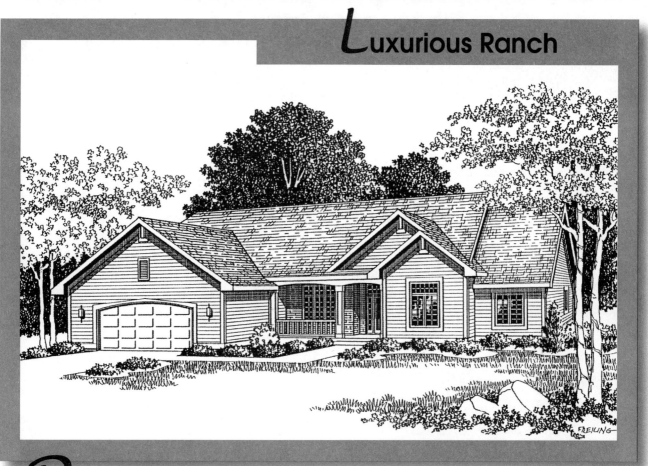

Plan #581-051D-0033

2,196 total square feet of living area

Special features

- Covered front porch leads to the vaulted foyer which invites guests into the great room
- Master bedroom features walk-in closet, private bath with double vanity, spa tub and linen closet
- Large open kitchen
- 3 bedrooms, 2 1/2 baths, 3-car garage
- Basement foundation

Price Code C

Plan #581-030D-0002

1,429 total square feet of living area

Special features

- ◆ Master suite with sitting area and private bath includes double walk-in closets
- ◆ Kitchen and dining area overlook living room
- ◆ Living room has fireplace, media center and access to covered porch
- ◆ 3 bedrooms, 2 baths, 2-car garage
- ◆ Slab or crawl space foundation, please specify when ordering

Price Code A

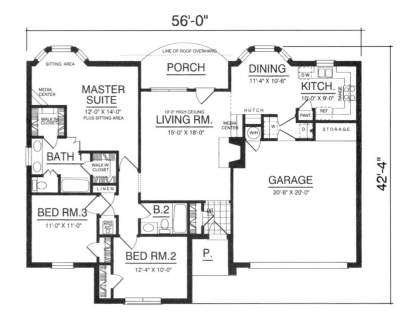

Plan #581-027D-0002

3,796 total square feet of living area

Special features

◆ Entry foyer leads directly to great room with fireplace and wonderful view through wall of windows

◆ Kitchen and breakfast room feature large island cooktop, pantry and easy access outdoors

◆ Master bedroom includes vaulted ceiling and pocket door entrance into master bath that features double-bowl vanity and a large tub

◆ 4 bedrooms, 3 1/2 baths, 2-car garage

◆ Basement foundation

Price Code F

First Floor
2,436 sq. ft.

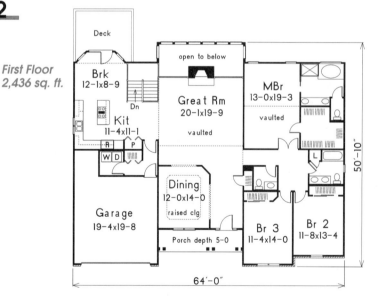

Lower Level
1,360 sq. ft.

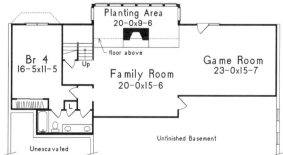

Plan #581-022D-0025

2,847 total square feet of living area

Special features

◆ Master bedroom includes skylighted bath, deck access and double closets

◆ Bedroom #2 converts to guest room with private bath

◆ Impressive foyer and gallery opens into large living room with fireplace

◆ Formal dining and living rooms, casual family and breakfast rooms

◆ Kitchen features desk area, center island, adjacent bayed breakfast area and access to laundry room with half bath

◆ 4 bedrooms, 3 1/2 baths, 2-car side entry garage

◆ Basement foundation

Price Code E

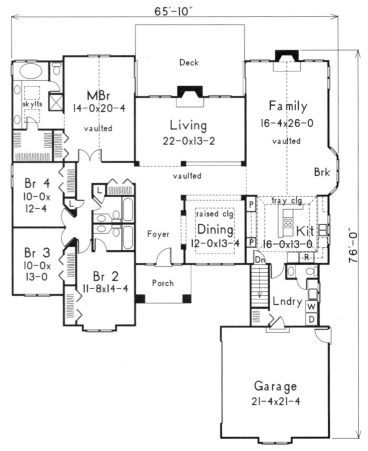

Vaulted Living Area

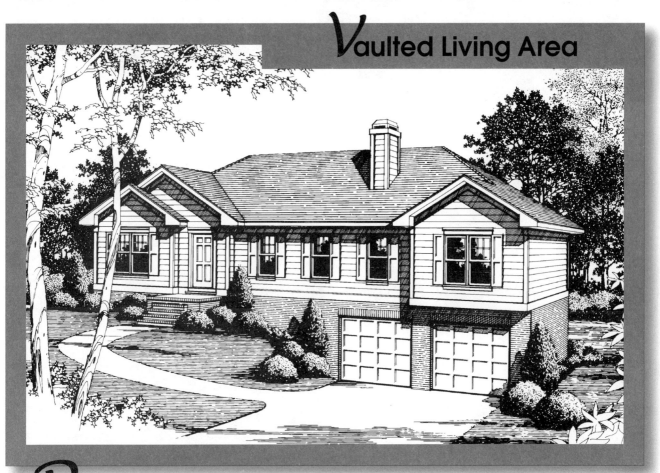

Plan #581-053D-0048

1,697 total square feet of living area

Special features

- ◆ Secondary bedrooms share bath with private dressing area
- ◆ Large living room with fireplace and vaulted ceiling
- ◆ Secluded master bedroom boasts a private deluxe bath
- ◆ Open kitchen and breakfast area includes a pantry and rear access to sun deck
- ◆ 3 bedrooms, 2 baths, 2-car drive under garage
- ◆ Basement foundation

Price Code B

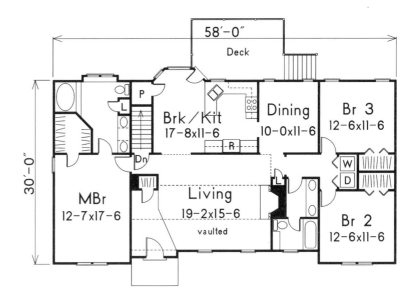

Luxurious Master Bath

Plan #581-034D-0002

1,456 total square feet of living area

Special features

- Open floor plan adds spaciousness to this design
- Bayed dining area creates a cheerful setting
- Corner fireplace in great room is a terrific focal point
- 3 bedrooms, 2 baths, 2-car garage
- Basement foundation

Price Code A

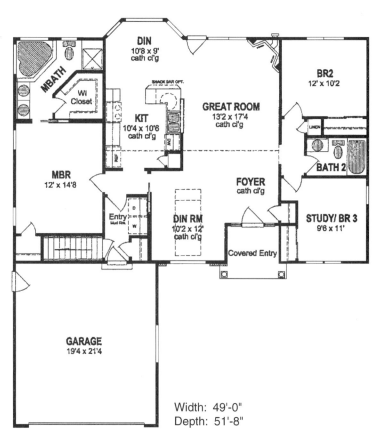

Width: 49'-0"
Depth: 51'-8"

Dramatic Atrium Views

Plan #581-007D-0136

1,533 total square feet of living area

Special features

- ◆ Multiple gables and stonework deliver a warm and inviting exterior
- ◆ The vaulted great room has a fireplace and spectacular views accomplished with a two-story atrium window wall
- ◆ A covered rear porch is easily accessed from the breakfast room or garage
- ◆ The atrium provides an ideal approach to an optional finished walk-out basement
- ◆ 3 bedrooms, 2 baths, 2-car garage
- ◆ Walk-out basement foundation

Price Code B

Rear View

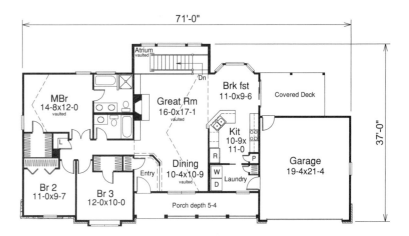

71'-0"

37'-0"

Atrium
vaulted

Dn

MBr
14-8x12-0
vaulted

Great Rm
16-0x17-1
vaulted

Brk fst
11-0x9-6

Covered Deck

Kit
10-9x
11-0

Garage
19-4x21-4

Entry

Dining
10-4x10-9
vaulted

R

W D

P

Laundry

Br 2
11-0x9-7

Br 3
12-0x10-0

Porch depth 5-4

Formal Country Charm

Plan #581-052D-0011

1,325 total square feet of living area

Special features

- ◆ Sloped ceiling and a fireplace in living area creates a cozy feeling
- ◆ Formal dining and breakfast areas have an efficiently designed kitchen between them
- ◆ Master bedroom has a walk-in closet with luxurious private bath
- ◆ 3 bedrooms, 2 baths, 2-car drive under garage
- ◆ Basement or crawl space foundation, please specify when ordering

Price Code A

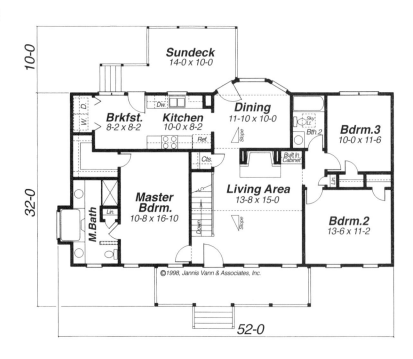

*P*lan #581-047D-0059

3,556 total square feet of living area

Special features

◆ Curved portico welcomes guests

◆ The master bedroom has a see-through fireplace, wet bar, private bath and sitting area opening to covered patio

◆ Cozy family room with fireplace has adjacent summer kitchen outdoors on patio

◆ 4 bedrooms, 3 1/2 baths, 3-car side entry garage

◆ Slab foundation

Price Code F

Width: 85'-0"
Depth: 85'-0"

Vaulted Rear Porch

Plan #581-039D-0014

1,849 total square feet of living area

Special features

◆ Open floor plan creates an airy feeling

◆ Kitchen and breakfast area include center island, pantry and built-in desk

◆ Master bedroom has private entrance off breakfast area and a view of vaulted porch

◆ 3 bedrooms, 2 baths, 2-car garage

◆ Crawl space or slab foundation, please specify when ordering

Price Code C

Width: 66'-5"
Depth: 60'-0"

Plan #581-019D-0011

1,955 total square feet of living area

Special features

- ◆ Porch adds outdoor area to this design
- ◆ Dining and great rooms are visible from foyer through a series of elegant archways
- ◆ Kitchen overlooks great room and breakfast room
- ◆ 3 bedrooms, 2 baths, 2-car side entry garage
- ◆ Crawl space foundation, drawings also include slab foundation

Price Code C

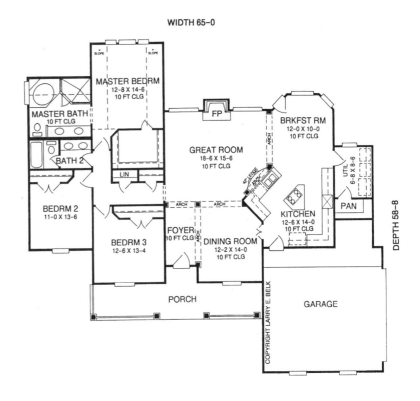

Plan #581-007D-0126

1,365 total square feet of living area

Special features

◆ Home is easily adaptable to physical accessibility featuring no stairs and extra wide hall baths, laundry and garage

◆ Living room has separate entry and opens to a spacious dining room with views of rear patio

◆ L-shaped kitchen is well-equipped and includes a built-in pantry

◆ All bedrooms are spaciously sized and offer generous closet storage

◆ 3 bedrooms, 2 baths, 1-car garage

◆ Slab foundation

Price Code A

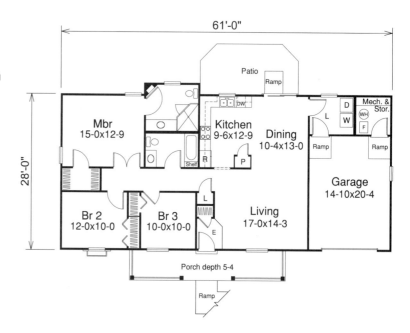

Plan #581-058D-0043

1,277 total square feet of living area

Special features

◆ Vaulted ceilings in master bedroom, great room, kitchen and dining room

◆ Laundry closet is located near bedrooms for convenience

◆ Compact, but efficient kitchen

◆ 3 bedrooms, 2 baths, 2-car garage

◆ Basement foundation

Price Code A

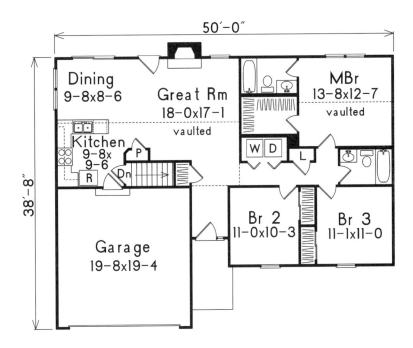

Plan #581-051D-0064

1,490 total square feet of living area

Special features

- ◆ Arch soffit frames the entrance of the kitchen
- ◆ Living room has fireplace with surrounding windows
- ◆ Bay window in master bedroom adds light and beauty
- ◆ Den can easily be converted to a third bedroom
- ◆ 2 bedrooms, 2 baths, 3-car garage
- ◆ Basement foundation

Price Code A

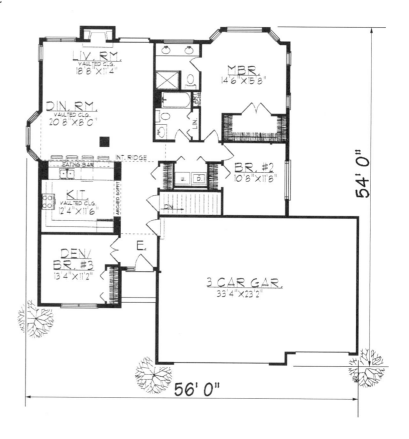

Plan #581-056D-0009

1,606 total square feet of living area

Special features

- ◆ Kitchen has snack bar which overlooks dining area for convenience
- ◆ Master bedroom has lots of windows with a private bath and large walk-in closet
- ◆ Cathedral vault in great room adds spaciousness
- ◆ 3 bedrooms, 2 baths, 2-car garage
- ◆ Slab foundation

Price Code B

Width: 50'-0"
Depth: 42'-0"

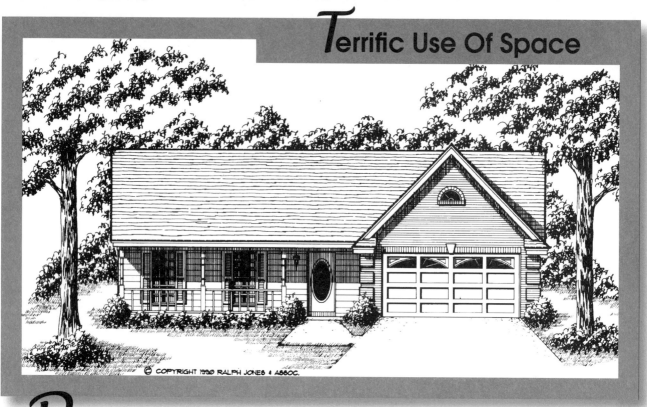

© COPYRIGHT 1990 RALPH JONES & ASSOC.

Plan #581-060D-0022

1,436 total square feet of living area

Special features

◆ Corner fireplace in great room warms home

◆ Kitchen and breakfast room combine for convenience

◆ Centrally located utility room

◆ 3 bedrooms, 2 baths, 2-car garage

◆ Slab foundation

Price Code A

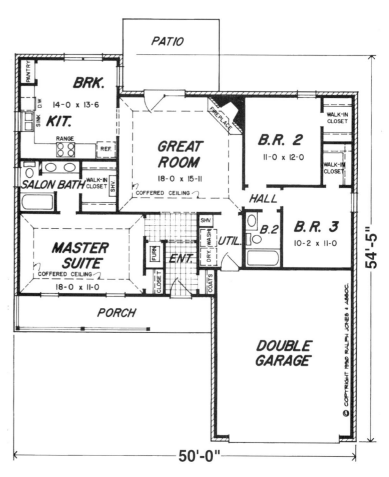

Plan #581-037D-0008

1,707 total square feet of living area

Special features

- The formal living room off the entry hall has a high sloping ceiling and prominent fireplace
- Kitchen and breakfast area allow access to oversized garage and rear porch
- Master bedroom has an impressive vaulted ceiling, luxurious bath, large walk-in closet and separate tub and shower
- Utility room conveniently located near bedrooms
- 3 bedrooms, 2 baths, 2-car garage
- Slab foundation

Price Code C

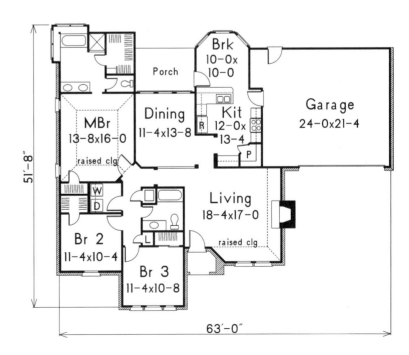

*P*lan #581-048D-0002

2,467 total square feet of living area

Special Features

- ◆ Tiled foyer leads into living room with vaulted ceiling and large bay window
- ◆ Kitchen features walk-in pantry and adjacent breakfast nook
- ◆ Master bedroom includes bay window and bath with large walk-in closet
- ◆ Varied ceiling heights throughout
- ◆ 3 bedrooms, 3 baths, 2-car garage
- ◆ Slab foundation

Price Code D

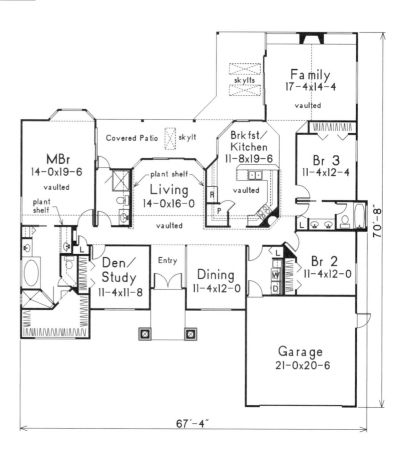

Plan #581-039D-0022

2,158 total square feet of living area

Special features

- Private master suite has walk-in closet and bath
- Sloped ceiling in family room adds drama
- Secondary bedrooms include 9' ceilings and walk-in closets
- Covered porch adds a charming touch
- 4 bedrooms, 3 baths, 2-car side entry garage
- Crawl space or slab foundation, please specify when ordering

Price Code C

Width: 65'-1"
Depth: 69'-0"

Scalloped Porch Cornice

Plan #581-052D-0036

1,772 total square feet of living area

Special features

- Dramatic palladian window and scalloped porch are attention grabbers
- Island kitchen sink allows for easy access and views into the living and breakfast areas
- Washer and dryer closet is easily accessible from all bedrooms
- 3 bedrooms, 2 baths, 3-car drive under garage
- Basement foundation

Price Code B

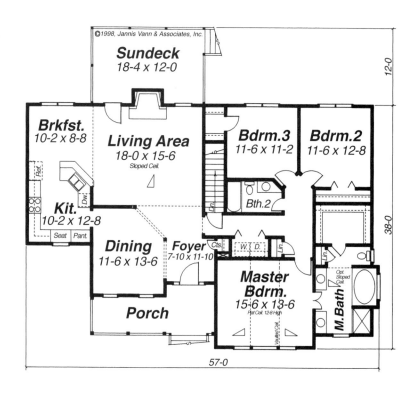

©1998, Jannis Vann & Associates, Inc.

Sundeck
18-4 x 12-0

Brkfst.
10-2 x 8-8

Living Area
18-0 x 15-6
Sloped Ceil.

Bdrm.3
11-6 x 11-2

Bdrm.2
11-6 x 12-8

Kit.
10-2 x 12-8

Bth.2

Dining
11-6 x 13-6

Foyer
7-10 x 11-10

W/D

Master
Bdrm.
15-6 x 13-6

M.Bath

Porch

12-0

38-0

57-0

Plan #581-067D-0005

1,698 total square feet of living area

Special features

- ◆ Large and open great room adds spaciousness to the living area
- ◆ Cheerful bayed sitting area in the master bedroom
- ◆ Compact, yet efficient kitchen
- ◆ 3 bedrooms, 2 1/2 baths, 2-car side entry garage
- ◆ Basement, crawl space or slab foundation, please specify when ordering

Price Code B

Plan #581-067D-0001

1,200 total square feet of living area

Special features

- ◆ Large great room extends the entire depth of the home and also accesses the outdoors
- ◆ U-shaped kitchen keeps everything within reach
- ◆ Convenient laundry room is located just off the kitchen
- ◆ 3 bedrooms, 2 baths, 2-car garage
- ◆ Basement, crawl space or slab foundation, please specify when ordering

Price Code A

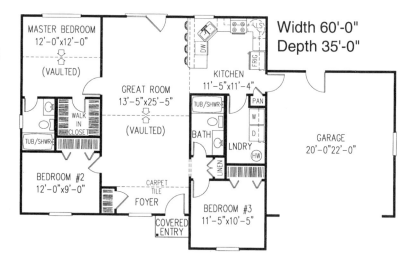

Width 60'-0"
Depth 35'-0"

© COPYRIGHT 1990 RALPH JONES & ASSOC.

*P*lan #581-060D-0014

1,021 total square feet of living area

Special features

- ◆ 11' ceiling in great room expands living area
- ◆ Kitchen and breakfast room combine allowing easier preparation and cleanup
- ◆ Master suite features private bath and an oversized walk-in closet
- ◆ 3 bedrooms, 2 baths, optional 2-car garage
- ◆ Slab or crawl space foundation, please specify when ordering

Price Code AA

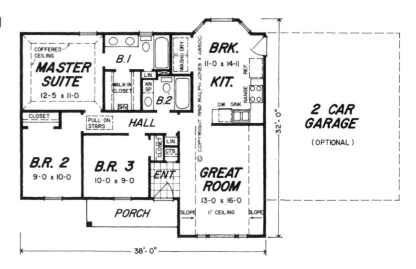

*W*indowed Dining Room

*P*lan #581-041D-0001

2,003 total square feet of living area

Special features

- Octagon-shaped dining room with tray ceiling and deck overlook
- L-shaped island kitchen serves living and dining rooms
- Master bedroom boasts luxury bath and walk-in closet
- Living room features columns, elegant fireplace and 10' ceiling
- 3 bedrooms, 2 baths, 2-car garage
- Basement foundation

Price Code D

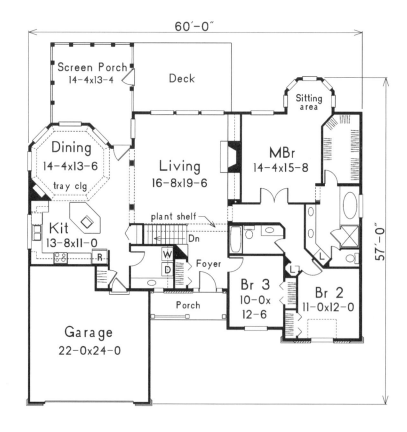

Plan #581-014D-0005

1,314 total square feet of living area

Special features

- ◆ Energy efficient home with 2" x 6" exterior walls
- ◆ Covered porch adds appeal and welcoming charm
- ◆ Functional kitchen complete with pantry and eating bar
- ◆ Cozy fireplace in the living room
- ◆ Master bedroom features a large walk-in closet and bath
- ◆ 3 bedrooms, 2 baths, 2-car garage
- ◆ Basement foundation

Price Code A

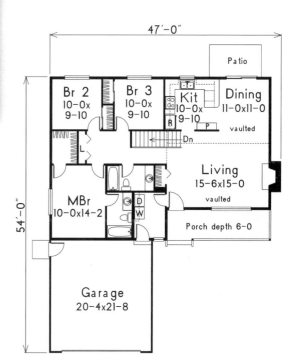

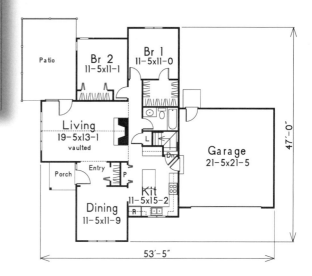

Plan #581-045D-0019

1,134 total square feet of living area

Special features

- ◆ Kitchen has plenty of counterspace, an island worktop, large pantry and access to the garage
- ◆ Living room features a vaulted ceiling, fireplace and access to an expansive patio
- ◆ Bedroom #1 has a large walk-in closet
- ◆ Convenient linen closet in the hall
- ◆ 2 bedrooms, 1 bath, 2-car garage
- ◆ Basement foundation

Price Code AA

*B*ayed Breakfast Room

*P*lan #581-035D-0048

1,915 total square feet of living area

Special features

- ◆ Large breakfast area overlooks vaulted great room
- ◆ Master suite has cheerful sitting room and a private bath
- ◆ Plan features unique in-law suite with private bath and walk-in closet
- ◆ 4 bedrooms, 3 baths, 2-car garage
- ◆ Walk-out basement, slab or crawl space foundation, please specify when ordering

Price Code C

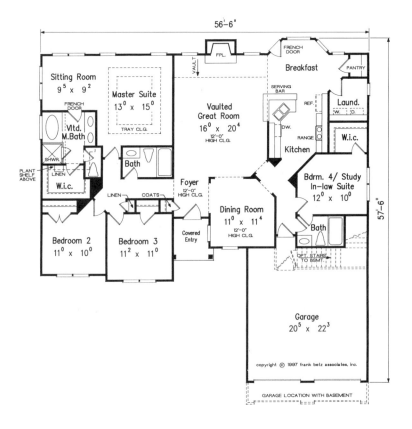

Elegant Family Room

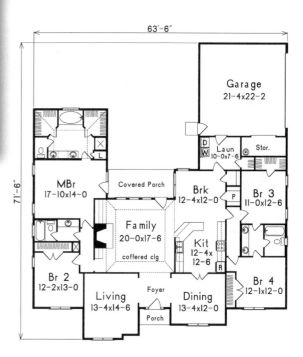

Plan #581-023D-0010

2,558 total square feet of living area

Special features

◆ 9' ceilings throughout home

◆ Angled counter in kitchen serves breakfast and family rooms

◆ Entry foyer flanked by formal living and dining rooms

◆ 4 bedrooms, 3 baths, 2-car side entry garage

◆ Slab foundation, drawings also include crawl space foundation

Price Code D

Secluded Master Suite

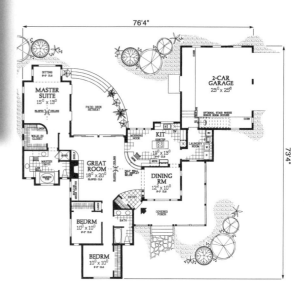

Plan #581-049D-0008

1,937 total square feet of living area

Special features

◆ Great room offers a sloped ceiling, fireplace with extended hearth and built-in shelves for an entertainment center

◆ Gourmet kitchen includes a cooktop island counter and a quaint morning room

◆ Master suite features a sloped ceiling, cozy sitting room, walk-in closet and a private bath with whirlpool tub

◆ 3 bedrooms, 2 baths, 2-car side entry garage

◆ Crawl space foundation

Price Code C

Distinctive Turret

Plan #581-018D-0006

1,742 total square feet of living area

Special features

- ◆ Efficient kitchen combines with breakfast area and great room creating a spacious living area
- ◆ Master bedroom includes a private bath with huge walk-in closet, shower and corner tub
- ◆ Great room boasts a fireplace and access outdoors
- ◆ Laundry room is conveniently located near the kitchen and garage
- ◆ 3 bedrooms, 2 baths, 2-car garage
- ◆ Slab foundation, drawings also include crawl space foundation

Price Code B

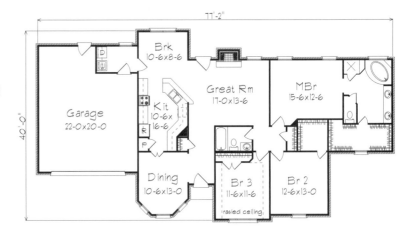

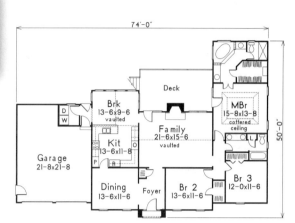

Plan #581-053D-0031

1,908 total square feet of living area

Special features

- Deck is nestled between living areas for easy access
- Vaulted ceiling and floor-to-ceiling windows in family and breakfast rooms create an open, unrestricted space
- Master bedroom with deluxe bath, large walk-in closet and recessed ceiling
- 3 bedrooms, 2 baths, 2-car garage
- Crawl space foundation, drawings also include slab foundation

Price Code C

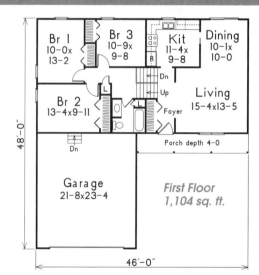

First Floor 1,104 sq. ft.

Plan #581-001D-0022

1,680 total square feet of living area

Special features

- Country facade and covered front porch
- Large basement area for family room, study or hobby area
- Plenty of closet space throughout this design
- 3 bedrooms, 2 baths, 2-car garage
- Basement foundation

Price Code B

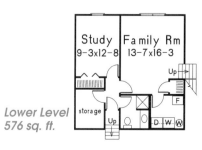

Lower Level 576 sq. ft.

Plan #581-023D-0019

1,539 total square feet of living area

Special features

- ◆ Large master bedroom has a private bath with access to patio
- ◆ Convenient laundry room is located between carport and kitchen
- ◆ Bedrooms are secluded from living areas for added privacy
- ◆ Private dining area features a bay window for elegant entertaining
- ◆ Attached carport offers additional roomy storage area
- ◆ 3 bedrooms, 2 baths, 2-car attached carport
- ◆ Slab foundation

Price Code B

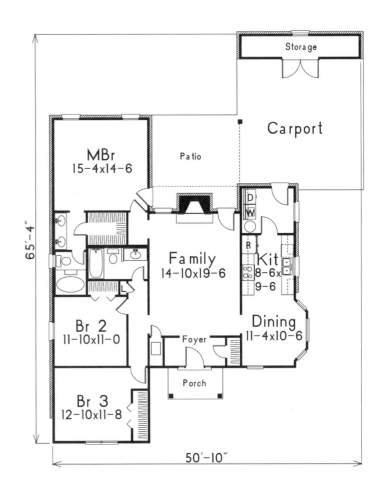

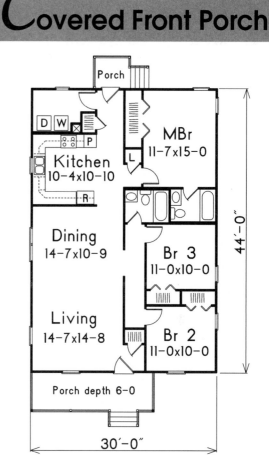

Plan #581-001D-0036

1,320 total square feet of living area

Special features

◆ Functional U-shaped kitchen features pantry

◆ Living and dining areas join creating an open atmosphere

◆ Secluded master bedroom includes private full bath

◆ Covered front porch opens into large living area

◆ Utility/laundry room located near the kitchen

◆ 3 bedrooms, 2 baths

◆ Crawl space foundation

Price Code A

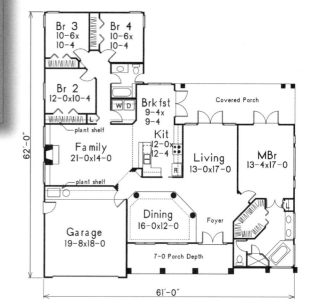

Plan #581-048D-0006

2,153 total square feet of living area

Special features

◆ Foyer leads directly into formal living room

◆ Master bedroom features wall of windows and also accesses porch

◆ Family room boasts 12' barrel vaulted ceiling and built-in bookshelves on each side of dramatic fireplace

◆ Varied ceiling heights throughout

◆ 4 bedrooms, 2 baths, 2-car garage

◆ Slab foundation

Price Code C

Bright, Spacious Plan

Plan #581-058D-0015

2,308 total square feet of living area

Special features

- ◆ Efficient kitchen designed with many cabinets and large walk-in pantry adjoins family/breakfast area featuring a beautiful fireplace
- ◆ Dining area has architectural colonnades that separate it from living area while maintaining spaciousness
- ◆ Enter master bedroom through double-doors and find double walk-in closets and a beautiful luxurious bath
- ◆ Living room includes vaulted ceiling, fireplace and a sunny atrium window wall creating a dramatic atmosphere
- ◆ 3 bedrooms, 2 baths, 2-car side entry garage
- ◆ Walk-out basement foundation

Price Code D

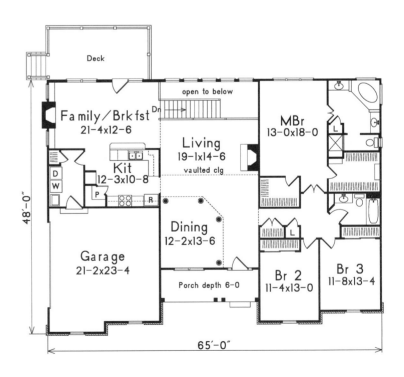

For A Small Family

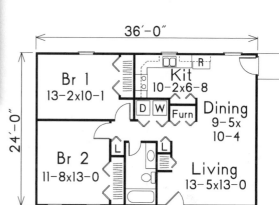

36'-0"

24'-0"

Br 1
13-2x10-1

Kit
10-2x6-8

R

D W Furn

Dining
9-5x
10-4

Br 2
11-8x13-0

L L

Living
13-5x13-0

Porch depth 4-0

Plan #581-001D-0040

864 total square feet of living area

Special features

♦ L-shaped kitchen with convenient pantry is adjacent to dining area

♦ Easy access to laundry area, linen closet and storage closet

♦ Both bedrooms include ample closet space

♦ 2 bedrooms, 1 bath

♦ Crawl space foundation, drawings also include basement and slab foundations

Price Code AAA

Columns Grace Entry

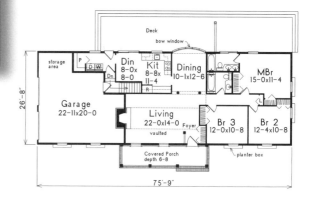

Deck

bow window

storage area

P D.W.

Din
8-0x
8-0

Dn

Kit
8-8x
11-4

Dining
10-1x12-6

MBr
15-0x11-4

26'-8"

Garage
22-11x20-0

R

Living
22-0x14-0
vaulted

Foyer

L

Br 3
12-0x10-8

Br 2
12-4x10-8

Covered Porch
depth 6-8

planter box

75'-9"

Plan #581-017D-0003

1,476 total square feet of living area

Special features

♦ Energy efficient home with 2" x 6" exterior walls

♦ Living room made more spacious by vaulted ceiling

♦ Master bedroom features bath and private deck

♦ Dining room defined by columns and a large bow window

♦ 3 bedrooms, 2 baths, 2-car side entry garage

♦ Basement foundation, drawings also include slab foundation

Price Code B

Expansive Family Room

Plan #581-043D-0002

3,671 total square feet of living area

Special features

- ◆ Grand entry features a 14' ceiling and display niches
- ◆ 11'-9" ceilings in nook, den, dining and sitting rooms
- ◆ Kitchen has island eating counter, pantry and built-in desk
- ◆ Fireplace in master bedroom
- ◆ 3 bedrooms, 2 full baths, 2 half baths, 4-car garage
- ◆ Crawl space foundation

Price Code F

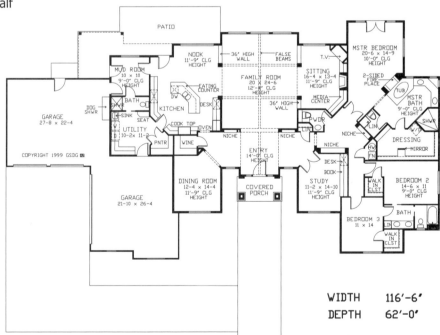

WIDTH 116'-6'
DEPTH 62'-0'

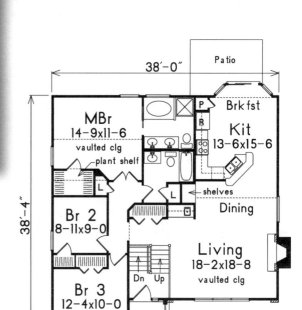

Plan #581-007D-0061

1,340 total square feet of living area

Special features

◆ Grand-sized vaulted living and dining rooms offer fire-place, wet bar and breakfast counter open to kitchen

◆ Vaulted master bedroom features double entry doors, walk-in closet and an elegant bath

◆ 3 bedrooms, 2 baths, 2-car drive under garage with storage area

◆ Basement foundation

Price Code A

Rooflines Add Interest

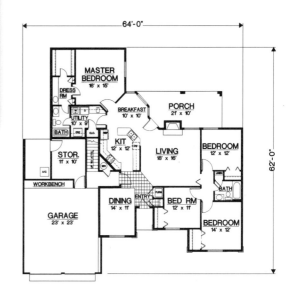

Plan #581-020D-0007

1,828 total square feet of living area

Special features

◆ Energy efficient home with 2" x 6" exterior walls

◆ Master bath features a giant walk-in closet, built-in linen storage with convenient access to utility room

◆ Kitchen has a unique design that is elegant and practical

◆ 4 bedrooms, 2 baths, 2-car garage

◆ Basement foundation, drawings also include crawl space and slab foundations

Price Code C

*P*lan #581-069D-0001

947 total square feet of living area

Special Features

- ◆ Efficiently designed kitchen/dining area accesses the outdoors onto a rear porch

- ◆ Future expansion plans included which allow the home to become 392 square feet larger with 3 bedrooms and 2 baths

- ◆ 2 bedrooms, 1 bath

- ◆ Crawl space or slab foundation, please specify when ordering

Price Code AA

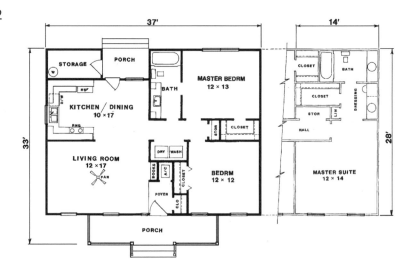

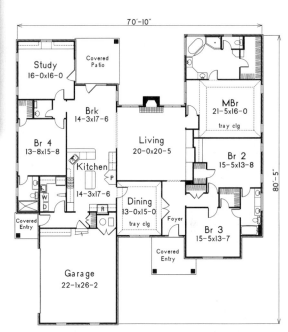

Plan #581-068D-0014

3,366 total square feet of living area

Special features

- Wonderful covered patio off secluded study and breakfast area
- Separate dining area for entertaining
- Spacious master bedroom has an enormous private bath with walk-in closet
- 4 bedrooms, 3 1/2 baths, 2-car side entry garage
- Crawl space foundation, drawings also include slab foundation

Price Code F

Two Bedroom Cottage

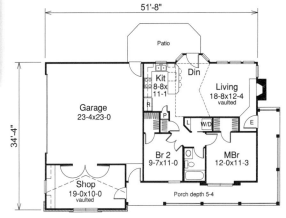

Plan #581-007D-0135

801 total square feet of living area

Special features

- A wrap-around porch, roof dormer and fancy stonework all contribute to a delightful and charming exterior
- The living room enjoys a separate entry, a stone fireplace, vaulted ceiling and lots of windows
- The well-equipped kitchen has a snack bar and dining area with bay which offers access to the rear patio
- 2 bedrooms, 1 bath, 2-car side entry garage
- Slab foundation

Price Code AAA

COPYRIGHT   LARRY E. BELK

*P*lan #581-019D-0009

1,862 total square feet of living area

Special features

- ◆ 10' ceilings throughout this home
- ◆ Comfortable traditional has all the amenities of a larger plan in a compact layout
- ◆ Angled eating bar separates kitchen and great room while leaving these areas open to one another for entertaining
- ◆ 3 bedrooms, 2 baths, 2-car garage
- ◆ Crawl space foundation, drawings also include slab foundation

Price Code C

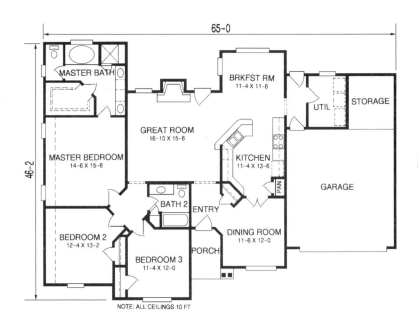

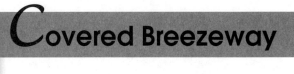

Plan #581-039D-0004

1,406 total square feet of living area

Special features

- ◆ Master bedroom has a sloped ceiling
- ◆ Kitchen and dining area merge becoming a gathering place
- ◆ Enter family room from charming covered front porch to find a fireplace and lots of windows
- ◆ 3 bedrooms, 2 baths, 2-car detached garage
- ◆ Slab or crawl space foundation, please specify when ordering

Price Code A

Dormers Add Appeal

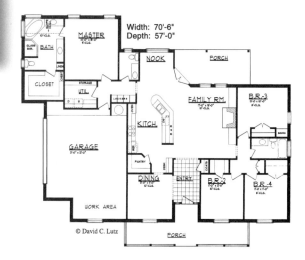

Plan #581-031D-0011

2,164 total square feet of living area

Special features

- ◆ Country-styled front porch adds charm
- ◆ Plenty of counterspace in kitchen
- ◆ Large utility area meets big families' laundry needs
- ◆ Double-doors lead to covered rear porch
- ◆ 4 bedrooms, 2 1/2 baths, 2-car side entry garage
- ◆ Slab foundation

Price Code C

Plan #581-034D-0012

2,278 total square feet of living area

Special features

- ◆ Octagon-shaped dining area is cheerful and bright
- ◆ Kitchen with eat-in breakfast bar overlooks family room with fireplace
- ◆ Unique box bay window in bedroom #2
- ◆ 3 bedrooms, 2 1/2 baths, 2-car garage
- ◆ Basement foundation

Price Code D

Width: 76'-0"
Depth: 58'-0"

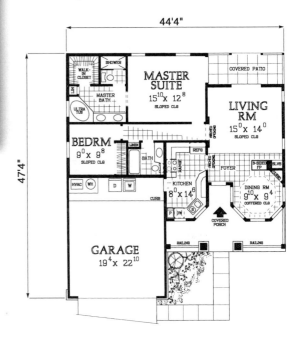

Plan #581-049D-0007

1,118 total square feet of living area

Special features

◆ Convenient kitchen has direct access into garage and looks out onto front covered porch

◆ The covered patio is enjoyed by both the living room and master suite

◆ Octagon-shaped dining room adds interest to the front exterior while the interior is sunny and bright

◆ 2 bedrooms, 2 baths, 2-car garage

◆ Slab foundation

Price Code AA

Impressive Foyer

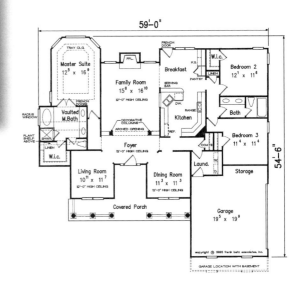

Plan #581-035D-0032

1,856 total square feet of living area

Special features

◆ Beautiful covered porch creates a Southern accent

◆ Kitchen has an organized feel with lots of cabinetry

◆ Large foyer has a grand entrance and leads into family room through columns and an arched opening

◆ 3 bedrooms, 2 baths, 2-car side entry garage

◆ Walk-out basement, crawl space or slab foundation, please specify when ordering

Price Code C

Gables Accent Facade

Plan #581-060D-0026

1,497 total square feet of living area

Special features

- ◆ Open living area with kitchen counter overlooking a cozy great room with fireplace
- ◆ Sloped ceiling accents dining room
- ◆ Master suite has privacy from other bedrooms
- ◆ 3 bedrooms, 2 baths, 2-car garage
- ◆ Slab foundation

Price Code A

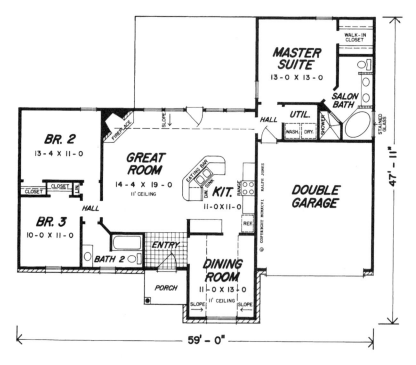

Plan #581-069D-0014

1,680 total square feet of living area

Special features

◆ Master suite has two walk-in closets and a private bath

◆ Kitchen has snack bar and connects to a dining area

◆ A covered porch extends the living area to the outdoors

◆ Extra storage in garage

◆ 3 bedrooms, 2 baths, 2-car garage

◆ Slab or crawl space foundation, please specify when ordering

Price Code B

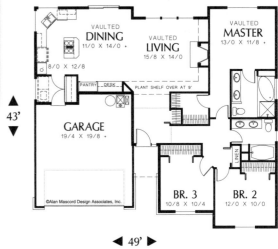

Plan #581-011D-0005

1,467 total square feet of living area

Special features

◆ Vaulted ceilings, an open floor plan and a wealth of windows create an inviting atmosphere

◆ Efficiently arranged kitchen has an island with built-in cooktop and a snack counter

◆ Plentiful storage and closetspace throughout this home

◆ 3 bedrooms, 2 baths, 2-car garage

◆ Crawl space foundation

Price Code C

Plan #581-045D-0014

987 total square feet of living area

Special features

- ◆ Galley kitchen opens into cozy breakfast room
- ◆ Convenient coat closets located by both entrances
- ◆ Dining/living room combine for an expansive open area
- ◆ Breakfast room has access to the outdoors
- ◆ Front porch great for enjoying outdoor living
- ◆ 3 bedrooms, 1 bath
- ◆ Basement foundation

Price Code AA

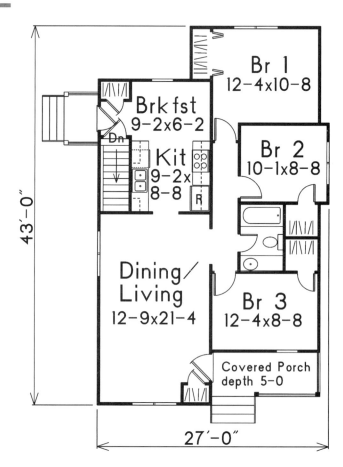

Plan #581-019D-0013

1,932 total square feet of living area

Special features

- Double arches form entrance to this elegantly styled home
- Two palladian windows add distinction to facade
- Kitchen has an angled eating bar opening to the breakfast and living rooms
- 3 bedrooms, 2 baths, 2-car side entry garage
- Crawl space foundation, drawings also include slab foundation

Price Code C

Plan #581-040D-0011

1,739 total square feet of living area

Special features

- Vaulted ceiling lends drama to the family room with fireplace and double French doors
- Island kitchen is enhanced by adjoining breakfast area with access to the patio
- Formal dining room features a 10' ceiling
- Private hallway separates bedrooms from living area
- 3 bedrooms, 2 baths, 2-car side entry garage
- Slab foundation

Price Code B

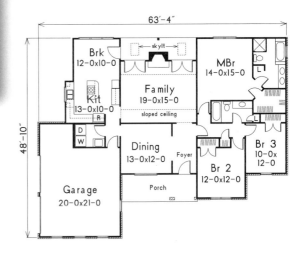

*G*raceful, Neat Floor Plan

*P*lan #581-001D-0020

1,416 total square feet of living area

Special features

- One-story simplicity affords convenient traffic flow
- Roomy master bedroom has large closet and a private bath
- Laundry is conveniently located adjacent to bedrooms
- Secluded living room for quiet and privacy
- 3 bedrooms, 2 baths, 2-car garage
- Basement foundation, drawings also include a crawl space foundation

Price Code A

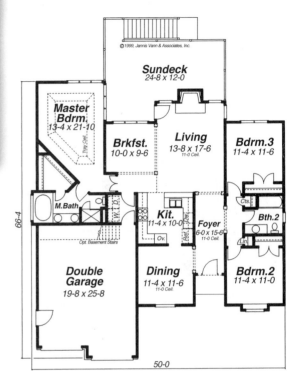

Plan #581-052D-0024

1,635 total square feet of living area

Special features

◆ Large sundeck extends the rear of the home outdoors

◆ Master bedroom is separate from other bedrooms

◆ A wall of windows brightens the interior of the breakfast room

◆ 3 bedrooms, 2 baths, 2-car garage

◆ Basement, crawl space or slab foundation, please specify when ordering

Price Code B

Grand Entrance

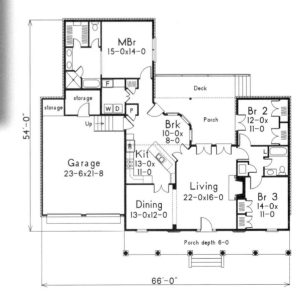

Plan #581-021D-0004

1,800 total square feet of living area

Special features

◆ Kitchen and breakfast area feature large windows

◆ Covered front and rear porches provide an added dimension to this home's living space

◆ Energy efficient home with 2" x 6" exterior walls

◆ Master bedroom has adjoining bath

◆ 3 bedrooms, 2 baths, 2-car garage

◆ Crawl space foundation, drawings also include slab foundation

Price Code C

*P*lan #581-036D-0048

1,830 total square feet of living area

Special features

- Inviting covered verandas in the front and rear of the home
- Great room has fireplace and cathedral ceiling
- Handy service porch allows easy access
- Master bedroom has vaulted ceiling and private bath
- 3 bedrooms, 2 baths, 3-car side entry garage
- Basement, crawl space or slab foundation, please specify when ordering

Price Code C

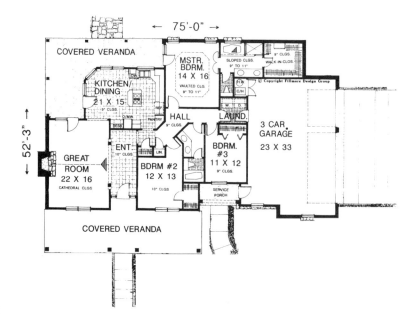

Plan #581-021D-0012

1,672 total square feet of living area

Special features

- Master bedroom has walk-in closet and adjoining bath
- Energy efficient home with 2" x 6" exterior walls
- 12' ceilings in living room, kitchen and bedroom #2
- Kitchen complete with pantry, angled bar and adjacent eating area
- 3 bedrooms, 2 baths, 2-car side entry garage
- Crawl space foundation, drawings also include basement and slab foundations

Price Code C

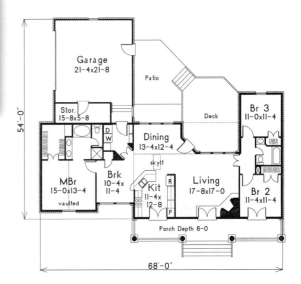

Plan #581-026D-0114

2,498 total square feet of living area

Special features

- Den could easily convert to a fourth bedroom
- Built-in bookshelves frame family room fireplace
- Elegant arched entry invites guests
- 3 bedrooms, 2 1/2 baths, 3-car garage
- Basement foundation

Price Code D

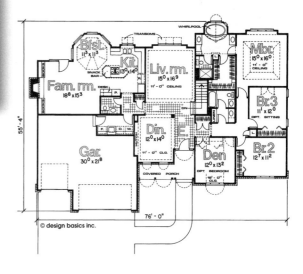

© design basics inc.

*E*asy Living

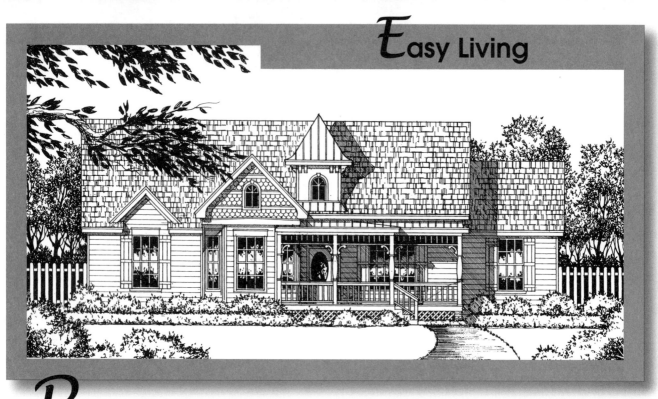

*P*lan #581-030D-0003

1,753 total square feet of living area

Special features

- ◆ Large front porch has charming appeal
- ◆ Kitchen with breakfast bar overlooks morning room and accesses covered porch
- ◆ Master suite has amenities such as a private bath, spacious closets and sunny bay window
- ◆ 3 bedrooms, 2 baths
- ◆ Slab or crawl space foundation, please specify when ordering

Price Code B

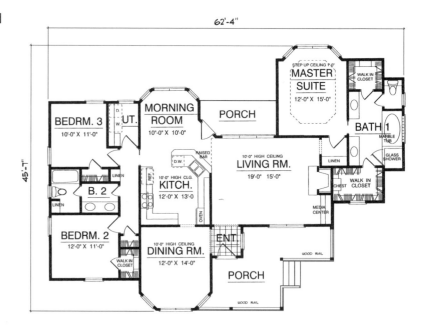

Plan #581-022D-0024

1,127 total square feet of living area

Special features

◆ Vaulted master bedroom has double walk-in closets, deck access and private bath

◆ Great room features vaulted ceiling, fireplace and sliding doors to covered deck

◆ Ideal home for a narrow lot

◆ 2 bedrooms, 2 baths, 2-car garage

◆ Basement foundation

Price Code AA

Plan #581-053D-0006

1,976 total square feet of living area

Special features

◆ Compact ranch features garage entry near front door

◆ Vaulted living area has large balcony above

◆ Isolated master bedroom with coffered ceiling and luxurious bath

◆ Loft area has access to plenty of attic storage and future play room

◆ 3 bedrooms, 2 baths, 2-car side entry garage

◆ Basement foundation

Price Code C

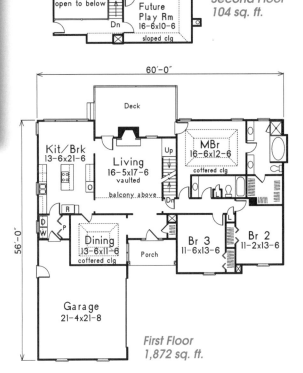

Plan #581-036D-0056

1,604 total square feet of living area

Special features

◆ Ideal design for a narrow lot

◆ Living and dining areas combine for a spacious feel

◆ Secluded study has double-doors for privacy

◆ Master bedroom has a spacious private bath

◆ 3 bedrooms, 2 baths, 2-car garage

◆ Slab foundation

Price Code B

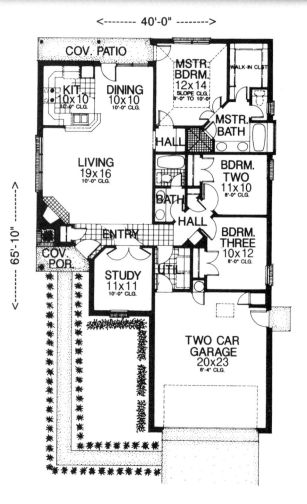

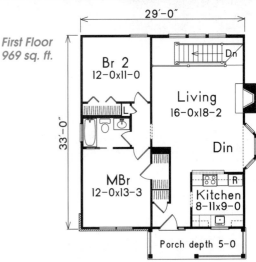

First Floor
969 sq. ft.

29'-0"

33'-0"

Br 2
12-0x11-0

Living
16-0x18-2

Dn

Din

MBr
12-0x13-3

Kitchen
8-11x9-0

Porch depth 5-0

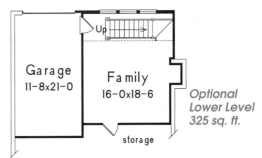

Garage
11-8x21-0

Up

Family
16-0x18-6

Optional
Lower Level
325 sq. ft.

storage

Plan #581-007D-0104

969 total square feet of living area

Special features

◆ Eye-pleasing facade enjoys stone accents with country porch for quiet evenings

◆ A bayed dining area, cozy fireplace and atrium with sunny two-story windows are the many features of the living room

◆ Step-saver kitchen includes a pass-through snack bar

◆ 2 bedrooms, 1 bath, 1-car rear entry garage

◆ Walk-out basement foundation

Price Code AA

Bonus Space

Optional
Second Floor
287 sq. ft.

Future Space
11' · 20'

First Floor
2,616 sq. ft.

Width: 70'-0"
Depth: 72'-0"

Plan #581-047D-0045

2,616 total square feet of living area

Special features

◆ Archway joins formal living and family rooms

◆ Master bedroom has private bath and accesses covered patio

◆ Breakfast nook overlooks family room with cozy corner fireplace

◆ 3 bedrooms, 3 baths, 2-car side entry garage

◆ Slab foundation

Price Code E

Comfortable Living

*P*lan #581-025D-0003

1,379 total square feet of living area

Special features

- ◆ Vaulted great room makes a lasting impression with corner fireplace and windows
- ◆ Formal dining room easily connects to kitchen making entertaining easy
- ◆ Master bath includes all the luxuries such as a spacious walk-in closet, oversized tub and separate shower
- ◆ 3 bedrooms, 2 baths, 2-car garage
- ◆ Slab foundation

Price Code A

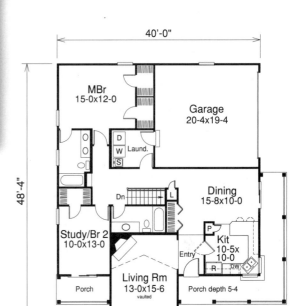

Plan #581-007D-0133

1,316 total square feet of living area

Special features

- Porches are accessible from entry, dining room and bedroom #2
- Vaulted living room enjoys a corner fireplace
- Kitchen has an outdoor plant shelf
- 2 bedrooms, 2 baths, 2-car side entry garage
- Basement foundation, drawings also include crawl space and slab foundations

Price Code A

Plan #581-039D-0024

2,361 total square feet of living area

Special features

- Enormous breakfast area and kitchen create a perfect gathering place
- Family room enhanced with wall of windows and a large fireplace
- Office/gameroom is easily accessible through separate side entrance
- 4 bedrooms, 3 baths, 2-car side entry garage
- Basement foundation

Price Code D

Cozy Cottage Style

Plan #581-052D-0018

1,514 total square feet of living area

Special features

- See-though fireplace warms the living and dining areas
- Handy computer station located near bedrooms
- Sliding glass doors in kitchen lead to a covered patio
- 3 bedrooms, 2 baths, 2-car garage
- Basement or crawl space foundation, please specify when ordering

Price Code B

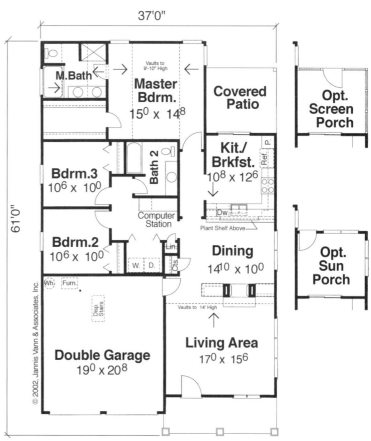

Plan #581-014D-0015

1,941 total square feet of living area

Special features

◆ Kitchen incorporates a cooktop island, a handy pantry and adjoins the dining and family rooms

◆ Formal living room lends a touch of privacy

◆ Both the dining and family rooms have access outdoors through sliding doors

◆ 3 bedrooms, 2 1/2 baths, 2-car garage

◆ Crawl space foundation

Price Code C

Plan #581-053D-0044

1,340 total square feet of living area

Special features

◆ Master bedroom has a private bath and walk-in closet

◆ Recessed entry leads to vaulted family room with see-through fireplace to dining area

◆ Garage includes handy storage area

◆ Convenient laundry closet in the kitchen

◆ 3 bedrooms, 2 baths, 2-car side entry garage

◆ Slab foundation, drawings also include crawl space foundation

Price Code A

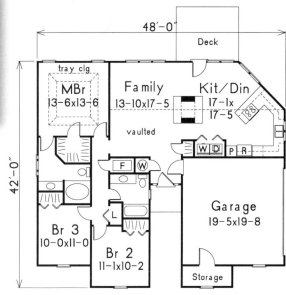

Plan #581-001D-0091

1,344 total square feet of living area

Special features

- Kitchen has side entry, laundry area, pantry and joins family/dining area
- Master bedroom includes a private bath
- Linen and storage closets in hall
- Covered porch opens to the spacious living room with a handy coat closet
- 3 bedrooms, 2 baths
- Crawl space foundation, drawings also include basement and slab foundations

Price Code A

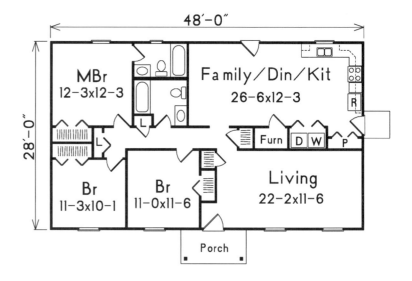

Width: 83'-0"
Depth: 40'-6"

Plan #581-062D-0051

1,578 total square feet of living area

Special features

- A fireplace warms the great room and is flanked by windows overlooking the rear deck
- Bedrooms are clustered on one side of the home for privacy from living areas
- Master bedroom has a unique art niche at its entry
- 3 bedrooms, 2 baths, 2-car side entry garage
- Basement or crawl space foundation, please specify when ordering

Price Code B

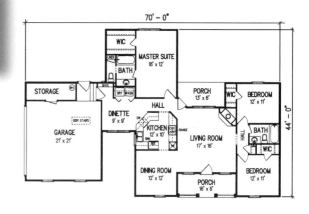

Plan #581-020D-0002

1,434 total square feet of living area

Special features

- Isolated master suite includes walk-in closet and bath
- Elegant formal dining room
- Efficient kitchen has an adjacent dining area which includes shelves and access to laundry facilities
- Extra storage in garage
- 3 bedrooms, 2 baths, 2-car side entry garage
- Crawl space foundation, drawings also include slab foundation

Price Code A

Plan #581-047D-0051

2,962 total square feet of living area

Special features

- ◆ Vaulted breakfast nook is adjacent to the kitchen for convenience
- ◆ Bedroom #4 is an ideal guest suite with private bath
- ◆ Master bedroom includes see-through fireplace, bayed vanity and massive walk-in closet
- ◆ 4 bedrooms, 3 baths, 3-car side entry garage
- ◆ Slab foundation

Price Code E

Width: 66'-8"
Depth: 76'-8"

*L*arge Living Area

*P*lan #581-001D-0081

1,160 total square feet of living area

Special features

- ◆ U-shaped kitchen includes breakfast bar and convenient laundry area
- ◆ Master bedroom features private half bath and large closet
- ◆ Dining room has outdoor access
- ◆ Dining and great rooms combine to create an open living atmosphere
- ◆ 3 bedrooms, 1 1/2 baths
- ◆ Crawl space foundation, drawings also include basement and slab foundations

Price Code AA

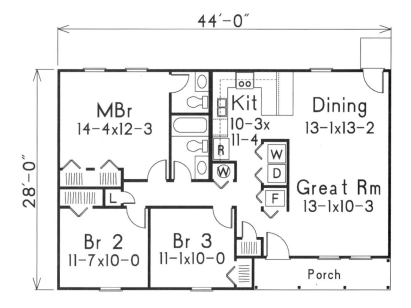

*D*ramatic Interior

*P*lan #581-014D-0009

1,428 total square feet of living area

Special features

- ◆ 10' ceiling in entry and hallway
- ◆ Vaulted dining room combines a desk area near the see-through fireplace
- ◆ Energy efficient home with 2" x 6" exterior walls
- ◆ Vaulted secondary bedrooms
- ◆ Kitchen loaded with amenities including an island with salad sink and pantry
- ◆ Master bedroom with vaulted ceiling includes large walk-in closet and private master bath
- ◆ 3 bedrooms, 2 baths, 2-car garage
- ◆ Basement foundation, drawings also include crawl space foundation

Price Code A

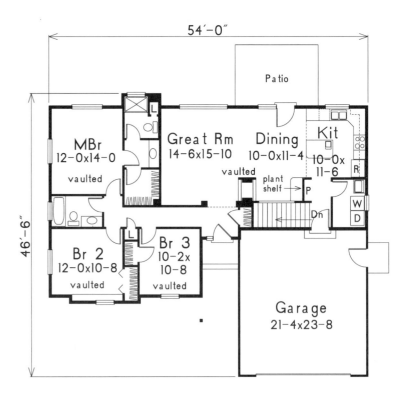

Plan #581-023D-0017

1,596 total square feet of living area

Special features

- Large corner fireplace enhances living area
- Centrally located utility room provides convenient access
- Master bath features double walk-in closets, oversized tub and plant shelves
- Both the living area and master bedroom are accented with raised ceilings
- Bay window in dining area adds interest and light
- 3 bedrooms, 2 baths
- Slab foundation

Price Code B

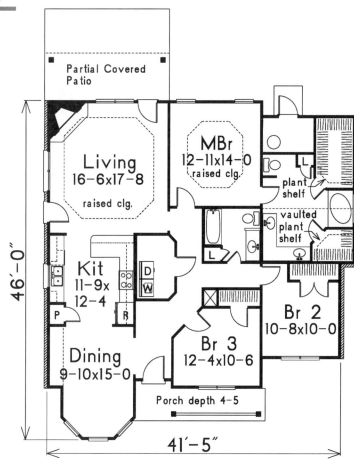

Partial Covered Patio

Living
16-6x17-8
raised clg.

MBr
12-11x14-0
raised clg.

plant shelf

vaulted plant shelf

Kit
11-9x 12-4

Br 2
10-8x10-0

Br 3
12-4x10-6

Dining
9-10x15-0

Porch depth 4-5

46'-0"

41'-5"

Appealing Facade

Plan #581-034D-0010

2,178 total square feet of living area

Special features

- ◆ Large foyer leads to a sunny great room with corner fireplace and expansive entertainment center
- ◆ Kitchen and dining area are efficiently designed
- ◆ Master bedroom has private bath with step-up tub and a bay window
- ◆ 3 bedrooms, 2 baths, 2-car side entry garage
- ◆ Basement foundation

Price Code C

Width: 59'-0"
Depth: 77'-8"

*O*ld-Fashioned Porch

*P*lan #581-001D-0074

1,664 total square feet of living area

Special features

- L-shaped country kitchen includes pantry and cozy breakfast area
- Bedrooms located on second floor for privacy
- Master bedroom includes walk-in closet, dressing area and bath
- 3 bedrooms, 2 1/2 baths, 2-car garage
- Crawl space foundation, drawings also include basement and slab foundations

Price Code B

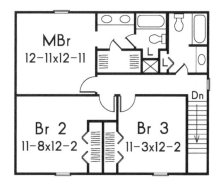

MBr
12-11x12-11

Br 2
11-8x12-2

Br 3
11-3x12-2

Dn

Second Floor
832 sq. ft.

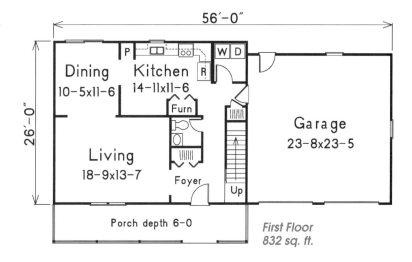

56'-0"

26'-0"

P

W D

Dining
10-5x11-6

Kitchen
14-11x11-6

R

Furn

Garage
23-8x23-5

Living
18-9x13-7

Foyer

Up

Porch depth 6-0

First Floor
832 sq. ft.

Plan #581-051D-0055

1,907 total square feet of living area

Special features

- Vaulted entry and great room
- Large three stall garage includes ample storage space for hobby materials
- Covered porch directly off eating nook provides easy access to the outdoors
- 3 bedrooms, 2 1/2 baths, 3-car garage
- Basement foundation

Price Code C

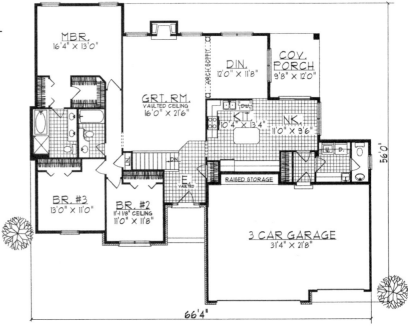

Large Family-Sized Kitchen

Plan #581-053D-0051

2,731 total square feet of living area

Special features

- ◆ Isolated master bedroom enjoys double walk-in closets, a coffered ceiling and elegant bath
- ◆ Both dining and living rooms feature coffered ceilings and bay windows
- ◆ Breakfast room includes dramatic vaulted ceiling and plenty of windows
- ◆ Family room features fireplace flanked by shelves, vaulted ceiling and access to rear deck
- ◆ Secondary bedrooms are separate from living areas
- ◆ 4 bedrooms, 3 1/2 baths, 2-car side entry garage
- ◆ Basement foundation

Price Code E

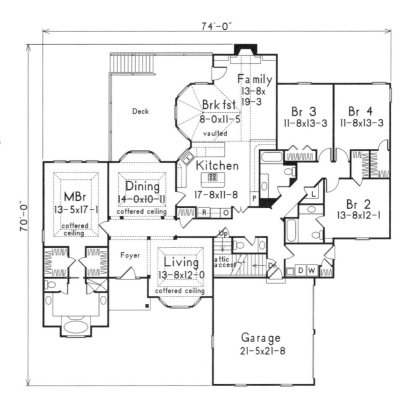

R. BRADSHAW

*P*lan #581-048D-0009

2,041 total square feet of living area

Special features

- ◆ Columned foyer projects past living and dining rooms into family room
- ◆ Kitchen conveniently accesses dining room and breakfast area
- ◆ Master bedroom features double-doors to patio and pocket door to master bath with walk-in closet, double-bowl vanity and tub
- ◆ 4 bedrooms, 2 baths, 2-car garage
- ◆ Slab foundation, drawings also include crawl space foundation

Price Code C

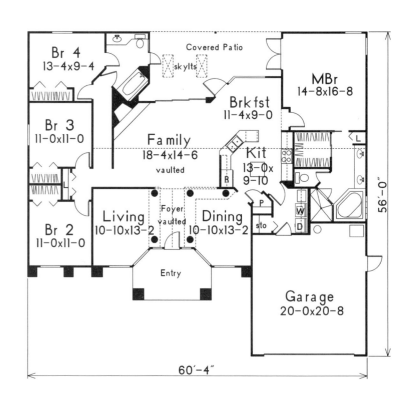

Plan #581-037D-0011

1,846 total square feet of living area

Special features

♦ Enormous living area combines with dining and breakfast rooms complemented by extensive windows and high ceilings

♦ Master bedroom has walk-in closet, display niche and deluxe bath

♦ Secondary bedrooms share a bath and feature large closet space and a corner window

♦ Oversized two-car garage has plenty of storage and work space with handy access to the kitchen through the utility area

♦ Breakfast nook has wrap-around windows adding to eating enjoyment

♦ 3 bedrooms, 2 baths, 2-car garage

♦ Slab foundation

Price Code C

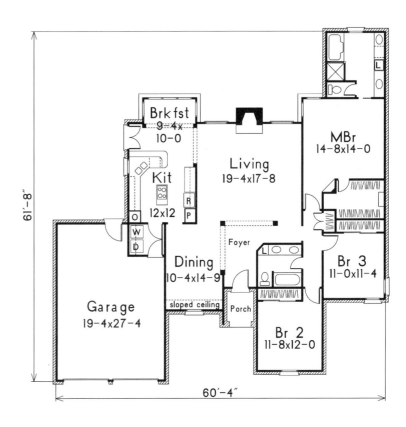

_P_lan #581-023D-0012

2,365 total square feet of living area

Special features

◆ 9' ceilings throughout home

◆ Expansive central living room complemented by corner fireplace

◆ Breakfast bay overlooks rear porch

◆ Master bedroom features bath with double walk-in closets and vanities, separate tub and shower and handy linen closet

◆ Peninsula keeps kitchen private

◆ 4 bedrooms, 2 baths, 2-car carport

◆ Slab foundation

Price Code D

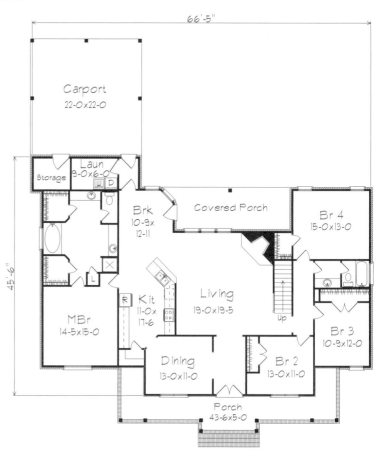

Elegant Starter Home

Plan #581-007D-0109

888 total square feet of living area

Special features

- Home features an eye-catching exterior and has a spacious porch
- The breakfast room with bay window is open to living room and adjoins kitchen with pass-through snack bar
- The bedrooms are quite roomy and feature walk-in closets
- The master bedroom has double entry doors and access to rear patio
- 2 bedrooms, 1 bath, 1-car garage
- Basement foundation

Price Code AAA

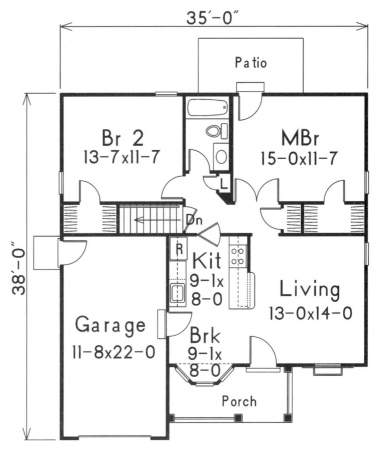

Patio

Br 2
13-7x11-7

MBr
15-0x11-7

Kit
9-1x
8-0

Living
13-0x14-0

Garage
11-8x22-0

Brk
9-1x
8-0

Porch

35'-0"

38'-0"

Dn

R

Plan #581-053D-0035

1,527 total square feet of living area

Special features

- ◆ Convenient laundry room is located off the garage
- ◆ Vaulted ceiling in living room slopes to foyer and dining area creating a spacious entrance
- ◆ Galley kitchen provides easy passage to both breakfast and dining areas
- ◆ Master bedroom is complete with a large master bath, platform tub and shower, plus roomy walk-in closets
- ◆ 3 bedrooms, 2 baths, 2-car side entry garage
- ◆ Basement foundation, drawings also include slab and crawl space foundations

Price Code B

Plan #581-001D-0045

1,197 total square feet of living area

Special features

- U-shaped kitchen includes ample workspace, breakfast bar, laundry area and direct access to the outdoors
- Large living room with convenient coat closet
- Bedroom #1 features a large walk-in closet
- 3 bedrooms, 1 bath
- Crawl space foundation, drawings also include basement and slab foundations

Price Code AA

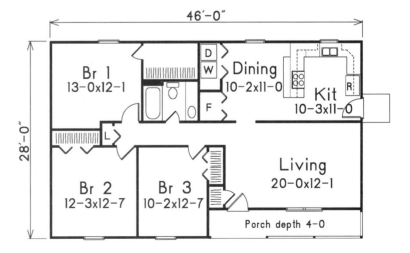

46'-0"

28'-0"

Br 1
13-0x12-1

D
W
F

Dining
10-2x11-0

Kit
10-3x11-0

L

Br 2
12-3x12-7

Br 3
10-2x12-7

Living
20-0x12-1

Porch depth 4-0

*F*oyer Is A Grand Entrance

*P*lan #581-015D-0044

2,148 total square feet of living area

Special features

- ◆ 9' ceilings throughout this home
- ◆ 11' ceilings in great room, kitchen, nook and foyer
- ◆ Eating bar in kitchen extends the dining space for extra guests or casual seating
- ◆ 3 bedrooms, 2 baths, 2-car side entry garage
- ◆ Basement foundation

Price Code C

Width: 65'-0"
Depth: 54'-6"

SCREENED PORCH 13/2 x 9/2

COVERED PATIO

BREAKFAST ROOM 10/10 x 13/0

MASTER 14/8 x 12/8

BDRM 2 11/0 x 12/0

TV

GREAT RM 16/4 x 20/6

EATING BAR

KIT 12/0 x 14/6

R

RAILING

DOWN

LINEN

8" DIAMETER COLUMNS

PANTRY

UTIL

ARCH

FOYER

BDRM 3 13/0 x 11/10

COVERED PORCH

DINING 12/6 x 13/8

GARAGE 21/2 x 21/8

Plan #581-065D-0020

1,315 total square feet of living area

Special features

- First floor laundry room and kitchen are convenient work spaces
- Windows on both sides of the fireplace make the great room very pleasant for relaxing and enjoying views outdoors
- Open stairs to the lower level make it simple to finish the basement
- 3 bedrooms, 2 baths, 2-car side entry garage
- Walk-out basement or basement foundation, please specify when ordering

Price Code A

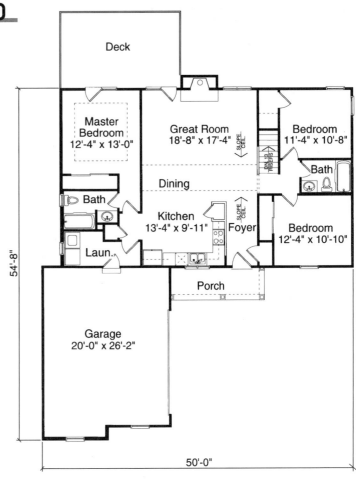

Rustic Stone Exterior

Plan #581-017D-0008

1,466 total square feet of living area

Special features

- ◆ Energy efficient home with 2" x 6" exterior walls
- ◆ Foyer separates the living room from the dining room and contains a generous coat closet
- ◆ Large living room with corner fireplace, bay window and pass-through to the kitchen
- ◆ Informal breakfast area opens to a large terrace through sliding glass doors which brightens area
- ◆ Master bedroom has a large walk-in closet and private bath
- ◆ 3 bedrooms, 2 baths, 2-car garage
- ◆ Basement foundation, drawings also include slab foundation

Price Code B

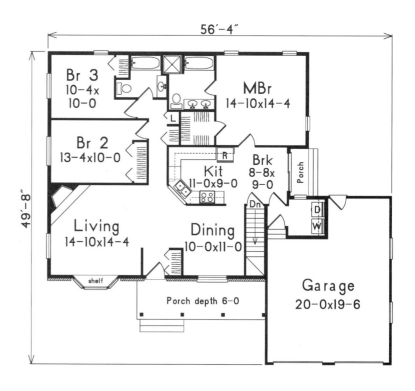

Plan #581-035D-0026

1,845 total square feet of living area

Special features

◆ Vaulted living room has cozy fireplace

◆ Breakfast area and kitchen are lovely gathering places

◆ Dining room overlooks living room

◆ 3 bedrooms, 2 1/2 baths, 2-car side entry garage

◆ Walk-out basement or crawl space foundation, please specify when ordering

Price Code C

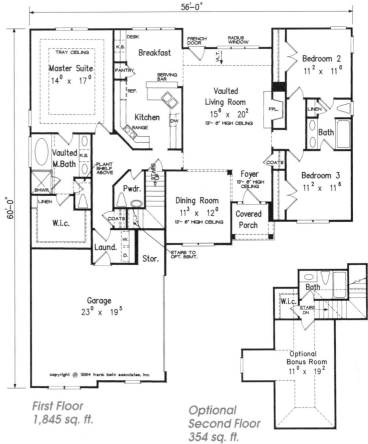

First Floor
1,845 sq. ft.

Optional
Second Floor
354 sq. ft.

Roomy Ranch

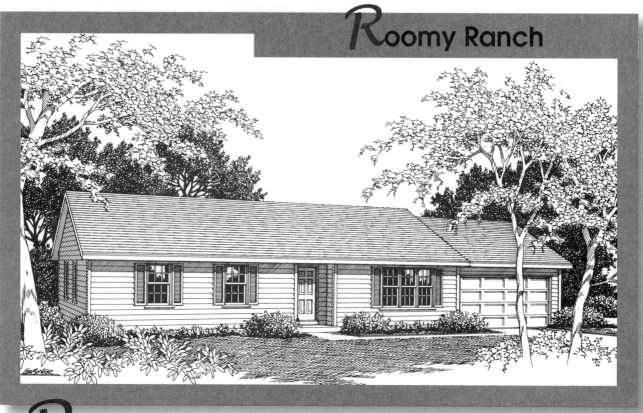

Plan #581-001D-0023

1,343 total square feet of living area

Special features

- Separate and convenient family and living/dining areas
- Nice-sized master bedroom suite with large closet and private bath
- Foyer with convenient coat closet opens into combined living and dining rooms
- Kitchen has access to the outdoors through sliding glass doors
- 3 bedrooms, 2 baths, 2-car garage
- Crawl space foundation, drawings also include basement foundation

Price Code A

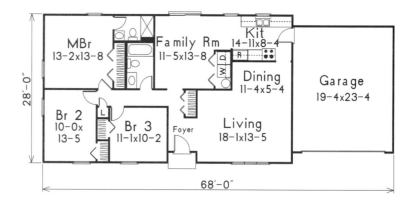

$\mathcal{P}$lan #581-069D-0019

2,162 total square feet of living area

Special features

- 10' ceilings in great room, dining room, master suite and foyer
- Enormous great room overlooks kitchen with oversized snack bar
- Luxurious master bath boasts a triangular whirlpool tub drenched in light from large windows
- 3 bedrooms, 2 baths, 2-car garage
- Crawl space or slab foundation, please specify when ordering

Price Code C

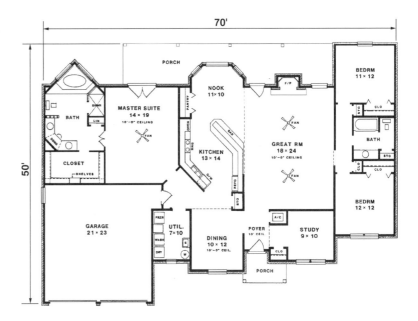

*P*lan #581-058D-0022

1,578 total square feet of living area

Special features

- Plenty of closet, linen and storage space
- Covered porches in the front and rear of home add charm to this design
- Open floor plan has unique angled layout
- 3 bedrooms, 2 baths, 2-car garage
- Basement foundation

Price Code B

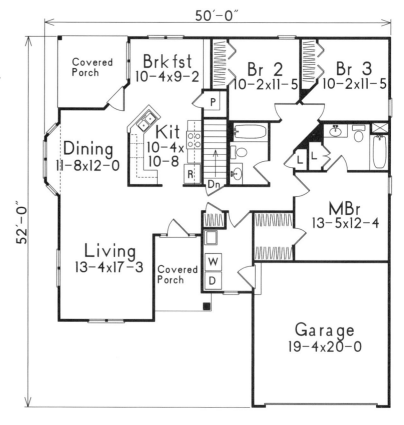

Plan #581-007D-0112

1,062 total square feet of living area

Special features

◆ Handsome appeal created by triple-gable facade

◆ An efficient U-shaped kitchen features a snack bar and breakfast room and is open to living room with bay window

◆ Both the master bedroom, with its own private bath, and bedroom #2/study enjoy access to rear patio

◆ 3 bedrooms, 2 baths, 2-car garage

◆ Basement foundation

Price Code AA

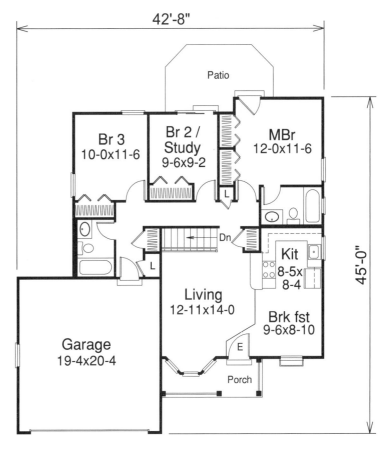

Plan #581-001D-0032

2,520 total square feet of living area

Special features

◆ Open hearth fireplace warms family and breakfast rooms

◆ Master bedroom features a private bath with deluxe tub, double-bowl vanity and large walk-in closet

◆ Vaulted living and dining rooms flank foyer

◆ Corner sink in kitchen overlooks family and breakfast rooms

◆ 4 bedrooms, 2 1/2 baths, 2-car side entry garage

◆ Basement foundation, drawings also include crawl space and slab foundations

Price Code D

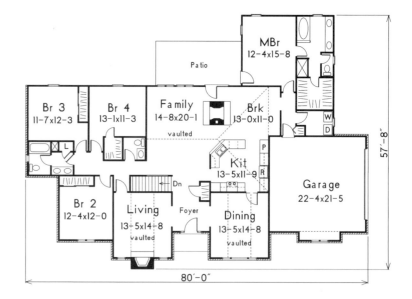

Affordable Simplicity

Plan #581-007D-0134

1,310 total square feet of living area

Special features

- ◆ The combination of brick quoins, roof dormers and an elegant porch creates a classic look
- ◆ Open-space floor plan has vaulted kitchen, living and dining rooms
- ◆ The master bedroom is vaulted and enjoys privacy from other bedrooms
- ◆ A spacious laundry room is convenient to the kitchen and master bedroom with access to an oversized garage
- ◆ 3 bedrooms, 2 baths, 2-car garage
- ◆ Basement foundation, drawings also include crawl space and slab foundations

Price Code A

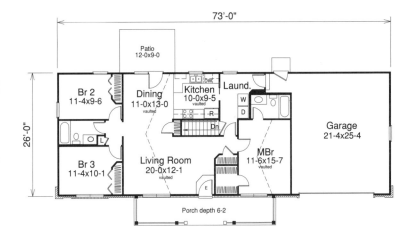

Charming Covered Porch

Plan #581-069D-0018

2,069 total square feet of living area

Special features

- 9' ceilings throughout this home
- Kitchen has many amenities including a snack bar
- Large front and rear porches
- 3 bedrooms, 2 1/2 baths, 2-car garage
- Slab or crawl space foundation, please specify when ordering

Price Code C

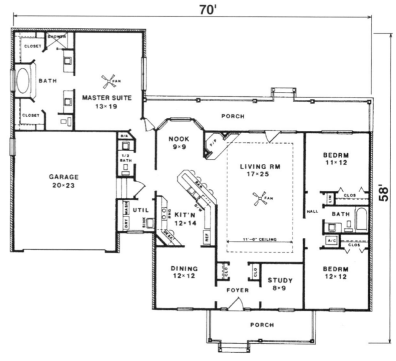

Old World Charm

COPYRIGHT LARRY E. BELK

Plan #581-019D-0020

2,745 total square feet of living area

Special features

- Country French styling
- Tall ceilings throughout
- See-through fireplace warms living areas
- 4 bedrooms, 2 1/2 baths, 2-car side entry garage
- Basement foundation, drawings also include crawl space and slab foundations

Price Code E

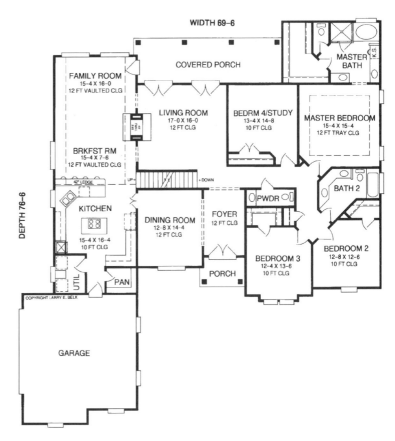

WIDTH 69-6

DEPTH 76-6

FAMILY ROOM
15-4 X 16-0
12 FT VAULTED CLG

BRKFST RM
15-4 X 7-6
12 FT VAULTED CLG

42" LEDGE

KITCHEN
15-4 X 16-4
10 FT CLG

UTIL

PAN

COPYRIGHT LARRY E. BELK

GARAGE

COVERED PORCH

LIVING ROOM
17-0 X 16-0
12 FT CLG

BEDRM 4/STUDY
13-4 X 14-8
10 FT CLG

DINING ROOM
12-8 X 14-4
12 FT CLG

FOYER
12 FT CLG

PWDR

PORCH

BEDROOM 3
12-4 X 13-6
10 FT CLG

MASTER BATH

MASTER BEDROOM
15-4 X 15-4
12 FT TRAY CLG

BATH 2

BEDROOM 2
12-8 X 12-6
10 FT CLG

Plan #581-040D-0012

2,988 total square feet of living area

Special features

◆ Bedrooms #2 and #3 share a common bath

◆ Energy efficient home with 2" x 6" exterior walls

◆ Rear porch has direct access to master bedroom, living and dining rooms

◆ Spacious utility room located off garage entrance features a convenient bath with shower

◆ Large L-shaped kitchen has plenty of workspace

◆ Oversized master bedroom is complete with a walk-in closet and master bath

◆ 3 bedrooms, 3 1/2 baths, 2-car side entry garage

◆ Partial basement/crawl space foundation

Price Code E

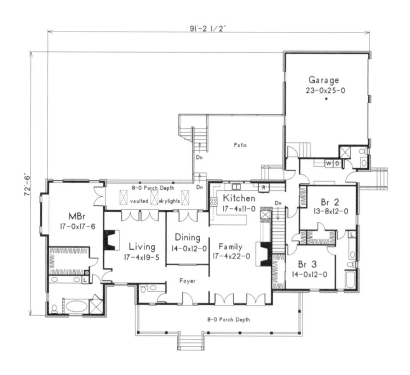

Cozy Covered Front Porch

Plan #581-035D-0045

1,749 total square feet of living area

Special features

- Tray ceiling in master bedroom
- Breakfast bar overlooks vaulted great room
- Additional bedrooms are located away from master suite for privacy
- Optional bonus room above the garage has an additional 308 square feet of living area
- 3 bedrooms, 2 baths, 2-car garage
- Walk-out basement, slab or crawl space foundation, please specify when ordering

Price Code B

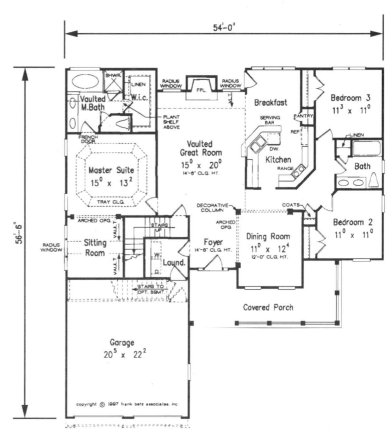

Plan #581-037D-0010

1,770 total square feet of living area

Special features

◆ Distinctive covered entrance leads into spacious foyer

◆ Master bedroom, living and dining rooms, all feature large windows for plenty of light

◆ Oversized living room has a high ceiling and large windows that flank the fireplace

◆ Kitchen includes pantry and large planning center

◆ Master bedroom has high vaulted ceiling, deluxe bath, and private access outdoors

◆ 3 bedrooms, 2 baths, 2-car garage

◆ Slab foundation

Price Code B

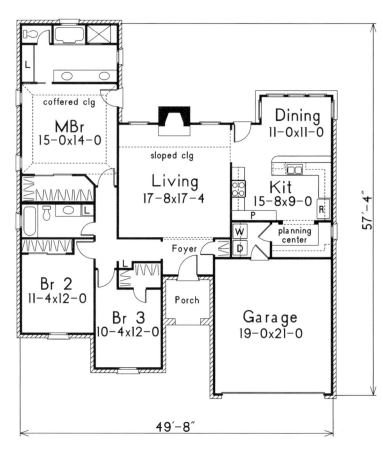

© COPYRIGHT 1990
RALPH JONES

Plan #581-060D-0015

1,192 total square feet of living area

Special features

◆ Kitchen eating bar overlooks a well-designed great room

◆ Private bath in master suite

◆ Extra storage space in garage

◆ 3 bedrooms, 2 baths, 2-car garage

◆ Slab or crawl space foundation, please specify when ordering

Price Code AA

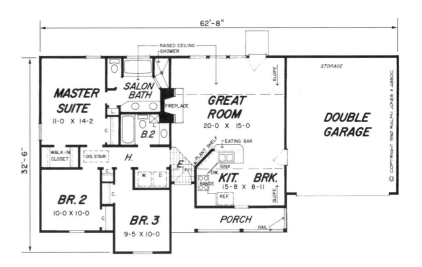

Exciting Split-Foyer

Plan #581-053D-0040

1,407 total square feet of living area

Special features

- ◆ Large living room has fireplace and access to the rear deck
- ◆ Kitchen and dining area combine to create open gathering area
- ◆ Convenient laundry room and broom closet
- ◆ Master bedroom includes private bath with large vanity and separate tub and shower
- ◆ 3 bedrooms, 2 baths, 2-car drive under garage
- ◆ Basement foundation

Price Code A

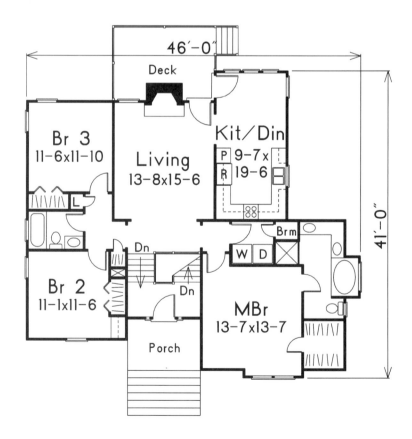

Plan #581-016D-0065

2,585 total square feet of living area

Special features

- Kitchen includes walk-in pantry and an angled serving counter
- Sensational master bedroom enjoys bayed sitting area, huge walk-in closet and large private bath
- Flanking the foyer, the formal living and dining rooms have pillar framed entrances and stepped ceilings
- 3 bedrooms, 2 1/2 baths, 2-car side entry garage
- Basement, slab or crawl space foundation, please specify when ordering

Price Code D

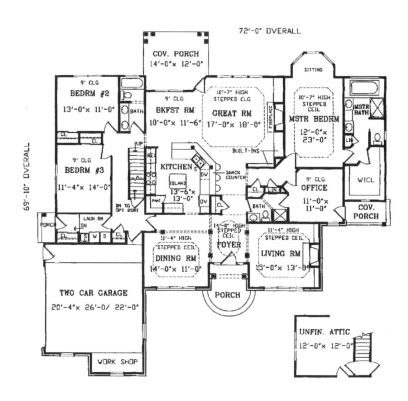

*P*lan #581-014D-0004

1,689 total square feet of living area

Special features

- ◆ Distinct covered entrance
- ◆ Large, open living and dining area include vaulted ceiling, corner fireplace and access to the rear deck
- ◆ Stylish angled kitchen offers large counter workspace and nook
- ◆ Master bedroom boasts a spacious bath with step-up tub, separate shower and large walk-in closet
- ◆ 3 bedrooms, 2 baths, 2-car garage
- ◆ Basement foundation, drawings also include slab and crawl space foundations

Price Code B

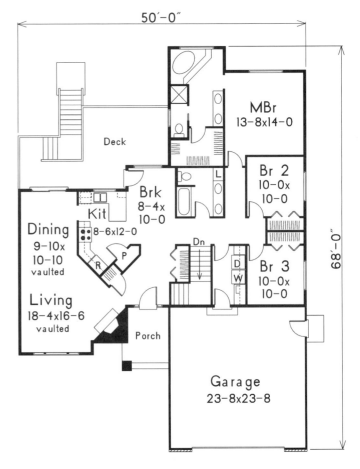

Amenity-Full Ranch

*P*lan #581-051D-0057

2,229 total square feet of living area

Special features

- ◆ Welcoming and expansive front porch
- ◆ Dining room has tray ceiling
- ◆ Sunny nook with arched soffit creates an inviting entry into this eating space
- ◆ 3 bedrooms, 2 baths, 2-car side entry garage
- ◆ Basement foundation

Price Code D

Dormers Add Accent

Plan #581-068D-0008

2,651 total square feet of living area

Special features

- ◆ Vaulted family room has a corner fireplace and access to breakfast room and outdoor patio
- ◆ Dining room has double-door entry from covered front porch and a beautiful built-in corner display area
- ◆ Master bedroom has 10' tray ceiling, private bath and two walk-in closets
- ◆ Kitchen has an enormous amount of counterspace with plenty of eating area and overlooks a cheerful breakfast room
- ◆ 3 bedrooms, 2 baths, 2-car side entry garage
- ◆ Basement foundation, drawings also include crawl space and slab foundations

Price Code E

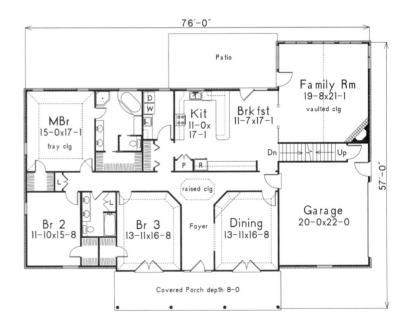

76'-0"

Patio

Family Rm
19-8x21-1
vaulted clg

MBr
15-0x17-1
tray clg

Kit
11-0x
17-1

Brkfst
11-7x17-1

Dn   Up

57'-0"

P R

raised clg

Br 2
11-10x15-8

Br 3
13-11x16-8

Foyer

Dining
13-11x16-8

Garage
20-0x22-0

Covered Porch depth 8-0

An Ideal Starter Home

*P*lan **#581-022D-0020**

988 total square feet of living area

Special features

◆ Great room features corner fireplace

◆ Vaulted ceiling and corner windows add space and light in great room

◆ Eat-in kitchen with vaulted ceiling accesses deck for outdoor living

◆ Master bedroom features separate vanities and private access to the bath

◆ 2 bedrooms, 1 bath, 2-car garage

◆ Basement foundation

Price Code AA

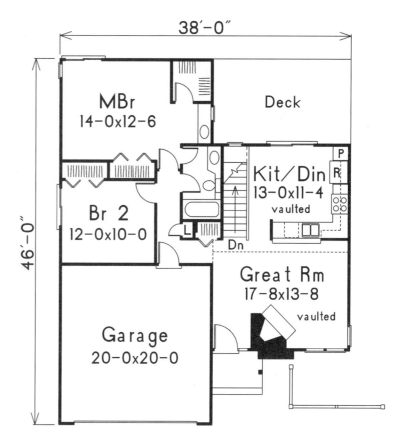

Plan #581-058D-0007

1,013 total square feet of living area

Special features

- ◆ Vaulted ceilings in both the family room and kitchen with dining area just beyond breakfast bar
- ◆ Plant shelf above kitchen is a special feature
- ◆ Oversized utility room has space for full-size washer and dryer
- ◆ Hall bath is centrally located with easy access from both bedrooms
- ◆ 2 bedrooms, 1 bath
- ◆ Slab foundation

Price Code AA

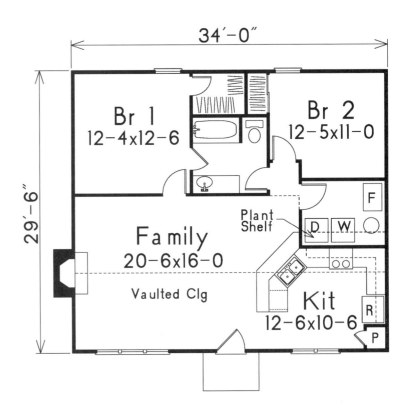

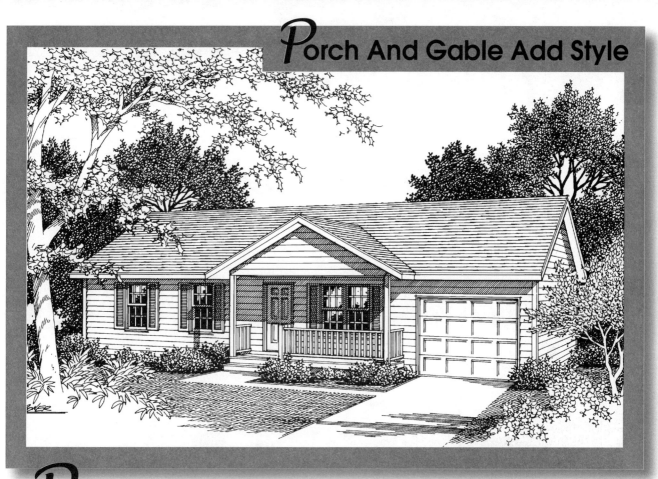

Plan #581-001D-0018

988 total square feet of living area

Special features

- ◆ Pleasant covered porch entry
- ◆ The kitchen, living and dining areas are combined to maximize space
- ◆ Entry has convenient coat closet
- ◆ Laundry closet is located adjacent to bedrooms
- ◆ 3 bedrooms, 1 bath, 1-car garage
- ◆ Basement foundation, drawings also include crawl space foundation

Price Code AA

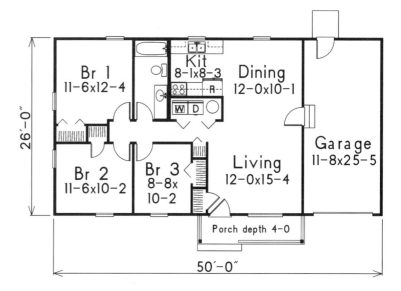

*S*tucco Adds Excitement

*P*lan #581-025D-0028

2,350 total square feet of living area

Special features

- ◆ Luxurious master suite with large bath and an enormous walk-in closet
- ◆ Built-in hutch in breakfast room is eye-catching
- ◆ Terrific study located in its own private hall with half bath includes two closets and a bookcase
- ◆ 3 bedrooms, 2 1/2 baths, 2-car side entry garage
- ◆ Walk-out basement, crawl space or slab foundation, please specify when ordering

Price Code D

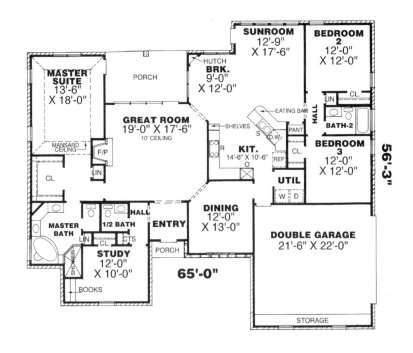

Plan #581-053D-0029

1,220 total square feet of living area

Special features

- ◆ Vaulted ceilings add luxury to the living room and master bed-room
- ◆ Spacious living room is accented with a large fireplace and hearth
- ◆ Gracious dining area is adjacent to the convenient wrap-around kitchen
- ◆ Washer and dryer are handy to the bedrooms
- ◆ Covered porch entry adds appeal
- ◆ Rear deck adjoins dining area
- ◆ 3 bedrooms, 2 baths, 2-car drive under garage
- ◆ Basement foundation

Price Code A

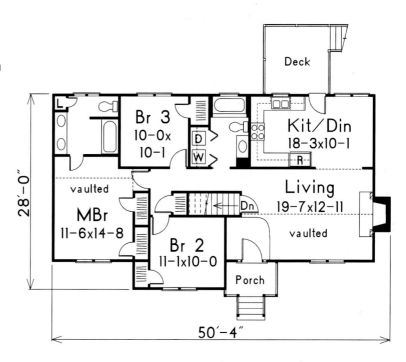

Prestige Abounds

Plan #581-007D-0050

2,723 total square feet of living area

Special features

- Large porch invites you into an elegant foyer which accesses a vaulted study with private hall and coat closet

- Great room is second to none, comprised of fireplace, built-in shelves, vaulted ceiling and a 1 1/2 story window wall

- A spectacular hearth room with vaulted ceiling and masonry fireplace opens to an elaborate kitchen featuring two snack bars, cooking island and walk-in pantry

- 3 bedrooms, 2 1/2 baths, 3-car side entry garage

- Basement foundation

Price Code E

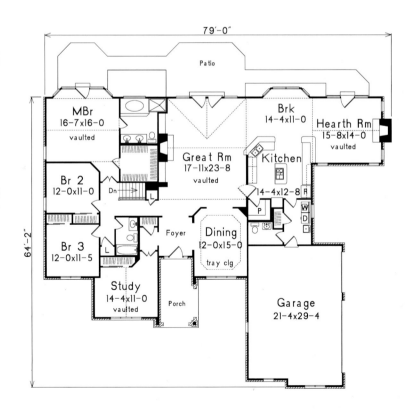

Plan #581-016D-0001

1,783 total square feet of living area

Special features

◆ The front to rear flow of the great room, with built-ins on one side is a furnishing delight

◆ Bedrooms are all quietly zoned on one side

◆ The master bedroom is separated for privacy

◆ Every bedroom features walk-in closets

◆ 3 bedrooms, 2 baths, 2-car side entry garage

◆ Basement, crawl space or slab foundation, please specify when ordering

Price Code D

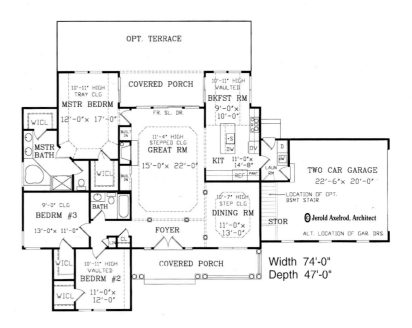

*P*lan #581-007D-0007

2,523 total square feet of living area

Special features

◆ Entry with high ceiling leads to massive vaulted great room with wet bar, plant shelves, pillars and fireplace with a harmonious window trio

◆ Elaborate kitchen with bay and breakfast bar adjoins morning room with fireplace-in-a-bay

◆ Vaulted master bedroom features fireplace, book and plant shelves, large walk-in closet and double baths

◆ 3 bedrooms, 2 baths, 3-car garage

◆ Basement foundation

Price Code D

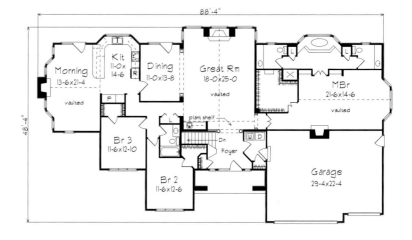

*F*ireplace Warms This Home

*P*lan #581-038D-0034

1,625 total square feet of living area

Special features

- ◆ Double-door in corner of den/guest room creates an interesting entry
- ◆ Spacious master bath has both a whirlpool tub and a shower
- ◆ Welcoming planter boxes in front add curb appeal
- ◆ 3 bedrooms, 2 baths, 2-car garage
- ◆ Basement or crawl space foundation, please specify when ordering

Price Code B

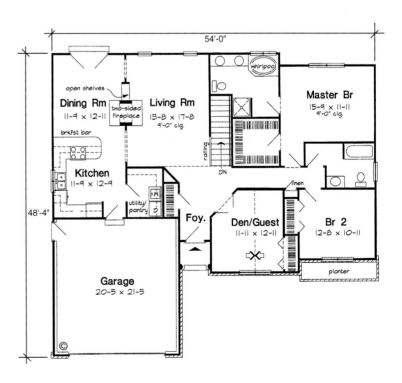

Focused On Patio Views

Plan #581-007D-0113

2,547 total square feet of living area

Special features

- Grand-sized great room features a 12' volume ceiling, fireplace with built-in wrap-around shelving and patio doors with sidelights and transom windows

- The walk-in pantry, computer desk, large breakfast island for seven and bayed breakfast area are the many features of this outstanding kitchen

- The master bedroom suite enjoys a luxurious bath, large walk-in closets and patio access

- 4 bedrooms, 2 1/2 baths, 3-car side entry garage

- Basement foundation

Price Code D

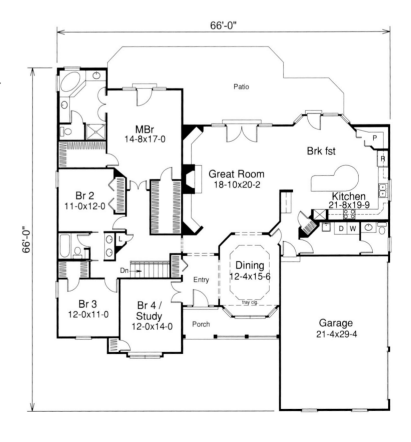

Lovely Pillars And Dormers

Plan #581-047D-0050

2,293 total square feet of living area

Special features

◆ Formal dining area flows into large family room making great use of space

◆ Cozy nook off kitchen would make an ideal breakfast dining area

◆ Covered patio attaches to master bedroom and family room

◆ Framing - only concrete block available

◆ 4 bedrooms, 2 baths, 2-car side entry garage

◆ Slab foundation

Price Code D

Bal. Bonus Rm.
21⁴ • 16⁴

*Optional
Second Floor
509 sq. ft.*

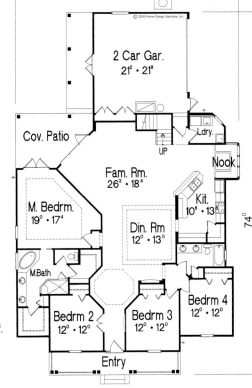

48⁰

2 Car Gar.
21² • 21⁸

Cov. Patio

Ldry.

UP

Nook

Fam. Rm.
26³ • 18⁴

Kit.
10⁸ • 13⁰

M. Bedrm.
19⁰ • 17⁴

Din. Rm
12⁰ • 13⁰

74⁰

M.Bath

*First Floor
2,293 sq. ft.*

Bedrm 2
12⁰ • 12⁰

Bedrm 3
12⁰ • 12⁰

Bedrm 4
12⁰ • 12⁰

Entry

Distinguished Styling

Plan #581-007D-0060

1,268 total square feet of living area

Special features

- Multiple gables, large porch and arched windows create classy exterior
- Innovative design provides openness in great room, kitchen and breakfast room
- Secondary bedrooms have private hall with bath
- 3 bedrooms, 2 baths, 2-car garage
- Basement foundation, drawings also include crawl space and slab foundations

Price Code B

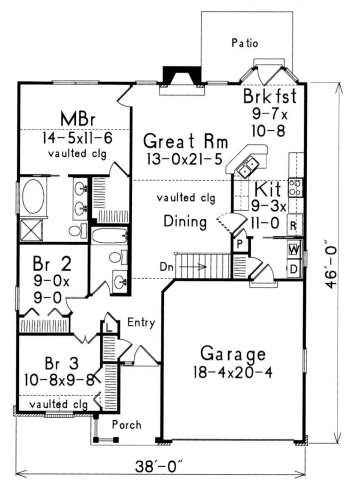

Plan #581-007D-0057

2,808 total square feet of living area

Special features

- ◆ An impressive front exterior show-cases three porches for quiet times
- ◆ Large living and dining rooms flank an elegant entry
- ◆ Bedroom #3 shares a porch with the living room and a spacious bath with bedroom #2
- ◆ Vaulted master bedroom enjoys a secluded screened porch and sumptuous bath with corner tub, double vanities and huge walk-in closet
- ◆ Living room can easily convert to an optional fourth bedroom
- ◆ 3 bedrooms, 2 1/2 baths, 3-car side entry garage
- ◆ Basement foundation

Price Code F

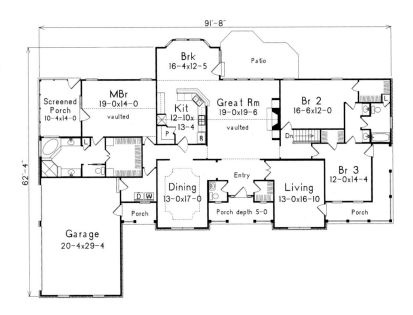

Plan #581-016D-0057

1,709 total square feet of living area

Special features

◆ The fireplace is flanked by a media center for convenient relaxation

◆ Dining room features a beautiful built-in cabinet to hold fine collect-ibles and china

◆ Centrally located kitchen is a great gathering place

◆ 3 bedrooms, 2 1/2 baths, 2-car side entry garage

◆ Basement, crawl space or slab foun-dation, please specify when ordering

Price Code C

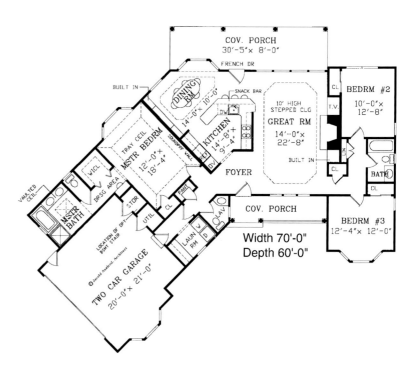

Width 70'-0"
Depth 60'-0"

Classic Three Bedroom

Plan #581-027D-0003

2,061 total square feet of living area

Special features

- Convenient entrance from garage into home through laundry room
- Master bedroom features walk-in closet and double-door entrance into master bath with oversized tub
- Formal dining room with tray ceiling
- Kitchen features island cooktop and adjacent breakfast room
- 3 bedrooms, 2 baths, 2-car garage
- Basement foundation

Price Code D

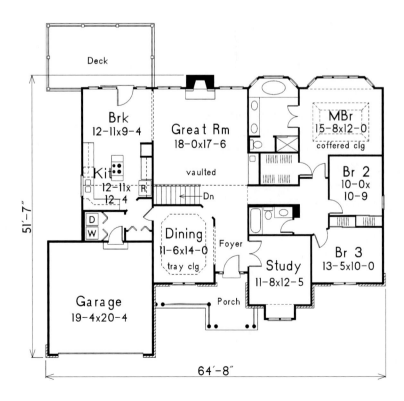

Plan #581-007D-0118

1,991 total square feet of living area

Special features

- A large porch with roof dormers and flanking stonework creates a distinctive country appeal
- The highly functional U-shaped kitchen is open to dining and living rooms defined by a colonnade
- Large bay windows are enjoyed by both the living room and master bedroom
- Every bedroom features spacious walk-in closets and its own private bath
- 3 bedrooms, 3 1/2 baths, 2-car side entry garage
- Basement foundation

Price Code C

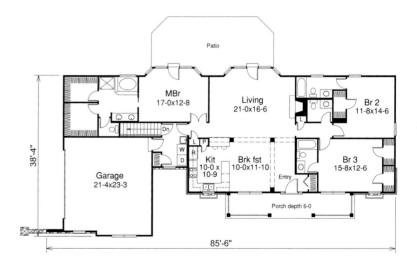

Gables Create Curb Appeal

Plan #581-026D-0111

2,254 total square feet of living area

Special features

- Built-in hutch in the formal dining room has a custom feel
- See-through fireplace from the kitchen into the great room is warm and well-designed
- Large master bath has a wonderful corner whirlpool tub
- 2 bedrooms, 2 baths, 3-car side entry garage
- Basement foundation

Price Code D

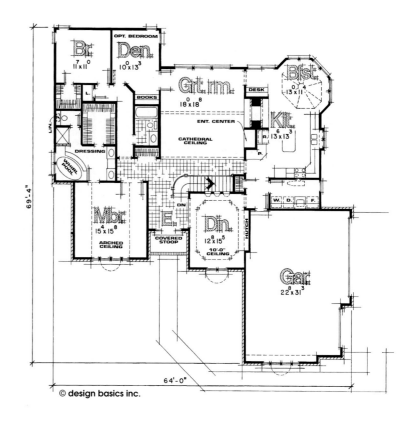

© design basics inc.

*P*lan #581-048D-0005

2,287 total square feet of living area

Special features

- ◆ Double-doors lead into an impressive master bedroom which accesses covered porch and features deluxe bath with double closets and step-up tub
- ◆ Kitchen easily serves formal and informal areas of home
- ◆ The spacious foyer opens into formal dining and living rooms
- ◆ 4 bedrooms, 2 1/2 baths, 2-car side entry garage
- ◆ Slab foundation

Price Code E

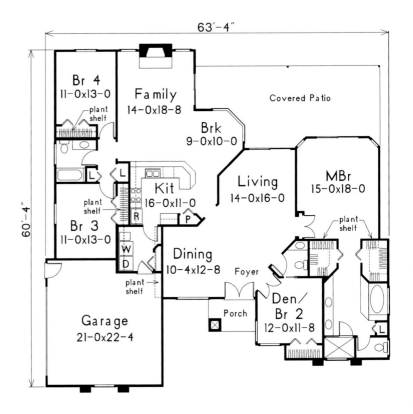

Plan #581-065D-0004

1,710 total square feet of living area

Special features

- Expansive kitchen provides an abundance of counterspace and a pantry for extra storage
- The great room enjoys a sloped ceiling, corner fireplace and access onto the rear patio
- Windows surround the breakfast area providing warm natural light
- 3 bedrooms, 2 baths, 2-car side entry garage
- Basement foundation

Price Code B

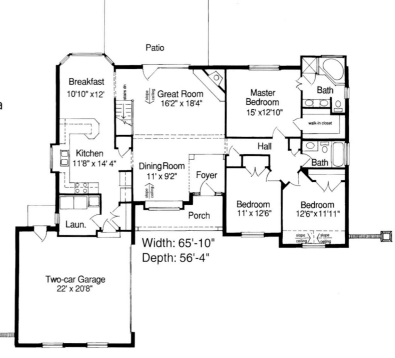

Patio

Breakfast
10'10" x 12'

Great Room
16'2" x 18'4"

Master Bedroom
15' x12'10"

Bath

walk-in closet

Kitchen
11'8" x 14' 4"

Hall

Bath

Dining Room
11' x 9'2"

Foyer

Laun.

Porch

Bedroom
11' x 12'6"

Bedroom
12'6"x 11'11"

Two-car Garage
22' x 20'8"

Width: 65'-10"
Depth: 56'-4"

*U*nique Craftsman-Style

*P*lan #581-011D-0014

3,246 total square feet of living area

Special features

- Private master bedroom has a sumptuous bath and large walk-in closet
- Lower level recreation room is a great casual family area
- L-shaped kitchen has a large center island with stove top and dining space
- 3 bedrooms, 2 1/2 baths, 3-car garage
- Crawl space foundation

Price Code G

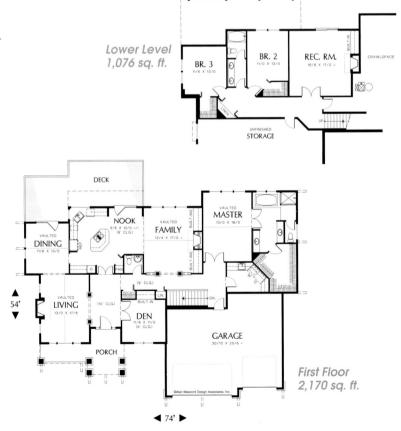

Lower Level 1,076 sq. ft.

First Floor 2,170 sq. ft.

*A*trium With True Pizzazz

*P*lan #581-007D-0098

2,397 total square feet of living area

Special features

- ◆ A grand entry porch leads to a dramatic vaulted foyer with plant shelf open to great room
- ◆ The great room enjoys a 12' vaulted ceiling, atrium featuring 2 1/2 story windows and fireplace with flanking bookshelves
- ◆ A conveniently located sunroom and side porch adjoin the breakfast room and garage
- ◆ 3 bedrooms, 2 baths, 3-car side entry garage
- ◆ Walk-out basement foundation

Price Code D

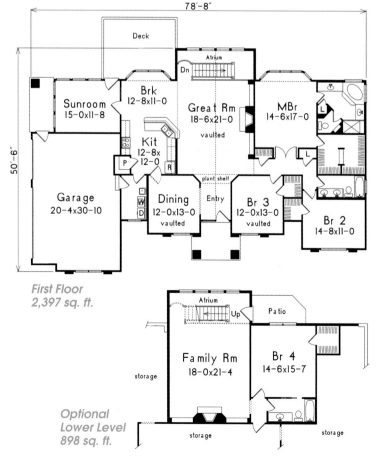

First Floor
2,397 sq. ft.

Optional
Lower Level
898 sq. ft.

Stunning All Brick Ranch

Plan #581-025D-0011

1,699 total square feet of living area

Special features

◆ Master suite is filled with luxury including a private bath with glass shower, oversized tub, large walk-in closet and double vanity

◆ Wonderful kitchen and breakfast room arrangement makes great use of space

◆ 3 bedrooms, 2 baths, 2-car side entry garage

◆ Slab foundation

Price Code B

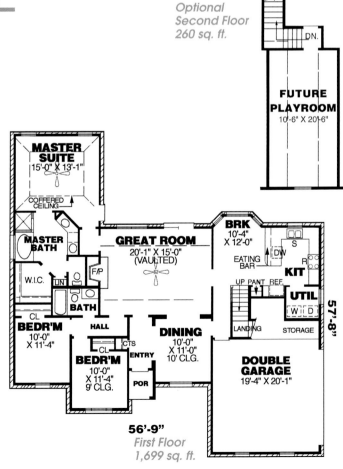

Optional
Second Floor
260 sq. ft.

FUTURE PLAYROOM
10'-6" X 20'-6"

56'-9"
First Floor
1,699 sq. ft.

Classic Contemporary

Plan #581-007D-0080

2,900 total square feet of living area

Special features

◆ The grandscale great room offers a vaulted ceiling and palladian windows flanking an 8' wide brick fireplace

◆ A smartly designed built-in-a-bay kitchen features a picture window above sink, huge pantry, cooktop island and is open to a large morning room with 12' of cabinetry

◆ All bedrooms include immense closet space

◆ 4 bedrooms, 2 1/2 baths, 3-car side entry garage

◆ Walk-out basement foundation

Price Code E

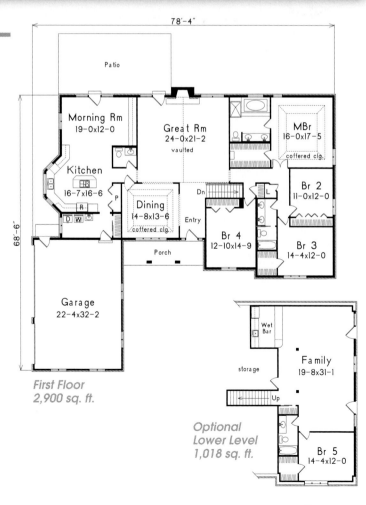

First Floor
2,900 sq. ft.

Optional
Lower Level
1,018 sq. ft.

Symmetry Dominates Design

Plan #581-007D-0046

1,712 total square feet of living area

Special features

- Stylish stucco exterior enhances curb appeal
- Sunken great room offers corner fireplace flanked by 9' wide patio doors
- Well-designed kitchen features ideal view of great room and fireplace through breakfast bar opening
- 3 bedrooms, 2 1/2 baths, 2-car garage
- Crawl space foundation

Price Code B

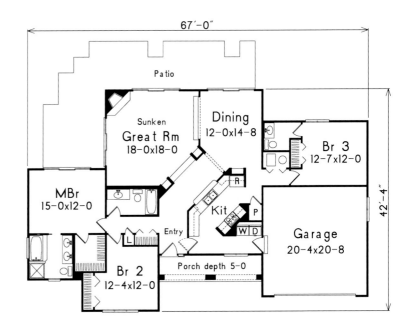

*P*lan #581-055D-0114

2,050 total square feet of living area

Special features

◆ Open living spaces allow for dining area, great room and breakfast room to flow together

◆ Bedroom #4 has unique design with double closets and a built-in desk

◆ Plenty of closet space throughout

◆ 4 bedrooms, 2 baths, 2-car garage

◆ Crawl space or slab foundation, please specify when ordering

Price Code C

Whirlpool With Skylight

Plan #581-026D-0112

1,911 total square feet of living area

Special features

- Large entry opens into a beautiful great room with an angled see-through fireplace
- Terrific design includes kitchen and breakfast area with adjacent sunny bayed hearth room
- Private master bedroom with bath features skylight and walk-in closet
- 3 bedrooms, 2 baths, 2-car garage
- Basement foundation

Price Code C

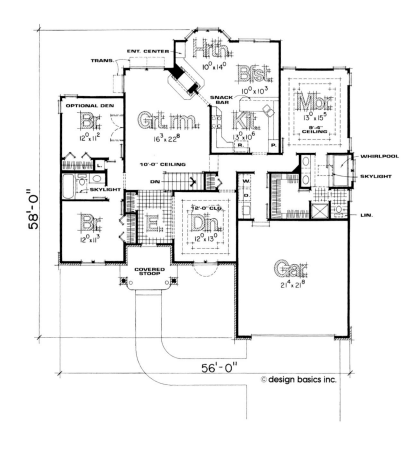

Central Fireplace

Plan #581-021D-0010

1,444 total square feet of living area

Special features

- 11' ceilings in living and dining rooms combine with a central fireplace to create large open living area
- Both secondary bedrooms have large walk-in closets
- Large storage area in garage suitable for a workshop or play area
- Front and rear covered porches add cozy touch
- U-shaped kitchen includes a laundry closet and serving bar
- 3 bedrooms, 2 baths, 2-car side entry garage
- Slab foundation, drawings also include crawl space foundation

Price Code A

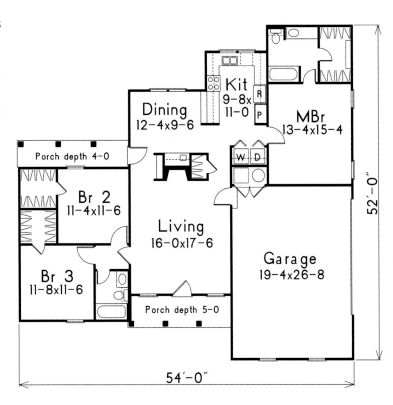

A Perfect Country Haven

*P*lan #581-007D-0067

1,761 total square feet of living area

Special features

- Exterior window dressing, roof dormers and planter boxes provide visual warmth and charm
- Great room boasts a vaulted ceiling, fireplace and opens to a pass-through kitchen
- Master bedroom is vaulted with luxury bath and walk-in closet
- Home features eight separate closets with an abundance of storage
- 4 bedrooms, 2 baths, 2-car side entry garage
- Basement foundation

Price Code B

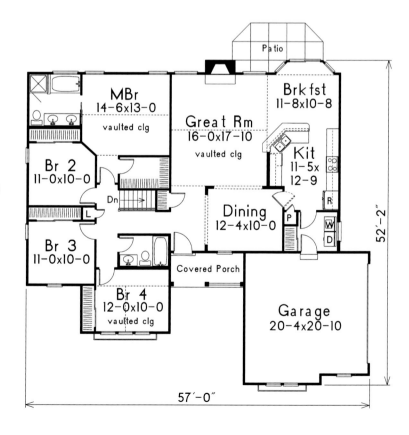

Craftsman Cottage

Plan #581-026D-0161

1,375 total square feet of living area

Special features

◆ Den can easily convert to a second bedroom

◆ A center island in the kitchen allows extra space for organizing and food preparation

◆ Centrally located laundry room

◆ 1 bedroom, 2 baths, 2-car rear entry garage

◆ Basement foundation

Price Code A

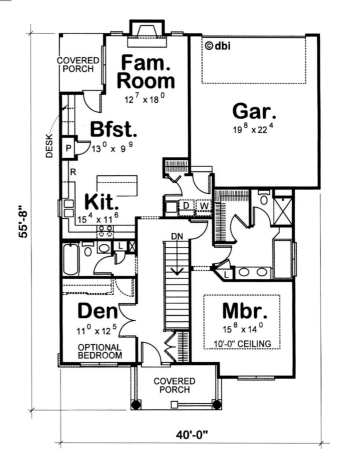

*P*lan #581-005D-0001

1,400 total square feet of living area

Special features

- Master bedroom is secluded for privacy
- Large utility room has additional cabinet space
- Covered porch provides an outdoor seating area
- Roof dormers add great curb appeal
- Living room and master bedroom feature vaulted ceilings
- Oversized two-car garage has storage space
- 3 bedrooms, 2 baths, 2-car garage
- Basement foundation, drawings also include crawl space foundation

Price Code B

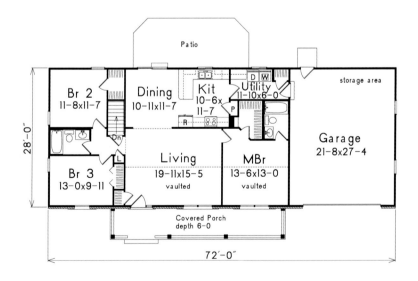

Relax In The Sunroom

Plan #581-070D-0011

2,198 total square feet of living area

Special features

- Double walk-in closets in the master bedroom as well as direct access to the laundry room
- Varied ceiling heights throughout this home
- Large study includes a walk-in closet and cathedral ceiling
- 2 bedrooms, 2 baths, 2-car garage
- Basement foundation

Price Code C

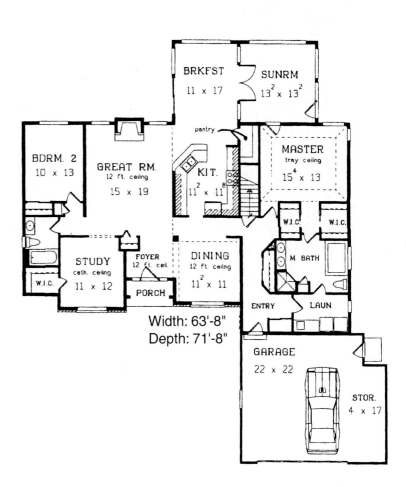

Width: 63'-8"
Depth: 71'-8"

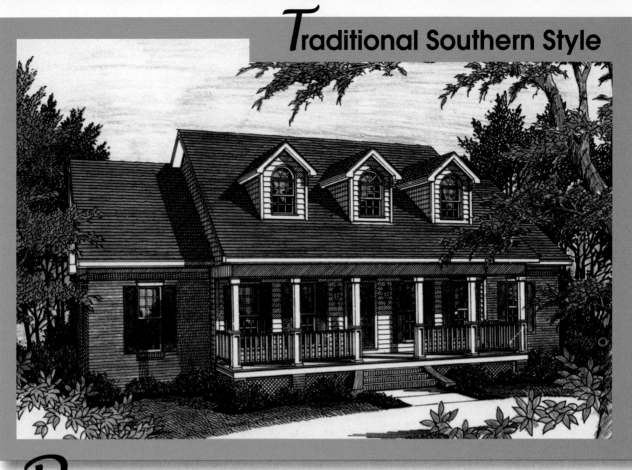

Traditional Southern Style

*P*lan #581-028D-0004

1,785 total square feet of living area

Special features

- ◆ 9' ceilings throughout home
- ◆ Luxurious master bath includes whirlpool tub and separate shower
- ◆ Cozy breakfast area is convenient to kitchen
- ◆ 3 bedrooms, 3 baths, 2-car detached garage
- ◆ Basement, crawl space or slab foundation, please specify when ordering

Price Code B

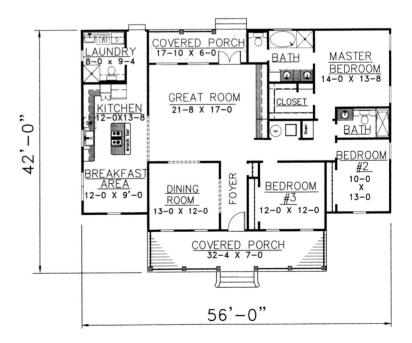

Comfortable Family Living

Plan #581-037D-0020

1,994 total square feet of living area

Special features

◆ Convenient entrance from the garage into the main living area through the utility room

◆ Standard 9' ceilings, bedroom #2 features a 12' vaulted ceiling and a 10' ceiling in the dining room

◆ Master bedroom offers a full bath with oversized tub, separate shower and walk-in closet

◆ Entry leads to formal dining room and attractive living room with double French doors and fireplace

◆ 3 bedrooms, 2 baths, 2-car garage

◆ Slab foundation

Price Code D

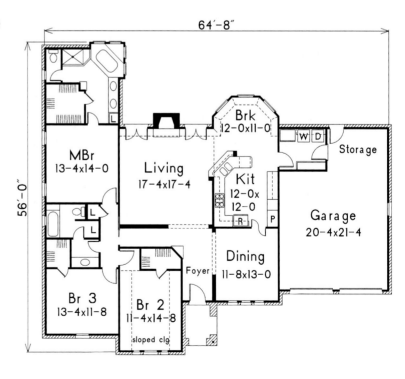

64'-8"

56'-0"

MBr
13-4x14-0

Living
17-4x17-4

Brk
12-0x11-0

Kit
12-0x
12-0

Garage
20-4x21-4

Storage

W D

Br 3
13-4x11-8

Br 2
11-4x14-8
sloped clg

Foyer

Dining
11-8x13-0

Plan #581-062D-0041

1,541 total square feet of living area

Special features

◆ Dining area offers access to a screened porch for outdoor dining and entertaining

◆ Country kitchen features a center island and a breakfast bay for casual meals

◆ Great room is warmed by a wood-stove

◆ 3 bedrooms, 2 baths, 2-car garage

◆ Basement or crawl space foundation, please specify when ordering

Price Code B

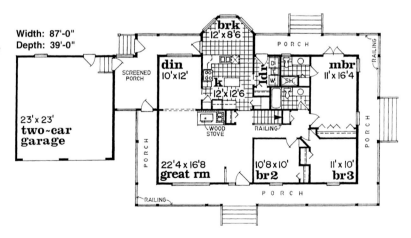

Width: 87'-0"
Depth: 39'-0"

SCREENED PORCH

23'x 23'
two-car garage

brk
12'x 8'6

din
10'x12'

k
12'x12'6

PORCH

ldr

mbr
11' x 16'4

RAILING

WOOD STOVE

RAILING

PORCH

22'4 x 16'8
great rm

10'8x10'
br2

11'x 10'
br3

PORCH

RAILING

Remarkably Spacious

Plan #581-007D-0042

914 total square feet of living area

Special features

◆ Large porch for leisure evenings

◆ Dining area with bay window, open stair and pass-through kitchen create openness

◆ Basement includes generous garage space, storage area, finished laundry and mechanical room

◆ 2 bedrooms, 1 bath, 2-car drive under garage

◆ Basement foundation

Price Code AA

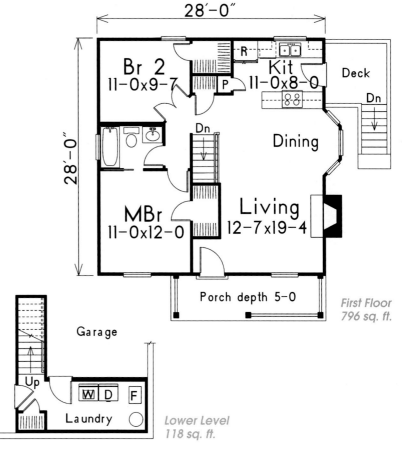

28'-0"

28'-0"

Br 2
11-0x9-7

Kit
11-0x8-0

Deck

Dn

P

Dn

Dining

MBr
11-0x12-0

Living
12-7x19-4

Porch depth 5-0

First Floor
796 sq. ft.

Garage

Garage

Up

W D F

Laundry

Lower Level
118 sq. ft.

Open Ranch Living

Plan #581-024D-0009

1,704 total square feet of living area

Special features

- ◆ Open floor plan combines foyer, dining and living rooms together for an open airy feeling
- ◆ Kitchen has island that adds workspace and storage
- ◆ Bedrooms are situated together and secluded from the rest of the home
- ◆ 3 bedrooms, 2 baths
- ◆ Slab foundation

Price Code B

Width: 58'-4"
Depth: 45'-0"

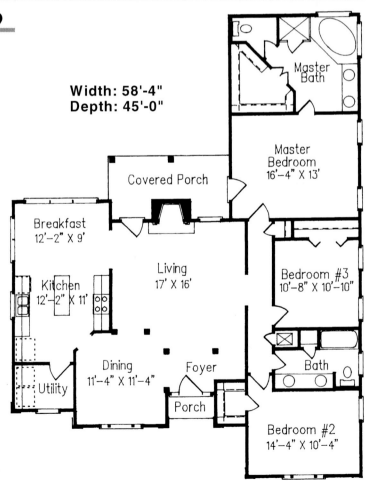

Master Bath

Master Bedroom
16'-4" X 13'

Covered Porch

Breakfast
12'-2" X 9'

Living
17' X 16'

Bedroom #3
10'-8" X 10'-10"

Kitchen
12'-2" X 11'

Dining
11'-4" X 11'-4"

Foyer

Bath

Utility

Porch

Bedroom #2
14'-4" X 10'-4"

Plan #581-013D-0010

1,593 total square feet of living area

Special features

◆ Large sitting area is enjoyed by the master bedroom which also features a walk-in closet and bath

◆ Centrally located kitchen accesses the family, dining and breakfast rooms with ease

◆ Storage/mechanical area is ideal for seasonal storage or hobby supplies

◆ 3 bedrooms, 2 baths, 2-car garage

◆ Basement, crawl space or slab foundation, please specify when ordering

Price Code C

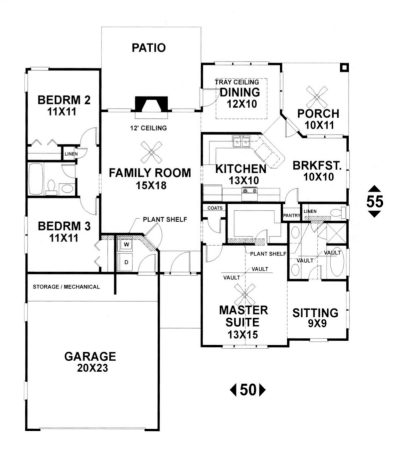

*A*ttractive Exterior

*P*lan #581-055D-0030

2,107 total square feet of living area

Special features

- ◆ Master bedroom is separate from other bedrooms for privacy
- ◆ Spacious breakfast room and kitchen include center island with eating space
- ◆ Centralized great room has fireplace and easy access to any area in the home
- ◆ 4 bedrooms, 2 1/2 baths, 2-car garage
- ◆ Crawl space, basement, walk-out basement or slab foundation, please specify when ordering

Price Code C

*P*lan #581-007D-0055

2,029 total square feet of living area

Special features

- Stonework, gables, roof dormer and double porches create a country flavor
- Kitchen enjoys extravagant cabinetry and counterspace in a bay, island snack bar, built-in pantry and cheery dining area with multiple tall windows
- Angled stair descends from large entry with wood columns and is open to vaulted great room with corner fireplace
- Master bedroom boasts two walk-in closets, double-doors leading to an opulent master bath and a private porch
- 3 bedrooms, 2 baths, 2-car side entry garage
- Basement foundation, drawings also include crawl space and slab foundations

Price Code D

A Great Plan With Charm

*P*lan #581-016D-0021

1,892 total square feet of living area

Special features

◆ Victorian home includes folk charm

◆ This split bedroom plan places a lovely master bedroom on the opposite end of the other two bedrooms for privacy

◆ Central living and dining areas combine creating a great place for entertaining

◆ 3 bedrooms, 2 1/2 baths, 2-car side entry garage

◆ Basement, crawl space or slab foundation, please specify when ordering

Price Code D

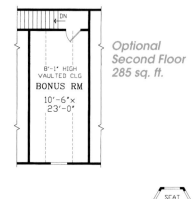

Optional Second Floor 285 sq. ft.

DN

8'-1" HIGH VAULTED CLG
BONUS RM
10'-6"x 23'-0"

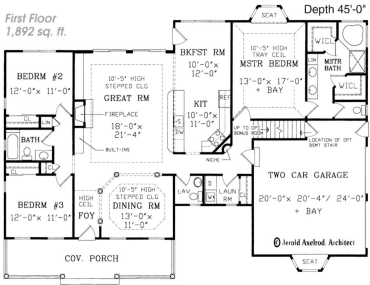

First Floor 1,892 sq. ft.

Width 65'-0"
Depth 45'-0"

© Jerold Axelrod. Architect

Cozy Corner Patio

*P*lan #581-007D-0031

1,092 total square feet of living area

Special features

◆ Box window and inviting porch with dormers create a charming facade

◆ Eat-in kitchen offers a pass-through breakfast bar, corner window wall to patio, pantry and convenient laundry with half bath

◆ Master bedroom features double entry doors and walk-in closet

◆ 3 bedrooms, 1 1/2 baths, 1-car garage

◆ Basement foundation

Price Code AA

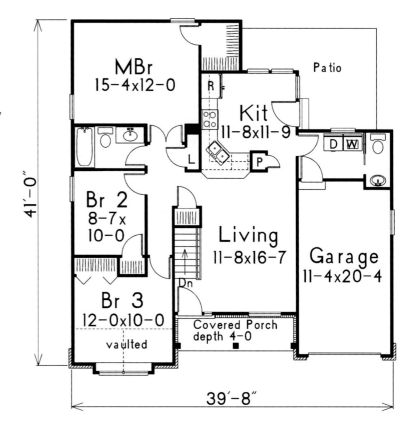

MBr
15-4x12-0

Patio

Kit
11-8x11-9

L
P

Br 2
8-7x
10-0

Living
11-8x16-7

Garage
11-4x20-4

Dn

Br 3
12-0x10-0
vaulted

Covered Porch
depth 4-0

41'-0"

39'-8"

Plan #581-011D-0004

1,997 total square feet of living area

Special features

- Corner fireplace warms the vaulted family room located near the kitchen
- A spa tub and shower enhance the master bath
- Plenty of closet space throughout
- 4 bedrooms, 2 1/2 baths, 3-car garage
- Crawl space foundation

Price Code D

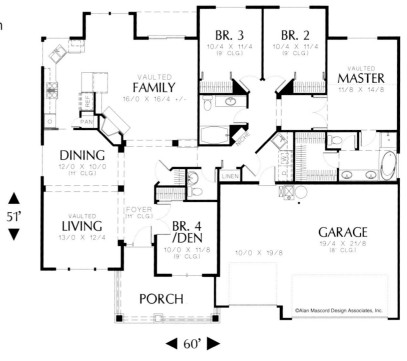

Home With Much To Offer

Plan #581-055D-0109

2,217 total square feet of living area

Special features

- ◆ Great room features a fireplace and is open to the foyer, breakfast and dining rooms
- ◆ Laundry room and storage closet are located off the garage
- ◆ Secluded master suite includes a bath with a corner whirlpool tub, split vanities, corner shower and a large walk-in closet
- ◆ 4 bedrooms, 2 baths, 2-car garage
- ◆ Crawl space or slab foundation, please specify when ordering

Price Code C

Plan #581-007D-0102

1,452 total square feet of living area

Special features

◆ Large living room features cozy corner fireplace, bayed dining area and access from entry with guest closet

◆ Forward master bedroom suite enjoys having its own bath and linen closet

◆ Three additional bedrooms share a bath with double-bowl vanity

◆ 4 bedrooms, 2 baths

◆ Basement foundation

Price Code A

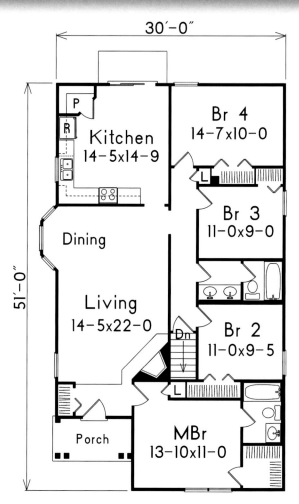

30'-0"

51'-0"

P

R

Kitchen
14-5x14-9

Br 4
14-7x10-0

L

Dining

Br 3
11-0x9-0

Living
14-5x22-0

Dn

Br 2
11-0x9-5

L

Porch

MBr
13-10x11-0

Plan #581-016D-0002

2,243 total square feet of living area

Special features

- An angled floor plan allows for flexible placement on any lot
- Great room has a 16' high tray ceiling, a fireplace and an entertainment center
- The luxurious master bedroom is separated for privacy
- The secondary bedrooms are in a private wing and share a common bath
- 3 bedrooms, 2 1/2 baths, 2-car side entry garage
- Basement, crawl space or slab foundation, please specify when ordering

Price Code E

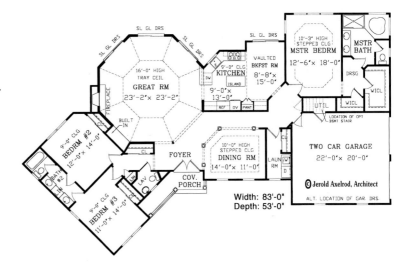

*P*lan #581-047D-0060

3,570 total square feet of living area

Special features

◆ Casual living areas combine creating lots of space for living

◆ Spacious master bedroom includes sitting area and an oversized bath

◆ Framing - only concrete block available

◆ 4 bedrooms, 4 baths, 3-car side entry garage

◆ Slab foundation

Price Code F

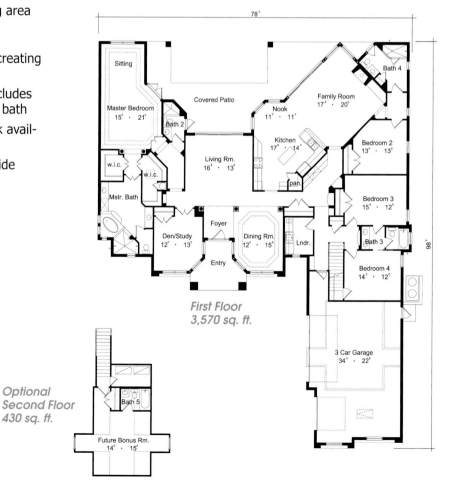

First Floor
3,570 sq. ft.

Optional
Second Floor
430 sq. ft.

Plan #581-028D-0015

2,421 total square feet of living area

Special features

- ◆ Charming courtyard on the side of the home easily accesses the porch leading into the breakfast area
- ◆ French doors throughout home create a sunny atmosphere
- ◆ Master bedroom accesses covered porch
- ◆ 4 bedrooms, 2 baths, optional 2-car detached garage
- ◆ Crawl space or slab foundation, please specify when ordering

Price Code D

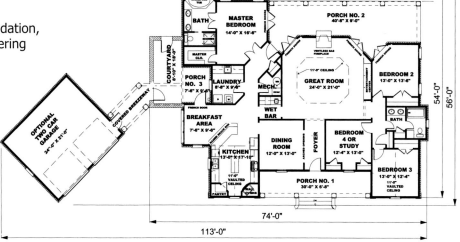

Stone And Stucco Facade

Plan #581-025D-0010

1,677 total square feet of living area

Special features

◆ Master suite has a secluded feel with a private and remote location from other bedrooms

◆ Great room is complete with fireplace and beautiful windows

◆ 3 bedrooms, 2 baths, 2-car side entry garage

◆ Slab foundation

Price Code B

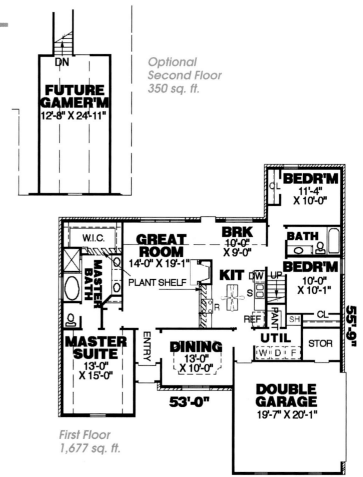

Optional Second Floor 350 sq. ft.

DN

FUTURE GAMER'M
12'-8" X 24'-11"

W.I.C.

GREAT ROOM
14'-0" X 19'-1"

PLANT SHELF

BRK
10'-0" X 9'-0"

BEDR'M
11'-4" X 10'-0"

BATH

MASTER BATH

KIT

BEDR'M
10'-0" X 10'-1"

REF

PANT

SH

CL

MASTER SUITE
13'-0" X 15'-0"

ENTRY

DINING
13'-0" X 10'-0"

UTIL
W D F

STOR

DOUBLE GARAGE
19'-7" X 20'-1"

55'-9"

53'-0"

First Floor 1,677 sq. ft.

Private Breakfast Room

Plan #581-003D-0005

1,708 total square feet of living area

Special features

- ◆ Massive family room enhanced with several windows, fireplace and access to porch
- ◆ Deluxe master bath accented by step-up corner tub flanked by double vanities
- ◆ Closets throughout maintain organized living
- ◆ Bedrooms isolated from living areas
- ◆ 3 bedrooms, 2 baths, 2-car garage
- ◆ Basement foundation, drawings also include crawl space foundation

Price Code B

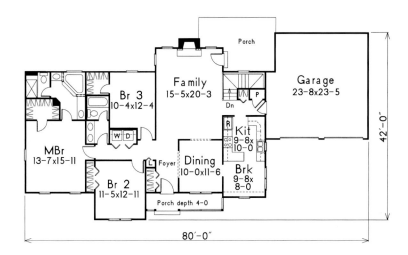

*P*lan #581-070D-0004

1,791 total square feet of living area

Special features

◆ A whirlpool tub adds luxury to the master bath

◆ Breakfast nook leads to a covered porch

◆ Double closets create plenty of storage in the foyer

◆ 3 bedrooms, 2 baths, 2-car side entry garage

◆ Basement foundation

Price Code B

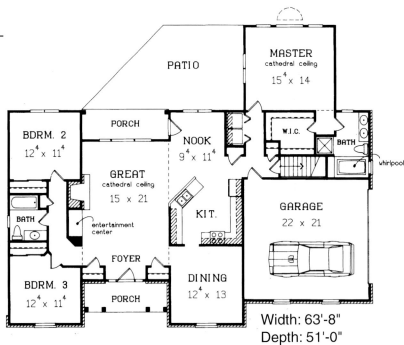

Width: 63'-8"
Depth: 51'-0"

*C*ountry Cottage

© 2003, Garrell Associates, Inc.

Christine Canova 9/02

*P*lan #581-056D-0001

1,624 total square feet of living area

Special features

◆ Large covered deck leads to two uncovered decks accessible by the master bedroom and bedroom #3

◆ Well-organized kitchen overlooks into the breakfast area and family room

◆ Laundry closet located near secondary bedrooms

◆ 3 bedrooms, 2 baths

◆ Crawl space or slab foundation, please specify when ordering

Price Code E

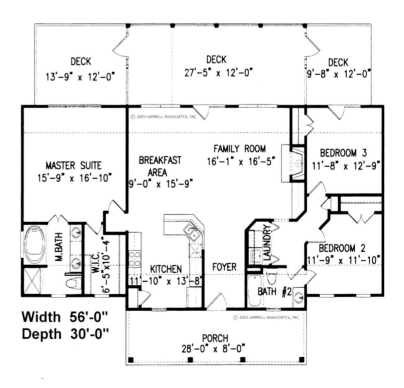

DECK
13'-9" x 12'-0"

DECK
27'-5" x 12'-0"

DECK
9'-8" x 12'-0"

© 2003 GARRELL ASSOCIATES, INC.

MASTER SUITE
15'-9" x 16'-10"

BREAKFAST
AREA
9'-0" x 15'-9"

FAMILY ROOM
16'-1" x 16'-5"

BEDROOM 3
11'-8" x 12'-9"

M.BATH

W.I.C.
6'-5" x 10'-4"

KITCHEN
11'-10" x 13'-8"

FOYER

LAUNDRY

BEDROOM 2
11'-9" x 11'-10"

BATH #2

Width 56'-0"
Depth 30'-0"

© 2003 GARRELL ASSOCIATES, INC.

PORCH
28'-0" x 8'-0"

Stylish Retreat

$\mathcal{P}$lan #581-007D-0105

1,084 total square feet of living area

Special features

- ◆ Delightful country porch for quiet evenings
- ◆ The living room offers a front feature window which invites the sun and includes a fireplace and dining area with private patio
- ◆ The U-shaped kitchen features lots of cabinets and bayed breakfast room with built-in pantry
- ◆ Both bedrooms have walk-in closets and access to their own bath
- ◆ 2 bedrooms, 2 baths
- ◆ Basement foundation

Price Code AA

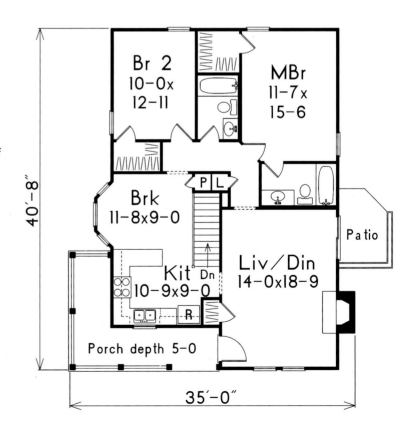

Br 2
10-0x 12-11

MBr
11-7 x 15-6

Brk
11-8x9-0

P L

Patio

Kit
10-9x9-0

Dn

R

Liv/Din
14-0x18-9

40'-8"

Porch depth 5-0

35'-0"

Plan #581-062D-0047

1,230 total square feet of living area

Special features

- ◆ Full-width deck creates plenty of outdoor living area
- ◆ The master bedroom accesses the deck through sliding glass doors and features a private bath
- ◆ Vaulted living room has a woodstove
- ◆ 3 bedrooms, 2 baths
- ◆ Crawl space or basement foundation, please specify when ordering

Price Code A

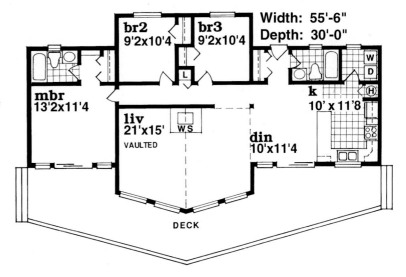

Width: 55'-6"
Depth: 30'-0"

br2 9'2x10'4

br3 9'2x10'4

mbr 13'2x11'4

liv 21'x15' VAULTED

W S

din 10'x11'4

k 10' x 11'8

DECK

Duo Atrium For Fantastic View

Plan #581-007D-0089

2,125 total square feet of living area

Special features

- A cozy porch leads to the vaulted great room with fireplace through the entry which has a walk-in closet and bath

- Large and well-arranged kitchen offers spectacular views from its cantilevered sink cabinetry through a two-story atrium window wall

- Master bedroom boasts a sitting room, large walk-in closet and bath with garden tub overhanging a brightly lit atrium

- Optional living area on the lower level features a study and family room with walk-in bar and full bath below the kitchen

- 3 bedrooms, 2 1/2 baths, 2-car side entry garage

- Walk-out basement foundation

Price Code C

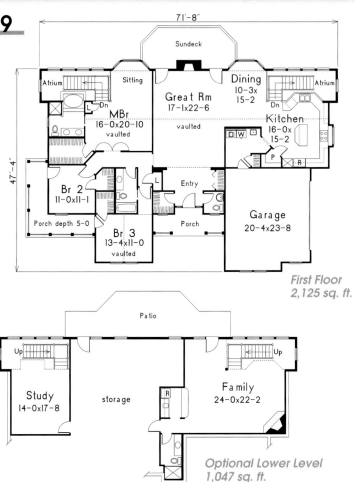

First Floor
2,125 sq. ft.

Optional Lower Level
1,047 sq. ft.

Cozy And Convenient

Plan #581-065D-0035

1,798 total square feet of living area

Special features

- The expansive great room enjoys a fireplace and has access onto the rear patio
- The centrally located kitchen is easily accessible to the dining room and breakfast area
- The master bedroom boasts a sloped ceiling and deluxe bath with a corner whirlpool tub and large walk-in closet
- A screened porch offers relaxing outdoor living
- 3 bedrooms, 2 baths, 2-car garage
- Basement foundation

Price Code B

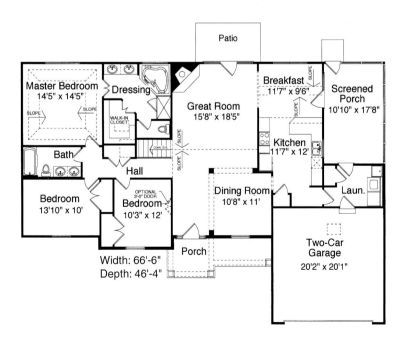

Patio

Master Bedroom
14'5" x 14'5"

Dressing

Great Room
15'8" x 18'5"

Breakfast
11'7" x 9'6"

Screened Porch
10'10" x 17'8"

WALK-IN CLOSET

Bath

Kitchen
11'7" x 12'

Hall

OPTIONAL 3'-0" DOOR

Bedroom
13'10" x 10'

Bedroom
10'3" x 12'

Dining Room
10'8" x 11'

Laun.

Porch

Two-Car Garage
20'2" x 20'1"

Width: 66'-6"
Depth: 46'-4"

*I*rresistible Paradise Retreat

*P*lan #581-007D-0039

1,563 total square feet of living area

Special features

◆ Enjoyable wrap-around porch and lower sundeck

◆ Vaulted entry is adorned with palladian window, plant shelves, stone floor and fireplace

◆ Huge vaulted great room has magnificient views through a two-story atrium window wall

◆ 2 bedrooms, 1 1/2 baths

◆ Basement foundation

Price Code B

Rear View

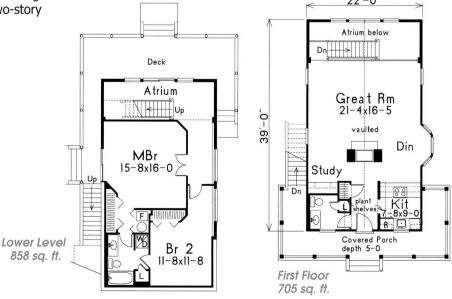

Lower Level 858 sq. ft.

Deck

Atrium — Up

MBr
15-8x16-0

Up

Br 2
11-8x11-8

22'-0"

Atrium below — Dn

Great Rm
21-4x16-5
vaulted

Din

Study

Dn

plant shelves

Kit
7-8x9-0

Covered Porch depth 5-0

39'-0"

First Floor 705 sq. ft.

© 2003, Garrell Associates, Inc.

Christine Canova 03/02

Plan #581-056D-0013

1,404 total square feet of living area

Special features

◆ Dining area and kitchen connect allowing for convenience and ease

◆ Well-located laundry area is within steps of bedrooms and baths

◆ Vaulted grand room creates a feeling of spaciousness for this gathering area

◆ 3 bedrooms, 2 1/2 baths, 2-car garage

◆ Slab foundation

Price Code E

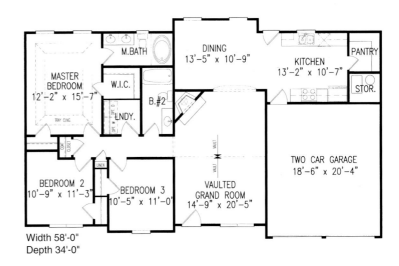

M.BATH

MASTER BEDROOM
12'-2" x 15'-7"

W.I.C.

B.#2

LNDY.

DINING
13'-5" x 10'-9"

KITCHEN
13'-2" x 10'-7"

PANTRY

STOR.

BEDROOM 2
10'-9" x 11'-3"

BEDROOM 3
10'-5" x 11'-0"

VAULTED GRAND ROOM
14'-9" x 20'-5"

TWO CAR GARAGE
18'-6" x 20'-4"

Width 58'-0"
Depth 34'-0"

*R*anch Of Enchantment

*P*lan #581-007D-0121

1,559 total square feet of living area

Special features

- ◆ A cozy country appeal is provided by a spacious porch, masonry fireplace, roof dormers and a perfect balance of stonework and siding
- ◆ Large living room enjoys a fireplace, bayed dining area and separate entry
- ◆ A U-shaped kitchen is adjoined by a breakfast room with bay window and large pantry
- ◆ 3 bedrooms, 2 1/2 baths, 2-car drive under side entry garage
- ◆ Basement foundation

Price Code B

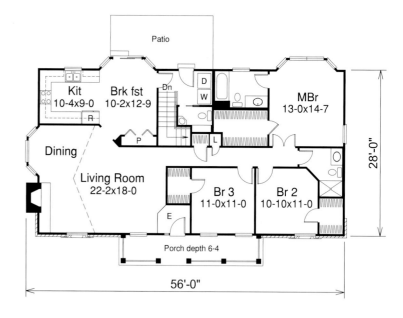

Luxurious Ranch Has It All

Plan #581-026D-0163

3,312 total square feet of living area

Special features

◆ Impressive front entry commands attention with an enormous living room straight ahead

◆ A casual family room and breakfast area combine to create a terrific gathering place just off the kitchen

◆ A second entry near the master bedroom is a convenient way into the home directly from the garage

◆ 3 bedrooms, 2 1/2 baths, 3-car side entry garage

◆ Slab foundation

Price Code F

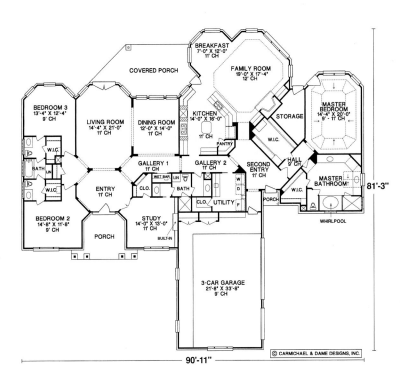

*P*lan #581-001D-0024

1,360 total square feet of living area

Special features

- ◆ Kitchen/dining room features island workspace and plenty of dining area
- ◆ Master bedroom has a large walk-in closet and private bath
- ◆ Laundry room is adjacent to the kitchen for easy access
- ◆ Convenient workshop in garage
- ◆ Large closets in secondary bedrooms
- ◆ 3 bedrooms, 2 baths, 2-car side entry garage
- ◆ Basement foundation, drawings also include crawl space and slab foundations

Price Code A

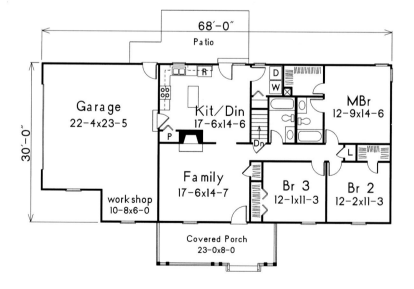

Plan #581-055D-0104

2,542 total square feet of living area

Special features

- ◆ Nice-sized guest room/study has walk-in closet and direct access to a full bath
- ◆ Columns grace foyer adding an elegant touch
- ◆ Center island makes food preparation easy
- ◆ 4 bedrooms, 3 baths, 2-car side entry garage
- ◆ Crawl space or slab foundation, please specify when ordering

Price Code D

First Floor
2,542 sq. ft.

Optional
Second Floor
473 sq. ft.

Plan #581-028D-0010

2,214 total square feet of living area

Special features

◆ Great room has built-in cabinets for entertainment system, fireplace and French doors leading to private rear covered porch

◆ Dining room has an arched opening from foyer

◆ Breakfast room has lots of windows for a sunny open feel

◆ 3 bedrooms, 2 baths, 2-car side entry garage

◆ Crawl space or slab foundation, please specify when ordering

Price Code D

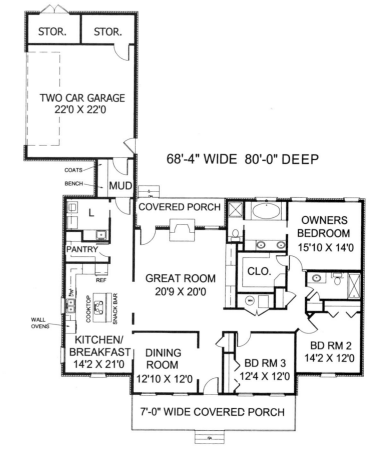

68'-4" WIDE 80'-0" DEEP

STOR. STOR.

TWO CAR GARAGE
22'0 X 22'0

COATS
BENCH MUD

COVERED PORCH

OWNERS BEDROOM
15'10 X 14'0

L

PANTRY

CLO.

GREAT ROOM
20'9 X 20'0

REF

WALL OVENS

COOKTOP SNACK BAR

KITCHEN/ BREAKFAST
14'2 X 21'0

DINING ROOM
12'10 X 12'0

BD RM 3
12'4 X 12'0

BD RM 2
14'2 X 12'0

7'-0" WIDE COVERED PORCH

Our Blueprint Packages Include...

Quality plans for building your future, with extras that provide unsurpassed value, ensure good construction and long-term enjoyment.

A quality home - one that looks good, functions well, and provides years of enjoyment - is a product of many things - design, materials, craftsmanship.

But it's also the result of outstanding blueprints - the actual plans and specifications that tell the builder exactly how to build your home.

And with our BLUEPRINT PACKAGES you get the absolute best. A complete set of blueprints is available for every design in this book. These "working drawings," are highly detailed, resulting in two key benefits:

- Better understanding by the contractor of how to build your home and...

- More accurate construction estimates.

When you purchase one of our designs, you'll receive all of the BLUEPRINT components shown here - elevations, foundation plan, floor plans, sections, and/or details. Other helpful building aids are also available to help make your dream home a reality.

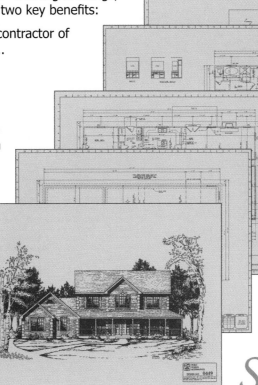

Cover Sheet
The cover sheet is the artist's rendering of the exterior of the home. It will give you an idea of how your home will look when completed and landscaped.

Interior Elevations
Interior elevations provide views of special interior elements such as fireplaces, kitchen cabinets, built-in units and other features of the home.

Foundation Plan
The foundation plan shows the layout of the basement, crawl space, slab or pier foundation. All necessary notations and dimensions are included. See plan page for the foundation types included. If the home plan you choose does not have your desired foundation type, our Customer Service Representatives can advise you on how to customize your foundation to suit your specific needs or site conditions.

Details
Details show how to construct certain components of your home, such as the roof system, stairs, deck, etc.

Sections
Sections show detail views of the home or portions of the home as if it were sliced from the roof to the foundation. This sheet shows important areas such as load-bearing walls, stairs, joists, trusses and other structural elements, which are critical for proper construction.

Floor Plans
The floor plans show the placement of walls, doors, closets, plumbing fixtures, electrical outlets, columns, and beams for each level of the home.

Exterior Elevations
Exterior elevations illustrate the front, rear and both sides of the house, with all details of exterior materials and the required dimensions.

Home Plan Index

Plan #	Square Feet	Price Code	Page	Material List / Price	Right Reading Reverse / Price	Use Canada Shipping
581-001D-0001	1,605	B	66	•/$60.00		
581-001D-0007	2,874	E	11	•/$70.00		
581-001D-0013	1,882	D	226	•/$65.00		
581-001D-0018	988	AA	415	•/$55.00		
581-001D-0020	1,416	A	364	•/$60.00		
581-001D-0021	1,416	A	84	•/$60.00		
581-001D-0022	1,680	B	347	•/$60.00		
581-001D-0023	1,343	A	396	•/$60.00		
581-001D-0024	1,360	A	472	•/$60.00		
581-001D-0029	1,260	A	174	•/$60.00		
581-001D-0030	1,416	A	137	•/$60.00		
581-001D-0031	1,501	B	23	•/$60.00		
581-001D-0032	2,520	D	400	•/$65.00		
581-001D-0033	1,624	B	80	•/$60.00		
581-001D-0034	1,642	B	286	•/$60.00		
581-001D-0035	1,396	A	129	•/$60.00		
581-001D-0036	1,320	A	349	•/$60.00		
581-001D-0040	864	AAA	351	•/$50.00		
581-001D-0041	1,000	AA	205	•/$55.00		
581-001D-0043	1,104	AA	121	•/$55.00		
581-001D-0044	1,375	A	90	•/$60.00		
581-001D-0045	1,197	AA	391	•/$55.00		
581-001D-0048	1,400	A	293	•/$60.00		
581-001D-0053	1,344	A	180	•/$60.00		
581-001D-0058	1,720	B	128	•/$60.00		
581-001D-0067	1,285	B	239	•/$60.00		
581-001D-0069	1,504	B	69	•/$60.00		
581-001D-0071	1,440	A	103	•/$60.00		
581-001D-0072	1,288	A	313	•/$60.00		
581-001D-0074	1,664	B	383	•/$60.00		
581-001D-0076	1,584	B	261	•/$60.00		
581-001D-0079	2,080	C	149	•/$65.00		
581-001D-0080	1,832	C	170	•/$65.00		
581-001D-0081	1,160	AA	379	•/$55.00		
581-001D-0085	720	AAA	273	•/$50.00		
581-001D-0088	800	AAA	79	•/$50.00		
581-001D-0089	1,000	AA	158	•/$55.00		
581-001D-0090	1,300	A	278	•/$60.00		
581-001D-0091	1,344	A	376	•/$60.00		
581-001D-0093	1,120	AA	197	•/$55.00		
581-003D-0002	1,676	B	238	•/$60.00		
581-003D-0005	1,708	B	461	•/$60.00		
581-004D-0002	1,823	C	276	•/$65.00		
581-005D-0001	1,400	B	442	•/$60.00		
581-006D-0001	1,643	B	266	•/$60.00		
581-006D-0003	1,674	B	51	•/$60.00		
581-007D-0002	3,814	G	4	•/$75.00		
581-007D-0004	2,531	D	231	•/$65.00		
581-007D-0007	2,523	D	420	•/$65.00		
581-007D-0008	2,452	D	245	•/$65.00		
581-007D-0010	1,721	C	249	•/$65.00		
581-007D-0017	1,882	C	34	•/$65.00		
581-007D-0018	1,941	C	86	•/$65.00		
581-007D-0029	576	AAA	58	•/$50.00		
581-007D-0030	1,140	AA	252	•/$55.00		
581-007D-0031	1,092	AA	453	•/$55.00		
581-007D-0037	1,403	A	61	•/$60.00		
581-007D-0039	1,563	B	468	•/$60.00		
581-007D-0042	914	AA	447	•/$55.00		
581-007D-0043	647	AAA	40	•/$50.00		
581-007D-0044	1,516	B	112	•/$60.00		
581-007D-0045	1,321	A	303	•/$60.00		
581-007D-0046	1,712	B	436	•/$60.00		
581-007D-0048	2,758	E	243	•/$70.00		
581-007D-0049	1,791	C	63	•/$65.00		
581-007D-0050	2,723	E	418	•/$70.00		
581-007D-0053	2,334	D	54	•/$65.00		
581-007D-0055	2,029	D	451	•/$65.00		
581-007D-0056	3,199	E	59	•/$70.00		
581-007D-0057	2,808	F	425	•/$70.00		
581-007D-0058	4,826	G	42	•/$75.00		
581-007D-0060	1,268	B	424	•/$60.00		
581-007D-0061	1,340	A	353	•/$60.00		
581-007D-0062	2,483	D	16	•/$65.00		
581-007D-0065	2,218	D	214	•/$65.00		
581-007D-0066	2,408	D	247	•/$65.00		
581-007D-0067	1,761	B	440	•/$60.00		
581-007D-0068	1,384	B	46	•/$60.00		
581-007D-0069	2,070	C	316	•/$65.00		
581-007D-0075	1,684	B	251	•/$60.00		
581-007D-0077	1,977	C	19	•/$65.00		
581-007D-0078	2,514	D	156	•/$65.00		
581-007D-0080	2,900	E	435	•/$70.00		
581-007D-0085	1,787	B	36	•/$60.00		
581-007D-0089	2,125	C	466	•/$65.00		
581-007D-0090	1,826	C	125	•/$65.00		
581-007D-0098	2,397	D	433	•/$65.00		
581-007D-0101	2,384	D	32	•/$65.00		
581-007D-0102	1,452	A	456	•/$60.00		
581-007D-0103	1,231	A	233	•/$60.00		
581-007D-0104	969	AA	371	•/$55.00		
581-007D-0105	1,084	AA	464	•/$55.00		
581-007D-0106	1,200	A	167	•/$60.00		
581-007D-0107	1,161	AA	48	•/$55.00		
581-007D-0108	983	AA	195			
581-007D-0109	888	AAA	389	•/$50.00		
581-007D-0110	1,169	AA	229	•/$55.00		
581-007D-0112	1,062	AA	399			
581-007D-0113	2,547	D	422	•/$65.00		
581-007D-0115	588	AAA	94			
581-007D-0116	2,100	C	176			
581-007D-0117	2,695	E	26	•/$70.00		
581-007D-0118	1,991	C	428	•/$65.00		
581-007D-0119	1,621	B	52	•/$60.00		
581-007D-0120	1,914	C	148			
581-007D-0121	1,559	B	470	•/$60.00		
581-007D-0124	1,944	C	115			
581-007D-0125	1,302	A	288			
581-007D-0126	1,365	A	330	•/$60.00		
581-007D-0133	1,316	A	373			
581-007D-0134	1,310	A	401			
581-007D-0135	801	AAA	355			
581-007D-0136	1,533	B	325			
581-007D-0137	1,568	B	179			
581-007D-0139	1,348	A	88			
581-007D-0140	1,591	B	204	•/$60.00		
581-007D-0149	1,929	C	117			
581-007D-0150	2,420	D	77			
581-010D-0003	1,560	B	97	•/$60.00		
581-010D-0005	1,358	A	187	•/$60.00		
581-010D-0006	1,170	AA	43	•/$55.00		
581-011D-0001	1,275	C	235		•/$150.00	
581-011D-0002	1,557	C	53		•/$150.00	
581-011D-0004	1,997	D	454		•/$150.00	
581-011D-0005	1,467	C	361	•/$125.00	•/$150.00	
581-011D-0007	1,580	C	12	•/$125.00	•/$150.00	
581-011D-0009	2,840	F	245		•/$150.00	
581-011D-0010	2,197	C	225	•/$125.00	•/$150.00	
581-011D-0013	2,001	D	15		•/$150.00	
581-011D-0014	3,246	G	432	•/$125.00	•/$150.00	
581-013D-0001	1,050	AA	253			
581-013D-0003	1,296	B	49			
581-013D-0010	1,593	C	449	•/$125.00		
581-013D-0015	1,787	B	71			
581-013D-0021	1,982	C	18			
581-013D-0022	1,992	C	111	•/$125.00		
581-013D-0025	2,097	C	120	•/$125.00		
581-013D-0030	2,288	D	194			
581-014D-0001	2,159	C	74	•/$65.00		
581-014D-0002	2,070	C	147	•/$65.00		
581-014D-0003	3,003	E	306	•/$70.00		
581-014D-0004	1,689	B	410	•/$60.00		
581-014D-0005	1,314	A	343	•/$60.00		
581-014D-0006	1,588	B	109	•/$60.00		
581-014D-0007	1,453	A	100	•/$60.00		
581-014D-0008	1,135	AA	290	•/$55.00		
581-014D-0009	1,428	A	380	•/$60.00		
581-014D-0010	2,563	D	192	•/$65.00		
581-014D-0015	1,941	C	375	•/$60.00		
581-015D-0003	2,255	D	213	•/$125.00		
581-015D-0008	1,785	B	308	•/$125.00		
581-015D-0030	1,588	B	172			
581-015D-0044	2,148	C	392			
581-016D-0001	1,783	D	419	•/$125.00		
581-016D-0002	2,243	E	457	•/$125.00		
581-016D-0005	2,347	E	254	•/$125.00		
581-016D-0011	1,815	D	242	•/$125.00		
581-016D-0021	1,892	D	452	•/$125.00		
581-016D-0040	1,595	C	56	•/$125.00		
581-016D-0049	1,793	B	215	•/$125.00		
581-016D-0053	1,466	B	229	•/$125.00		
581-016D-0057	1,709	C	426	•/$125.00		
581-016D-0062	1,380	A	104	•/$125.00		
581-016D-0065	2,585	D	409	•/$125.00		
581-017D-0003	1,476	B	351	•/$60.00		
581-017D-0004	1,315	B	312	•/$60.00		
581-017D-0005	1,367	B	105	•/$60.00		
581-017D-0007	1,567	C	29	•/$65.00		
581-017D-0008	1,466	B	394	•/$60.00		
581-018D-0001	2,517	D	220	•/$65.00		
581-018D-0005	2,598	D	133	•/$65.00		
581-018D-0006	1,742	B	346	•/$60.00		
581-018D-0008	2,109	C	131	•/$65.00		
581-019D-0003	1,310	A	299			

Home Plan Index

Plan #	Square Feet	Price Code	Page	Material List / Price	Right Reading Reverse / Price	Use Canada Shipping
581-019D-0009	1,862	C	356			
581-019D-0010	1,890	C	155			
581-019D-0011	1,955	C	329			
581-019D-0013	1,932	C	363			
581-019D-0016	2,678	E	317			
581-019D-0020	2,745	E	403			
581-020D-0002	1,434	A	377			
581-020D-0003	1,420	A	106			
581-020D-0005	1,770	B	216			
581-020D-0007	1,828	C	353			
581-020D-0008	1,925	C	191			
581-020D-0015	1,191	AA	210			
581-021D-0001	2,396	D	151	•/$65.00		
581-021D-0002	1,442	A	70	•/$60.00		
581-021D-0004	1,800	C	365	•/$65.00		
581-021D-0005	2,177	C	201	•/$65.00		
581-021D-0006	1,600	C	64	•/$65.00		
581-021D-0007	1,868	D	188	•/$65.00		
581-021D-0008	1,266	A	81	•/$60.00		
581-021D-0009	2,252	D	135	•/$65.00		
581-021D-0010	1,444	A	439	•/$60.00		
581-021D-0011	1,800	D	236	•/$65.00		
581-021D-0012	1,672	C	367	•/$65.00		
581-021D-0013	2,648	E	143	•/$70.00		
581-021D-0014	1,856	C	130	•/$65.00		
581-022D-0005	1,360	A	73	•/$60.00		
581-022D-0011	1,630	B	65	•/$60.00		
581-022D-0018	1,368	A	57	•/$60.00		
581-022D-0019	1,283	B	185	•/$60.00		
581-022D-0020	988	AA	413	•/$55.00		
581-022D-0021	1,020	AA	76	•/$55.00		
581-022D-0022	1,270	A	160	•/$60.00		
581-022D-0023	950	AA	263	•/$55.00		
581-022D-0024	1,127	AA	369	•/$55.00		
581-022D-0025	2,847	E	322	•/$70.00		
581-022D-0026	1,993	D	45	•/$65.00		
581-022D-0027	1,847	C	85	•/$65.00		
581-022D-0030	3,412	F	307	•/$70.00		
581-023D-0010	2,558	D	345	•/$65.00		
581-023D-0012	2,365	D	388	•/$65.00		
581-023D-0017	1,596	B	381	•/$60.00		
581-023D-0018	1,556	B	275	•/$60.00		
581-023D-0019	1,539	B	348	•/$60.00		
581-024D-0002	1,405	A	281			
581-024D-0004	1,500	B	41			
581-024D-0009	1,704	B	448			
581-024D-0017	2,697	E	239			
581-024D-0018	2,246	D	116			
581-025D-0003	1,379	A	372			
581-025D-0008	1,609	B	22			
581-025D-0009	1,680	B	228			
581-025D-0010	1,677	B	460			
581-025D-0011	1,699	B	434			
581-025D-0019	2,074	C	60			
581-025D-0020	2,095	C	237			
581-025D-0028	2,350	D	416			
581-026D-0111	2,254	D	429	•/$125.00		
581-026D-0112	1,911	C	438	•/$125.00		
581-026D-0114	2,498	D	367	•/$125.00		
581-026D-0122	1,850	C	6	•/$125.00		
581-026D-0138	1,853	C	211	•/$125.00		
581-026D-0161	1,375	A	441	•/$125.00		
581-026D-0163	3,112	F	471	•/$125.00		
581-026D-0166	2,126	C	150	•/$125.00		
581-027D-0002	3,796	F	321	•/$70.00		
581-027D-0003	2,061	D	427	•/$65.00		
581-027D-0006	2,076	C	125	•/$65.00		
581-027D-0008	3,411	F	91	•/$70.00		
581-027D-0009	3,808	F	153	•/$70.00		
581-028D-0002	1,377	A	38			
581-028D-0003	1,716	B	234			
581-028D-0004	1,785	B	444			
581-028D-0005	1,856	C	13			
581-028D-0006	1,700	B	162			
581-028D-0008	2,156	C	20			
581-028D-0010	2,214	D	474			
581-028D-0011	2,123	C	231			
581-028D-0014	2,340	D	55			
581-028D-0015	2,421	D	459			
581-028D-0017	2,669	E	298			
581-030D-0001	1,374	A	136			
581-030D-0002	1,429	A	320			
581-030D-0003	1,753	B	368			
581-030D-0004	1,791	B	157			
581-030D-0007	2,050	C	318			
581-031D-0003	1,665	B	95			
581-031D-0005	1,735	B	141			
581-031D-0011	2,164	C	357			
581-031D-0013	2,380	D	285			
581-034D-0001	1,436	A	118			
581-034D-0002	1,456	A	324			
581-034D-0008	1,875	C	301			
581-034D-0010	2,178	C	382			
581-034D-0012	2,278	D	358			
581-035D-0003	2,115	C	119	•/$125.00		
581-035D-0005	1,281	A	165	•/$125.00		
581-035D-0011	1,945	C	83	•/$125.00		
581-035D-0014	2,236	D	207	•/$125.00		
581-035D-0026	1,845	C	395	•/$125.00		
581-035D-0028	1,779	B	223	•/$125.00		
581-035D-0032	1,856	C	359	•/$125.00		
581-035D-0035	2,322	D	107	•/$125.00		
581-035D-0036	2,193	C	189	•/$125.00		
581-035D-0039	2,201	D	124	•/$125.00		
581-035D-0042	2,311	D	181	•/$125.00		
581-035D-0045	1,749	B	405	•/$125.00		
581-035D-0046	1,080	AA	287	•/$125.00		
581-035D-0048	1,915	C	344	•/$125.00		
581-035D-0050	1,342	A	161	•/$125.00		
036D-0046	1,653	B	123			
036D-0048	1,830	C	366			
036D-0051	2,911	E	221			
036D-0053	2,528	D	282			
036D-0056	1,604	B	370			
036D-0057	2,578	D	272			
036D-0058	2,529	D	212			
036D-0060	1,760	B	107			
581-037D-0003	1,996	D	109	•/$65.00		
581-037D-0006	1,772	C	144	•/$65.00		
581-037D-0008	1,707	C	335	•/$65.00		
581-037D-0010	1,770	B	406	•/$60.00		
581-037D-0011	1,846	C	387	•/$65.00		
581-037D-0012	1,661	B	67	•/$60.00		
581-037D-0017	829	AAA	159	•/$50.00		
581-037D-0020	1,994	D	445	•/$65.00		
581-037D-0021	2,260	D	277	•/$65.00		
581-037D-0022	1,539	B	137	•/$60.00		
581-037D-0025	2,481	D	131	•/$65.00		
581-037D-0026	1,824	C	101	•/$65.00		
581-037D-0029	1,736	B	186	•/$60.00		
581-037D-0030	2,397	D	78	•/$65.00		
581-037D-0031	1,923	C	289	•/$65.00		
581-038D-0012	1,575	B	250	•/$125.00		
581-038D-0018	1,792	B	115	•/$125.00		
581-038D-0033	1,312	A	24	•/$125.00		
581-038D-0034	1,625	B	421	•/$125.00		
581-038D-0039	1,771	B	255	•/$125.00		
581-038D-0040	1,642	B	62	•/$125.00		
581-038D-0043	1,539	B	257	•/$125.00		
581-039D-0001	1,253	A	132	•/$125.00		
581-039D-0002	1,333	A	315	•/$125.00		
581-039D-0004	1,406	A	357	•/$125.00		
581-039D-0007	1,550	B	279	•/$125.00		
581-039D-0014	1,849	C	328	•/$125.00		
581-039D-0022	2,158	C	337	•/$125.00		
581-039D-0024	2,361	D	373	•/$125.00		
581-040D-0003	1,475	B	248	•/$60.00		
581-040D-0008	1,631	B	169	•/$60.00		
581-040D-0009	2,468	D	68	•/$65.00		
581-040D-0010	1,496	A	122	•/$60.00		
581-040D-0011	1,739	B	363	•/$60.00		
581-040D-0012	2,988	E	404	•/$70.00		
581-040D-0013	1,304	A	145	•/$60.00		
581-040D-0014	1,595	B	203	•/$60.00		
581-040D-0015	1,655	B	82	•/$60.00		
581-040D-0026	1,393	B	310	•/$60.00		
581-041D-0001	2,003	D	342	•/$65.00		
581-041D-0004	1,195	AA	105	•/$55.00		
581-043D-0001	3,158	E	113			
581-043D-0002	3,671	F	352			
581-043D-0003	1,890	C	117			
581-043D-0004	2,086	C	178			
581-043D-0005	1,734	B	314			
581-043D-0006	2,355	D	218			
581-043D-0007	2,788	E	304			
581-043D-0008	1,496	A	139			
581-045D-0003	1,958	C	209	•/$65.00		
581-045D-0009	1,684	B	292	•/$60.00		
581-045D-0010	1,558	B	103	•/$60.00		
581-045D-0014	987	AA	362	•/$55.00		
581-045D-0015	1,134	AA	343	•/$55.00		
581-047D-0019	1,783	B	199	•/$125.00		
581-047D-0020	1,783	B	98			
581-047D-0036	2,140	C	217	•/$125.00		
581-047D-0045	2,616	E	371			
581-047D-0046	2,597	D	259	•/$125.00		

What Kind Of Plan Package Do You Need?

Once you find the home plan you've been looking for, here are some suggestions on how to make your Dream Home a reality. To get started, order the type of plans that fit your particular situation.

Your Choices:

The 1-set package - We offer a 1-set plan package so you can study your home in detail. This one set is considered a study set and is marked "not for construction." It is a copyright violation to reproduce blueprints.

The Minimum 5-set package - If you're ready to start the construction process, this 5-set package is the minimum number of blueprint sets you will need. It will require keeping close track of each set so they can be used by multiple subcontractors and tradespeople.

The Standard 8-set package - For best results in terms of cost, schedule and quality of construction, we recommend you order eight (or more) sets of blueprints. Besides one set for yourself, additional sets of blueprints will be required by your mortgage lender, local building department, general contractor and all subcontractors working on foundation, electrical, plumbing, heating/air conditioning, carpentry work, etc.

Reproducible Masters - If you wish to make some minor design changes, you'll want to order reproducible masters. These drawings contain the same information as the blueprints but are printed on erasable and reproducible paper which clearly indicates your right to copy or reproduce. This will allow your builder or a local design professional to make the necessary drawing changes without the major expense of redrawing the plans. This package also allows you to print copies of the modified plans as needed. The right of building only one structure from these plans is licensed exclusively to the buyer. You may not use this design to build a second or multiple dwelling(s) without purchasing another blueprint. Each violation of the Copyright Law is punishable in a fine.

Mirror Reverse Sets - Plans can be printed in mirror reverse. These plans are useful when the house would fit your site better if all the rooms were on the opposite side than shown. They are simply a mirror image of the original drawings causing the lettering and dimensions to read backwards. Therefore, when ordering mirror reverse drawings, you must purchase at least one set of right-reading plans. Some of our plans are offered mirror reverse right-reading. This means the plan, lettering and dimensions are flipped but read correctly. See the Home Plans Index on pages 476-478 for availability and pricing.

BUILDING A HOME?

It sounds like lots of fun and just might be the biggest purchase you will ever make. But the process of building a home can be a tricky one. This program walks you through the process step-by-step. Compiled by consumers who have built new homes and learned the hard way. This is not a "how-to" video, but a visual checklist to open your eyes to issues you would never think about until you have lived in your home for years. *Available in VHS or DVD.*

$19.97 VHS   **$26.97** DVD

Other Great Products...

The Legal Kit - Avoid many legal pitfalls and build your home with confidence using the forms and contract featured in this kit. Included are request for proposal documents, various fixed price and cost plus contracts, instructions on how and when to use each form, warranty statements and more. Save time and money before you break ground on your new home or start a remodeling project. All forms are reproducible. The kit is ideal for homebuilders and contractors.
Cost: $35.00

Detail Plan Packages - Three separate packages offer homebuilders details for constructing various foundations; numerous floor, wall and roof framing techniques; simple to complex residential wiring; sump and water softener hookups; plumbing connection methods; installation of septic systems, and more. Each package includes three-dimensional illustrations and a glossary of terms. Purchase one or all three.
Note: These drawings do not pertain to a specific home plan.
Cost: $20⁰⁰ each or all three for $40⁰⁰

More Helpful Building Aids...

Your Blueprint Package will contain the necessary construction information to build your home. We also offer the following products and services to save you time and money in the building process.

Express Delivery - Most orders are processed within 24 hours of receipt. Please allow 7-10 business days for delivery. If you need to place a rush order, please call us by 11:00 a.m. Monday-Friday CST and ask for express service (allow 1-2 business days).

Technical Assistance - If you have questions, please call our technical support line at 1-314-770-2228 between 8:00 a.m. and 5:00 p.m. Monday-Friday CST. Whether it involves design modifications or field assistance, our designers are extremely familiar with all of our designs and will be happy to help you. We want your home to be everything you expect it to be.

Material List - Material lists are available for many of our plans. Each list gives you the quantity, dimensions and description of the building materials necessary to construct your home. You'll get faster and more accurate bids from your contractor and material suppliers, and you'll save money by paying for only the materials you need. Refer to the Home Plan Index on pages 476-478 for availability.

How To Order

For fastest service, Call Toll-Free 1-800-DREAM HOME
(1-800-373-2646) day or night

Three Easy Ways To Order

1. CALL toll free 1-800-373-2646 for credit card orders. MasterCard, Visa, Discover and American Express are accepted.

2. FAX your order to 1-314-770-2226.

3. MAIL the Order Form to: **HDA, Inc.**
   4390 Green Ash Drive
   St. Louis, MO 63045

Order Form

Please send me -

PLAN NUMBER 581- _____

PRICE CODE _____ (see Plan Index)

Specify Foundation Type *(see plan page for availability)*
- ☐ Slab   ☐ Crawl space   ☐ Pier
- ☐ Basement ☐ Walk-out basement

☐ Reproducible Masters	$_____
☐ Eight-Set Plan Package	$_____
☐ Five-Set Plan Package	$_____
☐ One-Set Study Package *(no mirror reverse)*	$_____

Additional Plan Sets*
- ☐ _____ (Qty.) at $45.00 each $_____

Mirror Reverse*
- ☐ Right-reading $150 one-time charge
  (see index on pages 476-478 for availability) $_____
- ☐ Print in Mirror Reverse *(where right-reading is not available)*
  _____ (Qty.) at $15.00 each $_____

☐ Material List* *(see index)*	$_____
☐ Legal Kit (see page 479)	$_____

Detail Plan Packages: (see page 479)
- ☐ Framing ☐ Electrical ☐ Plumbing $_____

Building Smart: (see page 479)
- ☐ VHS $19.97 #FP00001 ☐ DVD $26.97 #FP00002 $_____

SUBTOTAL	$_____
SALES TAX (MO residents add 6%)	$_____
☐ Shipping / Handling (see chart at right)	$_____
TOTAL (US funds only - *sorry no CODs*)	$_____

I hereby authorize HDA, Inc. to charge this purchase to my credit card account (check one):

☐ MasterCard ☐ VISA ☐ DISCOVER ☐ American Express Cards

Credit Card number _____

Expiration date _____

Signature _____

Name _____
(Please print or type)

Street Address _____
*(Please **do not** use PO Box)*

City _____

State _____

Zip _____

Daytime phone number (_____) - _____

E-mail address _____

I'm a ☐ Builder/Contractor ☐ Homeowner ☐ Renter
I ☐ have ☐ have not selected my general contractor

480 *Thank you for your order!*

- **Exchange Policies** - Since blueprints are printed in response to your o we cannot honor requests for refunds. However, if for some reason you that the plan you have purchased does not meet your requirements, may exchange that plan for another plan in our collection within 90 da purchase. At the time of the exchange, you will be charged a proces fee of 25% of your original plan package price, plus the difference in between the plan packages (if applicable) and the cost to ship the new to you.

  Please note: Reproducible drawings can only be exchanged i package is unopened.

- **Building Codes & Requirements** - At the time the construction draw were prepared, every effort was made to ensure that these plans specifications meet nationally recognized codes. Our plans conform to national building codes. Because building codes vary from area to area, s drawing modifications and/or the assistance of a professional design architect may be necessary to comply with your local codes or to ac modate specific building site conditions. We advise you to consult with local building official for information regarding codes governing your a

Questions? Call Our Customer Service Numbe
314-770-2228

Blueprint Price Schedule — BEST VALUE

Price Code	1-Set	SAVE $110 5-Sets	SAVE $200 8 Sets	Reproducible Masters
AAA	$225	$295	$340	$440
AA	$325	$395	$440	$540
A	$385	$455	$500	$600
B	$445	$515	$560	$660
C	$500	$570	$615	$715
D	$560	$630	$675	$775
E	$620	$690	$735	$835
F	$675	$745	$790	$890
G	$765	$835	$880	$980
H	$890	$960	$1005	$1105

Plan prices guaranteed through January 1, 2006.
Please note that plans are not refundable.

- **Additional Sets*** - Additional sets of the plan ordered are available fo additional cost (see order form at left). Five-set, eight-set, and reprodu packages offer considerable savings.

- **Mirror Reverse Plans*** - Available for an additional $15.00 per set, th plans are simply a mirror image of the original drawings causing dimensions and lettering to read backwards. Therefore, when ordering m reverse plans, you must purchase at least one set of right-reading pl Some of our plans are offered mirror reverse right-reading. This mean plan, lettering and dimensions are flipped but read correctly. See the H Plans Index on pages 476-478 for availability and pricing.

- **One-Set Study Package** - We offer a one-set plan package so you can s your home in detail. This one set is considered a study set and is ma "not for construction." It is a copyright violation to reproduce blueprints

Available only within 90 days after purchase of plan package or reproducible masters of same plan.

Shipping & Handling Charges

	1-4 Sets	5-7 Sets	8 Sets or Reproducibles
U.S. SHIPPING			
Regular *(allow 7-10 business days)*	$15.00	$17.50	$25.00
Priority *(allow 3-5 business days)*	$25.00	$30.00	$35.00
Express* *(allow 1-2 business days)*	$35.00	$40.00	$45.00
CANADA SHIPPING (to/from) - *Plans with suffix 032D & 062D - see index*			
Standard *(allow 8-12 business days)*	$25.00	$30.00	$35.00
Express* *(allow 3-5 business days)*	$40.00	$40.00	$45.00

Overseas Shipping/International - Call, fax, or e-mail (plans@hdainc.com) for shipping costs.
* For express delivery please call us by 11:00 a.m. Monday-Friday C